T0215320

Lecture Notes in Computer Science 12072

More information about this series at http://www.springer.com/series/7409

Valentina Janev · Damien Graux ·
Hajira Jabeen · Emanuel Sallinger (Eds.)

Knowledge Graphs and Big Data Processing

Springer

Editors
Valentina Janev
Institute Mihajlo Pupin
University of Belgrade
Belgrade, Serbia

Hajira Jabeen
CEPLAS, Botanical Institute
University of Cologne
Cologne, Germany

Damien Graux
ADAPT SFI Centre, O'Reilly Institute
Trinity College Dublin
Dublin, Ireland

Emanuel Sallinger
Institute of Logic and Computation
Faculty of Informatics
TU Wien
Wien, Austria

University of Oxford
Oxford, UK

ISSN 0302-9743   ISSN 1611-3349   (electronic)
Lecture Notes in Computer Science
ISBN 978-3-030-53198-0   ISBN 978-3-030-53199-7   (eBook)
https://doi.org/10.1007/978-3-030-53199-7

LNCS Sublibrary: SL3 – Information Systems and Applications, incl. Internet/Web, and HCI

This Springer imprint is published by the registered company Springer Nature Switzerland AG
The registered company address is: Gewerbestrasse 11, 6330 Cham, Switzerland

Preface

Data Analytics involves applying algorithmic processes to derive insights. Nowadays it is used in many industries to allow organizations and companies to make better decisions as well as to verify or disprove existing theories or models. The term data analytics is often used interchangeably with intelligence, statistics, reasoning, data mining, knowledge discovery, and others. Being in the era of big data, **Big Data Analytics** thus refers to the strategy of analyzing large volumes of data gathered from a wide variety of sources, including social networks, transaction records, videos, digital images, and different kinds of sensors.

The goal of this book is to introduce some of the definitions, methods, tools, frameworks, and solutions for big data processing, starting from the process of information extraction and knowledge representation, via knowledge processing and analytics to visualization, sense-making, and practical applications. However, this book is not intended either to cover the whole set of big data analytics methods or to provide a complete collection of references. Each chapter in this book addresses some pertinent aspect of the data processing chain, with a specific focus on understanding **Enterprise Knowledge Graphs**, **Semantic Big Data Architectures**, and **Smart Data Analytics solutions**.

Chapter 1's purpose is to characterize the relevant aspects of the **Big Data Ecosystem** and to explain the ecosystem with respect to the big data characteristics, the components needed for implementing end-to-end big data processing and the need to use semantics to improve data management, integration, processing, and analytical tasks.

Chapter 2 gives an overview of different definitions of the term **Knowledge Graphs** (KGs). In this chapter, we are going to take the position that precisely in the multitude of definitions lies one of the strengths of the area. We will choose a particular perspective, which we will call the layered perspective, and three views on Knowledge Graphs to guide the reader in a structured way.

Chapter 3 introduces the key technologies and business drivers for building big data applications and presents in detail several open-source tools and **Big Data Frameworks** for handling Big Data.

The subsequent chapters discuss the knowledge processing chain from the perspective of Knowledge Graph Creation (**Chapter 4**), via Federated Query Processing (**Chapter 5**), to Reasoning in Knowledge Graphs (**Chapter 6**).

Chapter 7 brings to attention the SANSA framework, which combines distributed analytics and semantic technologies into a scalable semantic analytics stack.

Chapter 8 elaborates further the semantic data integration problems and presents COMET (**CO**ntextualized **M**olecul**E**-based matching **T**echnique and framework) for matching contextually equivalent RDF entities from different sources into a set of 1-1 perfect matches between entities.

As the goal of the LAMBDA Project is to study the potentials, prospects, and challenges of Big Data Analytics in real-world applications, in addition to Chapter 1 (traffic management example), **Chapter 9** discusses the role of big data in different industries.

Finally, in **Chapter 10**, one sector has been selected – the energy domain – and insight is given into some potential applications of big data-oriented tools and analytical technologies for the control and monitoring of electricity production, distribution, and consumption.

This book is addressed to graduate students from technical disciplines, to professional audiences following continuous education short courses, and to researchers from diverse areas following self-study courses. Basic skills in computer science, mathematics, and statistics are required.

June 2020

Valentina Janev
Damien Graux
Hajira Jabeen
Emanuel Sallinger

Acknowledgments

This book is prepared as part of the LAMBDA Project (Learning, Applying, Multiplying **B**ig **D**ata Analytics), funded by the European Union under grant agreement number 809965. The project aims at advancing state-of-the-art in Big Data Analytics and fostering excellence in the Big Data Ecosystem through a combination of training, research, and innovation activities. As the number of Big Data-related methods, tools, frameworks, and solutions are growing, there is a need to systematize knowledge about the domain. Hence, in the LAMBDA project framework, an effort has been made to develop a new set of lectures and training materials based on state-of-the-art analysis and education materials and courses offered by project partners.

The lectures were presented at the LAMBDA Big Data Analytics Summer School (the first edition was held in Belgrade during June 17–19, 2019; the second edition was held online during June 16–17, 2020). We are grateful to the esteemed keynote speakers Prof. Dr. Sören Auer, Director of the German National Library for Science and Technology and Professor of Data Science and Digital Libraries at Leibniz Universität Hannover; Mr. Atanas Kiryakov, Chief Executive Officer of OntoText; Prof. Dr. Maria-Esther Vidal, Head of Scientific Data Management Research Group, German National Library for Science and Technology; Prof. Dr. Georgios Paliouras, Head of the Division of Intelligent Information Systems of IIT of the National Centre of Scientific Research "Demokritos," Greece; Dr. Mariana Damova, Chief Executive Officer of Mozaika; and Dr. Gloria Bordogna, Senior Researcher at the Italian National Research Council IREA.

The authors acknowledge the infrastructure and support of the Ministry of Science and Technological Development of the Republic of Serbia.

D. Graux acknowledges the support of the ADAPT SFI Centre for Digital Media Technology funded by Science Foundation Ireland through the SFI Research Centres Programme and co-funded under the European Regional Development Fund (ERDF) through grant # 13/RC/2106.

E. Sallinger acknowledges the support of the Vienna Science and Technology (WWTF) grant VRG18-013 and the EPSRC program grant EP/M025268/1.

Acronyms and Definitions

ABD	After Big Data
AI	Artificial Intelligence
BBD	Before Big Data
BDA	Big Data Analytics
CC	Cloud Computing
COMET	COntextualized MoleculE-based matching Technique
DBMS	Database Management System
DL	Deep Learning
DM	Data Mining
EB	Exabyte
HDFS	Hadoop Distributed File System
IEEE	Institute of Electrical and Electronics Engineer
IoT	Internet of Things
ISA	Interoperability Solutions for European Public Administration
ISO	International Organization for Standardization
IT	Information Technology
KG	Knowledge Graph
LAMBDA	Learning, Applying, Multiplying Big Data Analytics
MB	Megabyte
ML	Machine Learning
NILM	Non-Intrusive Load Monitoring
NIST	National Institute of Standards and Technology
NoSQL	Not only SQL
OASIS	Organization for the Advancement of Structured Information Standards
OGC	Open Geospatial Consortium
PB	Petabyte
QPS	Queries Per Second
RDBMS	Relational Database Management System
RDF	Resource Description Framework
SANSA	Scalable Semantic Analytics Stack
SG	Smart Grid
SQL	Structured Query Language
TB	Terabyte
W3C	World Wide Web Consortium

Contents

Foundations

Chapter 1
Ecosystem of Big Data

Valentina Janev$^{(\boxtimes)}$ (iD)

Institute Mihajlo Pupin, University of Belgrade, Belgrade, Serbia
valentina.janev@institutepupin.com

Abstract. The rapid development of digital technologies, IoT products and connectivity platforms, social networking applications, video, audio and geolocation services has created opportunities for collecting/accumulating a large amount of data. While in the past corporations used to deal with static, centrally stored data collected from various sources, with the birth of the web and cloud services, cloud computing is rapidly overtaking the traditional in-house system as a reliable, scalable and cost-effective IT solution. The high volumes of structures and unstructured data, stored in a distributed manner, and the wide variety of data sources pose problems related to data/knowledge representation and integration, data querying, business analysis and knowledge discovery. This introductory chapter serves to characterize the relevant aspects of the Big Data Ecosystem with respect to big data characteristics, the components needed for implementing end-to-end big data processing and the need for using semantics for improving the data management, integration, processing, and analytical tasks.

1 Introduction

In 2001, in an attempt to characterize and visualize the changes that are likely to emerge in the future, Douglas Laney [271] of META Group (Gartner now) proposed three dimensions that characterize the challenges and opportunities of increasingly large data: Volume, Velocity, and Variety, known as the *3 Vs of big data*. Thus, according to Gartner

"Big data" is high-volume, velocity, and variety information assets that demand cost-effective, innovative forms of information processing for enhanced insight and decision making.

According to Manyika et al. [297] this definition is intentionally subjective and incorporates a moving definition of how big a dataset needs to be in order to be considered big data. Along this lines, big data to Amazon or Google (see Table 1) is quite different from big data to a medium-sized insurance or telecommunications organization. Hence, many different definitions have emerged over time (see Chap. 3), but in general, it refers to "datasets whose size is beyond the ability of typical database software tools to capture, store, manage, and analyze"

V. Janev et al. (Eds.): Knowledge Graphs and Big Data Processing, LNCS 12072, pp. 3–19, 2020.
https://doi.org/10.1007/978-3-030-53199-7_1

[297] and technologies that address "data management challenges" and process and analyze data to uncover valuable information that can benefit businesses and organizations. Additional "Vs" of data have been added over the years, but Volume, Velocity and Variety are the tree main dimensions that characterize the data.

The volume dimension refers to the largeness of the data. The data size in a big data ecosystem can range from dozens of terabytes to a few zettabytes and is still growing [484]. In 2010, the McKinsey Global Institute estimated that enterprises globally stored more than 7 exabytes of new data on disk drives, while consumers stored more than 6 exabytes of new data on devices such as PCs and notebooks. While more than 800,000 Petabytes (1 PB $= 10^{15}$ bytes) of data were stored in the year 2000, according to International Data Corporation expectations [346] this volume will exceed 175 zettabytes (1 PB $= 10^{21}$ bytes) by 2025 [85].

The velocity dimension refers to the increasing speed at which big data is created and the increasing speed at which the data need to be stored and analysed, while the variety dimension refers to increased diversity of data types.

Variety introduces additional complexity to data processing as more kinds of data need to be processed, combined and stored. While the 3 Vs have been continuously used to describe big data, the additional dimensions of veracity and value have been added to describe data integrity and quality, in what is called the *5 Vs of big data*. More Vs have been introduced, including validity, vulnerability, volatility, and visualization, which sums up to the *10 Vs of big data* [138] (see Table 1). Regardless of how many descriptors are isolated when describing the nature of big data, it is abundantly clear that the nature of big data is highly complex and that it, as such, requires special technical solutions for every step in the data workflow.

2   Big Data Ecosystem

The term **Ecosystem** is defined in scientific literature as a complex network or interconnected systems (see Table 2). While in the past corporations used to deal with static, centrally stored data collected from various sources, with the birth of the web and cloud services, cloud computing is rapidly overtaking the traditional in-house system as a reliable, scalable and cost-effective IT solution. Thus, large datasets – log files, social media sentiments, click-streams – are no longer expected to reside within a central server or within a fixed place in the cloud. To handle the copious amounts of data, advanced analytical tools are needed which can process and store billions of bytes of real-time data, with hundreds of thousands of transactions per second. Hence, the goal of this book is to introduce definitions, methods, tools, frameworks and solutions for big data processing starting from the process of information extraction, via knowledge processing and knowledge representation to storing and visualization, sense-making, and practical applications.

Table 1. Big data characteristics

3 Vs	Volume	Vast amount of data that has to be captured, stored, processed and displayed
	Velocity	Rate at which the data is being generated, or analyzed
	Variety	Differences in data structure (format) or differences in data sources themselves (text, images, voice, geospacial data)
5 Vs	Veracity	Truthfulness (uncertainty) of data, authenticity, provenance, accountability
	Validity	Suitability of the selected dataset for a given application, accuracy and correctness of the data for its intended use
7 Vs	Volatility	Temporal validity and fluency of the data, data currency and availability, and ensures rapid retrieval of information as required
	Value	Usefulness and relevance of the extracted data in making decisions and capacity in turning information into action
10 Vs	Visualization	Data representation and understandability of methods (data clustering or using tree maps, sunbursts, parallel coordinates, circular network diagrams, or cone trees)
	Vulnerability	Security and privacy concerns associated with data processing
	Variability	the changing meaning of data, inconsistencies in the data, biases, ambiguities, and noise in data

3 Components of the Big Data Ecosystem

In order to depict the information processing flow in just a few phases, in Fig. 1, from left to right, we have divided the processing workflow into three layers:

- Data sources;
- Data management (integration, storage and processing);
- Data analytics, Business intelligence (BI) and knowledge discovery (KD).

Table 2. Examples of big data ecosystems

Facebook	Facebook (2018) has more than two billion users on **millions of servers**, running thousands of **configuration changes** every day involving trillions of configuration checks [310]
LinkedIn	It takes a lot of horsepower to support LinkedIn's 467 million members worldwide (in 2017), especially when you consider that each member is getting a **personalized experience** and a **web page** that includes only their contacts. Supporting the load are some 100,000 servers spread across **multiple data centers** [215]
Alibaba	The 402,000 **web-facing computers** that Alibaba hosts (2017) from China-allocated IP addresses would alone be sufficient to make Alibaba the second largest **hosting company** in the world today [321]
Google	There's no official data on how many servers there are in Google's data centers, but Gartner estimated in a July 2016 report that Google at the time had 2.5 **million servers**. Google data centers process an average of 40 million searches per second, resulting in 3.5 billion searches per day and 1.2 **trillion searches per year**, Internet Live Stats reports [390]
Amazon	... an estimate of 87 AWS datacenters in total and a range of somewhere between 2.8 and 5.6 million servers in Amazon's **cloud** (2014) [301]
Twitter	Twitter (2013) now has 150M worldwide **active users**, handles 300K queries per second (QPS) to generate timelines, and a firehose that churns out 22 MB/s. Some 400 million tweets a day flow through the system and it can take up to 5 min for a tweet to flow from Lady Gaga's fingers to her 31 million followers [197]

Such partition will allow the authors of this book to discuss big data topics from different perspectives. For computer scientists and engineers, big data poses problems of data storage and management, communication, and computation. For data scientists and statisticians responsible for machine learning models development, the issues are how to get usable information out of datasets that are too huge and complex for many traditional or classical methods to handle. From an organizational viewpoint, business analysts are expected to select and deploy analytics services and solutions that contribute mostly to the organizational strategic goals, for instance, taking into consideration a framework for measuring the organizational performance.

Data Sources. In a modern data ecosystem, the data sources layer is composed of both private and public data sources – see the left side of Fig. 2. The corporate data originates from internal systems, cloud-based systems, as well as external data provided from partners and third parties. Within a modern data architecture, any type of data can be acquired and stored; however, the most challenging task is to capture the heterogeneous datasets from various service providers. In order to allow developers to create new applications on top of open datasets (see examples below), machine-readable formats are needed. As such, XML and JSON have quickly become the de facto format for the web and mobile applications due to their ease of integration into browser technologies and server technologies that support Javascript. Once the data has been acquired, the interlinking of diverse data sources is quite a complex and challenging process, especially for the acquired unstructured data. That is the reason why semantic technologies and Linked Data principles [51] have become popular over the last decade [222]. Using Linked Data principles and a set of agreed vocabularies for a domain, the input data is modeled in the form of resources, while the existing relationships are modeled as a set of (named) relationships between resources. In order to represent the knowledge of a specific domain, conceptual schemas are applied (also called ontologies). Automatic procedures are used to map the data to the target ontology, while standard languages are used to represent the mappings (see Chap. 4). Furthermore, in order to unify the knowledge representation and data processing, standardized hierarchical and multilingual schemas are used called taxonomies. Over the last decade, thousands of data repositories emerged on the web [48] that companies can use to improve their products and/or processes. The public data sources (statistics, trends, conversations, images, videos, audios, and podcasts for instance from Google Trends, Twitter, Instagram, and others [299]) provide real-time information and on-demand insights that enable businesses to analyse user interactions, draw patterns and conclusions. IoT devices have also created significant challenges in many industries and enabled the development of new business models. However, one of the main challenges associated with these repositories is automatically understanding the underlying structures and patterns of the data. Such an understanding is a prerequisite to the application of advanced analytics to the retrieved data [143]. Examples of Open Data Sources from different domains are:

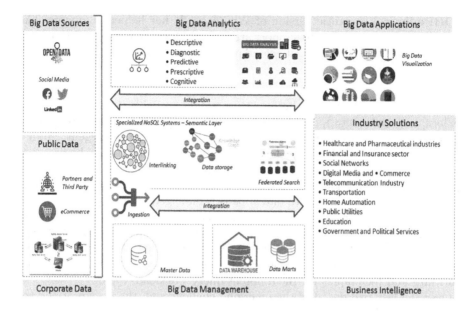

Fig. 1. From data to applications

- **Facebook** Graph API, curated by Facebook, is the primary way for apps to read and write to the Facebook social graph. It is essentially a representation of all information on Facebook now and in the past. For more info see here[1].
- **Open Corporates** is one of the largest open databases of companies in the world and holds hundreds of millions of datasets in essentially any country. For more info, see here[2].
- **Global Financial Data**'s API is recommended for analysts who require large amounts of data for broad research needs. It enables researchers to study the interaction between different data series, sectors, and genres of data. The API supports R and Python so that the data can be directly uploaded to the target application. For more info, see here[3].
- **Open Street Map** is a map of the world, created by people free to use under an open license. It powers map data on thousands of websites, mobile apps, and hardware devices. For more info, see here[4].
- **The National Centers for Environmental Information** (NCEI) is responsible for hosting and providing access to one of the most significant archives on Earth, with comprehensive oceanic, atmospheric, and geophysical data. For more info about the data access, see here[5].

---

[1] https://developers.facebook.com/docs/graph-api.
[2] https://opencorporates.com/.
[3] https://www.globalfinancialdata.com/.
[4] https://www.openstreetmap.org/.
[5] https://www.ncdc.noaa.gov/data-access.

- **DBPedia** is a semantic version of Wikipedia. It has helped companies like Apple, Google, and IBM to support artificial intelligence projects. DBpedia is in the center of the Linked Data cloud presented in Fig. 2, top-right quadrant[6]. For more info, see here[7].

Data Management. As data become increasingly available (from social media, web logs, IoT sensors etc.), the challenge of managing (selecting, combining, storing) and analyzing large and growing data sets is growing more urgent. From a data analytics point of view, that means that data processing has to be designed taking into consideration the diversity and scalability requirements of targeted data analytics applications. In modern settings, data acquisition via near real-time data streams in addition to batch loads is managed by different automated processes (see Fig. 2, top-left quadrant presents an example of monitoring and control of electric power facilities with the Supervisory, Control and Data Acquisition Systems[8] developed by the Mihajlo Pupin Institute. The novel architecture [471] is 'flexible enough to support different service levels as well as optimal algorithms and techniques for the different query workloads' [426].

Over the last two decades, the emerging challenges in the design of end-to-end data processing pipelines were addressed by computer scientists and software providers in the following ways:

- In addition to operational database management systems (present on the market since 1970s), different **NoSQL stores** appeared that lack adherence to the time-honored SQL principles of ACID (atomicity, consistency, isolation, durability), see Table 3.
- **Cloud computing** emerged as a paradigm that focuses on sharing data and computations over a scalable network of nodes including end user computers, data centers (see Fig. 2, bottom-left quadrant), and web services [23].
- The **Data Lake** concept as a new storage architecture was promoted where raw data can be stored regardless of source, structure and (usually) size. The *data warehousing* approach (based on a repository of structured, filtered data that has already been processed for a specific purpose) is thus perceived as outdated as it creates certain issues with respect to data integration and the addition of new data sources.

The wide availability of big data also means that there are many quality issues that need to be dealt with before using such data. For instance, data inherently contains a lot of noise and uncertainty or is compromised because of sensor malfunctioning or interferences, which may result in missing or conflicting data. Therefore, quality assessment approaches and methods applicable in open big data ecosystems have been developed [481].

---

[6] www.lod-cloud.net.

[7] https://wiki.dbpedia.org/.

[8] http://www.pupin.rs/en/products-services/process-management/.

Furthermore, in order to ensure interoperability between different processes and interconnected systems, the *semantic representation* of data sources/processes was introduced where a *knowledge graph*, from one side, meaningfully describes the data pipeline, and from the other, is used to generate new knowledge (see Chap. 4).

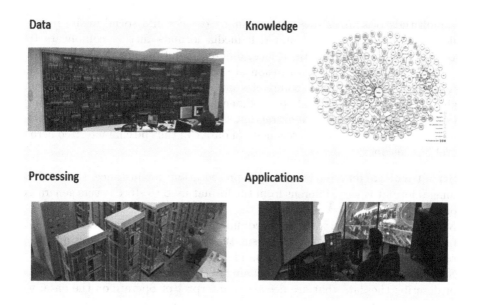

Fig. 2. Components of big data ecosystem

Data Analytics. Data analytics refers to technologies that are grounded mostly in data mining and statistical analysis [76]. The selection of an appropriate processing model and analytical solution is a challenging problem and depends on the business issues of the targeted domain [221], for instance e-commerce [416], market intelligence, e-government [220], healthcare, energy efficiency [47], emergency management [309], production management, and/or security (see Fig. 2, bottom-right quadrant, example of Simulators and training aids developed by the Mihajlo Pupin Institute). Depending on the class of problem that is being solved (e.g. risk assessment in banks and the financial sector, predictive maintenance of wind farms, sensing and cognition in production plants, automatic response in control rooms, etc.), the *data analytics* solution also relies on text/web/network/mobile analytical services. Here various machine learning techniques such as association rule mining, decision trees, regression, support vector machines, and others are used.

While simple reporting and business intelligence applications that generate aggregated measurements across different predefined dimensions based on the data-warehousing concept were enough in 1990s, since 1995 the focus has been on introducing parallelism into machine learning [435].

4   Using Semantics in Big Data Processing

Variety of Data Sources. In order to design and implement an adequate big data processing architecture, as well as volume and velocity companies also have to consider their ability to intercept the various available data sources. In addition to the existing enterprise resource management systems, data produced by a multitude of sources like sensors, smart devices and social media in raw, semi-structured, unstructured and rich media formats further complicate the processing and storage of data. Hence, different solutions for distributed storage, cloud computing, and data fusion are needed [286]. In order to make the data useful for data analysis, companies use different methods to reduce complexity, downsize the data scale (e.g. dimensional reduction, sampling, coding) and pre-process the data (data extraction, data cleaning, data integration, data transformation) [456]. The heterogeneity of data can thus be characterized across several dimensions:

– **Structural variety** refers to data representation; for instance, the satellite images format is very different from the format used to store tweets generated on the web;
– **Media variety** refers to the medium in which data gets delivered; for instance, the audio of a speech versus the transcript of the speech may represent the same information in two different media;
– **Semantic variety** refers to the meaning of the units (terms) used to measure or describe the data that are needed to interpret or operate on the data; for instance, a 'high' salary from a service in Ethiopia is very different from a 'high' salary from a similar service in the United States;
– **Availability variations** mean that the data can be accessed continuously; for instance, from traffic cameras, or intermediately, for instance, only when the satellite is over the region of interest.

Semantic Variety and the Need for Standards. Attempts to explain the uses of semantics in logic and computing date from the middle of the last century. In the information processing domain, *semantics* refers to the "meaning and meaningful use of data" [472], i.e., the effective use of a data object for representing a concept or object in the real world. Since 1980, the Artificial Intelligence community has been promoting the idea of feeding intelligent systems and agents with general, formalized knowledge of the world (see also the panel report from 1997 *Data Semantics: what, where and how?*) [398]. In 2001, Sir Tim Berners-Lee, the Director of the Wide Web Consortium, outlined his vision for the Semantic Web as an extension of the conventional Web and as a world-wide distributed architecture where data and services easily interoperate. Additionally, in 2006, Berners-Lee proposed the basic (Linked Data) principles for interlinking linking datasets on the Web through references to common concepts [51]. The standard for the representation of the information that describes the concepts is RDF (Resource Description Framework). In parallel, the wider adoption of standards for representing and querying semantic information, such as RDF(s) and SPARQL, along with increased functionalities and improved robustness of modern RDF stores, have established Linked Data and semantic technologies in the areas of data and knowledge management. As part of the EC'Interoperability Solutions for European Public Administrations' (ISA)[9] program, with cooperation with W3C, core vocabularies have been adopted to represent high-value datasets relevant for boosting innovative services.

Knowledge Engineering. Additionally, the scientific community has put a great deal of effort into showcasing how knowledge engineering [26,92,221] can take advantages from semantics-aware methods [222], which exploit knowledge kept in (big) data to better reasoning on data beyond the possibilities offered by more traditional data-instance-oriented approaches. With the announcement of the Google Knowledge Graph in 2012, representations of general world knowledge as graphs have drawn a lot of attention again [347].

To summarize, semantics principles can be used in big data processing for

- Representing (schema and schema-less) data;
- Representing metadata (about documentation, provenance, trust, accuracy, and other quality properties);
- Modeling data processes and flows, i.e., representing the entire pipeline making data representation shareable and verifiable.

The semantic representation of data in knowledge graphs (see Chap. 2), the semantic processing pipeline (see Chap. 3, Chap. 5, Chap. 8), reasoning in knowledge graphs (Chap. 6) and the semantic analysis of big data (Chap. 7) are the main topics of this book and will be explained in more detail in the subsequent chapters.

5 Big Data, Standards and Interoperability

Interoperability remains a major burden for the developers of the big data ecosystem. In its EU 2030 vision, the European Union has set out the creation of an internal single market through a standardised system of laws that apply in all member states and a single European data [85] space – a genuine single market for data where businesses have easy access to an almost infinite amount of high-quality industrial data. The vision is also supported by the EU Rolling Plan for ICT Standardisation [86] that identifies 170 actions organised around five priority domains—5G, cloud, cybersecurity, big data and Internet of Things. In order to enable broad data integration, data exchange and interoperability with the overall goal of fostering innovation based on data, standardisation at different levels (such as metadata schemata, data representation formats and licensing conditions of open data) is needed. This refers to all types of (multilingual) data, including both structured and unstructured data, and data from

---

[9] https://ec.europa.eu/isa2/.

different domains as diverse as geospatial data, statistical data, weather data, public sector information (PSI) and research data, to name just a few.

In the domain of big data, five different actions have been requested that also involve the following standardization organizations:

- CEN, the European Committee for Standardization, to support and assist the standardisation process and to coordinate with the relevant W3C groups on preventing incompatible changes and on the conditions for availability of the standard(s). The work will be in particular focused on the interoperability needs of data portals in Europe while providing semantic interoperability with other applications on the basis of reuse of established controlled vocabularies (e.g. EuroVoc) and mappings to existing metadata vocabularies (e.g. SDMX, INSPIRE metadata, Dublin Core, etc.);
- CENELEC (the European Committee for Electrotechnical Standardization) in particular in relation to personal data management and the protection of individuals' fundamental rights;
- ETSI (the European Telecommunications Standards Institute) to coordinate stakeholders and produce a detailed map of the necessary standards (e.g. for security, interoperability, data portability and reversibility) and together with CEN to work on various standardisation deliverables needed for the completion of the rationalised framework of e-signatures standards;
- IEEE has a series of new standards projects related to big data (mobile health, energy-efficient processing, personal agency and privacy) as well as pre-standardisation activities on big data and open data;
- ISO/IEC JTC1, WG 9—Big Data, formed at the November 2014 in relation to requirements, use cases, vocabulary and a reference architecture for big data;
- OASIS, in relation to querying and sharing data across disparate applications and multiple stakeholders for reuse in enterprise, cloud, and mobile devices. Specification development in the OASIS OData TC builds on the core OData Protocol V4 released in 2014 and addresses additional requirements identified as extensions in four directional white papers: data aggregation, temporal data, JSON documents, and XML documents as streams;
- OGC, the Open Geospatial Consortium defines and maintains standards for location-based, spatio-temporal data and services. The work includes, for instance, schema allowing descriptions of spatio-temporal sensors, images, simulations, and statistics data (such as "datacubes"), a modular suite of standards for Web services allowing ingestion, extraction, fusion, and (with the web coverage processing service (WCPS) component standard) analytics of massive spatio-temporal data like satellite and climate archives. OGC also contributes to the INSPIRE project;
- W3C, the W3C Semantic Web Activity Group has accepted numerous Web technologies as standards or recommendations for building semantic applications including RDF (Resource Description Framework) as a general-purpose language; RDF Schema as a meta-language or vocabulary to define properties

and classes of RDF resources; SPARQL as a standard language for querying RDF data: OWL, Web Ontology Language for effective reasoning. More about semantic standards can be found in [223].

Table 3. History of big data

Year	Description
1911	Computing-Tabulating-Recording Company was founded and renamed "International Business Machines" (**IBM**) in 1924
1929	The term "Super Computing" was first used in the New York World to refer to large custom-built tabulators that **IBM** had made for Columbia University
1937	Social security was introduced in the United States of America and the requirement arose for data management of 26 million residents
1945	John Von Neumann published a paper on the Electronic Discrete Variable Automatic Computer (EDVAC), the first "documented" discussion on program storage, and laid the foundations of computer architecture today
1957	A group of engineers established the Control Data Corporation (**CDC**) in Minneapolis, Minnesota
1960	Seymour Cray (**CDC**) completed the CDC 1604, one of the first solid-state computers, and the fastest computer in the world at a time when vacuum tubes were found in most large computers
1965	The first data center in the world was planned
1969	ARPANET set a message was sent from UCLA's host computer to Stanford's host computer
1970	Edgar Frank Codd invented the relational model for database management
1976	**SAS** Institute delivered the first version of the "Statistical Analysis System"
1977	**Oracle** Corporation was founded in Santa Clara, California, U.S
1998	**Google** was founded at the Stanford University in California
1999	**Apache** software foundation was established
1989	The invention of the World Wide Web at CERN
2003	**Google** File System was invented
2004	World Wide Web Consortium (**W3C**), the main international standards organization for the Web was founded
2005	The start of development on **Apache** Hadoop which came into production in 2008
2007	The first publicly available dataset on **DBpedia** was published by the Free University of Berlin and the Leipzig University
2009	**Yahoo** released Pig and Facebook created Hive
2011	Start of real-time processing as opposed to batch processing with **Apache** Storm and Spark
2012	Creation of Kafka by **LinkedIn**, **Google** introduced its Knowledge Graph project
2013	The definition of the Lambda architecture for efficient big data processing
2014	The definition of the Kappa architecture and the beginning of hybrid data processing

6   Big Data Analytics

6.1   The Evolution of Analytics

Over the last 50 years, **Data Analytics** has emerged as an important area of study for both practitioners and researchers. The **Analytics 1.0** era began in the 1950s and lasted roughly 50 years. As a software approach, this field evolved significantly with the invention of Relational Databases in the 1970s by Edgar

F. Codd, the development of artificial intelligence as a separate scientific discipline, and the invention of the Web by Sir Tim Berners-Lee in 1989. With the development of Web 2.0-based social and crowd-sourcing systems in the 2000s, the Analytics 2.0 era started. While the business solutions were tied to relational and multi-dimensional database models in the Analytics 1.0 era, the **Analytics 2.0** era brought NOSQL and big data database models that opened up new priorities and technical possibilities for analyzing large amounts of semi-structured and unstructured data. Companies and data scientists refer to these two periods in time as before big data (BBD) and after big data (ABD) [100]. The main limitations observed during the first era were that the potential capabilities of data were only utilised within organisations, i.e. the business intelligence activities addressed only what had happened in the past and offered no predictions about its future trends. The new generation of tools with fast-processing engines and NoSQL stores made possible the integration of internal data with externally sourced data coming from the internet, sensors of various types, public data initiatives (such as the human genome project), and captures of audio and video recordings. Also significantly developed in this period was the Data Science field (multifocal field consisting of an intersection of Mathematics & Statistics, Computer Science, and Domain Specific Knowledge), which delivered scientific methods, exploratory processes, algorithms and tools that can be easily leveraged to extract knowledge and insights from data in various forms.

The **Analytics 3.0** era started [23] with the development of the "Internet of Things" and cloud computing, which created possibilities for establishing hybrid technology environments for data storage, real-time analysis and intelligent customer-oriented services. Analytics 3.0 is also named *the Era of Impact* or *the Era of Data-enriched offerings* after the endless opportunities for capitalizing on analytics services. For creating value in the data economy, Davenport [100] suggests that the following factors need to be properly addressed:

- combining multiple types of data
- adoption of a new set of data management tools
- introduction of new "agile" analytical methods and machine-learning techniques to produce insights at a much faster rate
- embedding analytical and machine learning models into operational and decision processes
- requisite skills and processes to work with innovative discovery tools for data exploration
- requisite skills and processes to develop prescriptive models that involve large-scale testing and optimization and are a means of embedding analytics into key processes
- leveraging new approaches to decision making and management.

Nowadays, being in the **Analytics 4.0** era or *the Era of Consumer-controled data*, the goal is to enable the customers to have full or partial control over data. Also aligned with the Industry 4.0 movement, there are different possibilities for automating and augmenting human/computer communications by combining machine translation, smart reply, chat-bots, and virtual assistants.

6.2   Different Types of Data Analytics

In general, analytic problems and techniques can be classified into

- **Descriptive** - What happened?
- **Diagnostic** - Why did it happen?
- **Predictive** - What is likely to happen?
- **Prescriptive** - What should be done about it?
- **Cognitive** - What don't we know?

Descriptive analytics focus on analyzing historic data for the purpose of identifying patterns (*hindsights*) or trends. While statistical theory and descriptive methodologies [7] are well documented in scientific literature, that is not the case for other types of analytics, especially observing the big data and cloud computing context.

Diagnostic analytics [364] discloses the root causes of a problem and gives *insight*. The methods are treated as an extension to descriptive analytics that provide an explanation to the question "Why did it happen?".

Predictive analytics-based services apply forecasting and statistical modelling to give insight into "what is likely to happen" in the future (*foresight*) based on supervised, unsupervised, and semi-supervised learning models.

Prescriptive analytics-based services [281] answers the question "What should I do?". In order to provide automated, time-dependent and optimal decisions based on the provided constraints and context, the software tools utilize artificial intelligence, optimization algorithms and expert systems approaches.

Cognitive analytics is a term introduced recently in the context of cognitive computing (see also *Deloitte Tech Trends 2019*). Motivated by the capability of the human mind, and other factors such as changing technologies, smart devices, sensors, and cloud computing capabilities, the goal is to develop "AI-based services that are able to interact with humans like a fellow human, interpret the contextual meaning, analyze the past record of the user and draw deductions based on that interactive session" [174,176].

7   Challenges for Exploiting the Potential of Big Data

In order to exploit the full potential, big data professionals and researchers have to address different data and infrastructure management challenges that cannot be resolved with traditional approaches [72]. Hence, in the last decade, different techniques have emerged for acquisition, storing, processing and information derivation in the big data value chains.

In [404], the authors introduced three main categories of challenges as follows:

- **Data challenges** related to the characteristics of the data itself (e.g. data volume, variety, velocity, veracity, volatility, quality, discovery and dogmatism);
- **Process challenges** related to techniques (how to capture data, how to integrate data, how to transform data, how to select the right model for analysis and how to provide the results);

– **Management challenges** related to organizational aspects such as privacy, security, governance and ethical aspects.

Data, process and management challenges are interlinked and influence each other.

7.1 Challenges

The *3 Vs of big data* call for the integration of complex data sources (including complex types, complex structures, and complex patterns), as previously discussed. Therefore, *scalability* is considered to be a crucial bottleneck of big data solutions. Following the problem with processing, *storage* management is another unavoidable barrier regarding big data. Storing the huge quantity of data between its acquisition, processing and analysis requires gigantic memory capacity, thus rendering traditional solutions obsolete.

The inherent complexity of big data (*data complexity*) makes its perception, representation, understanding and computation far more challenging and results in sharp increases in the *computational complexity* required compared to traditional computing models based on total data. The design of system architectures, computing frameworks, processing modes, and benchmarks for highly energy-efficient big data processing platforms is the key issue to be addressed in *system complexity* [231]. Contemporary cloud-based solutions are also considered to be on the edge of feasibility since *responsiveness* can be a critical issue, especially in real-time applications, where upload speeds are considered the main bottleneck.

When simultaneously working with different data sources, the *reliability* of collected data will inevitably fluctuate with missed, partial and faulty measurements being unavoidable, resulting in serious potential trouble later on in the workflow, such as in the analytics stage. Hence, high-quality data management (i.e. data cleaning, filtering, transforming and other) actions are mandatory at the beginning of the process. Besides reliability, the *correctness* of the data is considered to be a key aspect of big data processing. High volumes, unstructured forms, the distributed nature of data in NoSQL data management systems and the necessity of near-to-real-time responses often lead to corrupted results with no method being able to guarantee their complete *validity*.

Other *quality* dimensions, that impact the design of a big data solution are *completeness, consistency, credibility, timeliness* and others.

For instance, in real-time applications (e.g. stock market, financial fraud detection and transactions parsing, traffic management, energy optimization etc.), quick responses are required and expected immediately because the retrieved information can be completely useless if it is derived with high latency with respect to the collected data.

An additional challenge from the human-computer perspective is the *visualization* of results. Although various ways in which the data can be displayed do not affect the data processing segment in any way, visualization is stated in the literature as a crucial factor because without adequate representation of the results, the derived knowledge is useless.

Depending on the type of data being processed, *security* can sometimes be a crucial component that requires special attention. When considering, for example, a weather forecast or public transport management use case, if a data loss or theft occurs, it can be considered practically irrelevant compared to a situation where personal information, names, addresses, location history, social security information or credit card PIN codes are stolen because in the latter case, data protection must be upheld at the highest possible standard.

7.2 Example: Analysis of Challenges and Solutions for Traffic Management

Smart transportation is one of the key big data vertical applications, and refers to the integrated application of modern technologies and management strategies in transportation systems. Big data platforms available on the market contribute to a great extent to smart management of cities and the implementation of intelligent transportation systems. In order to showcase the usage of different type of data analytics and to strengthen the discussion on challenges, we will point to the traffic management system used for monitoring highways in Serbia [366]. Highways and motorways control systems generate a high volume of data that is relevant for a number of stakeholder's from traffic and environmental departments to transport providers, citizens and the police. The Fig. 3 below points to (a) the European corridors, and (b) the Corridor 10 that is managed in Serbia by the public enterprise "Roads of Serbia" using a control system provided by Institute Mihajlo Pupin. Its holistic supervisory function and control includes (a) toll collection and motorway and highway traffic control, and (b) urban traffic control and management. The main challenges on EU level are related to:

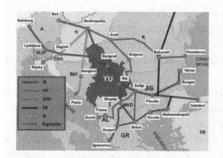

Fig. 3. Traffic management

- **Interoperability** of tolling services on the entire European Union road network because the ones introduced at local and national levels from the early 1990s onwards are still generally non-interoperable;
- **Smart mobility** and the need of users to be more informed about different options in real-time;
- the need for efficient and effective approaches for **assessment and management of air pollution** due to improved ambient air quality.

The main components of the traffic control system are:

- The toll **collection system**[10], which is hierarchically structured; it is fully modular, based on PC technology and up-to date real time operation systems, relational data base system and dedicated encryption of data transmission. Toll line controllers are based on industrial PC-technology and dedicated electronic interface boards. The toll plaza subsystem is the supervisory system for all line controllers. It collects all the data from lane controllers including financial transactions, digital images of vehicles, technical malfunctions, line operators' actions and failures. All data concerning toll collection processes and equipment status are permanently collected from the plaza computers and stored in a central system database. The toll collection system also comprises features concerning vehicle detection and classification, license plate recognition and microwave-based dedicated short-range communications.
- The Main **Control Centre** is connected through an optical communication link with the Plaza Control Centres. Also, the Control Centre is constantly exchanging data with various institutions such as: banks, insurance companies, institutions that handle credit and debit cards, RF tags vendors, etc. through a computer network. **Data analytics** is based on data warehouse architecture enabling optimal performances in near real time for statistical and historical analysis of large data volumes. Reporting is based on optimized data structures, allowing both predefined (standardized) reports as well as ad hoc (dynamic) reports, which are generated efficiently using the Oracle BI platform. Data analytics includes scenarios, such as
  - **Predicting and preventing road traffic congestion** analytics is used to improve congestion diagnosis and to enable traffic managers to proactively manage traffic and to organize the activities at toll collection stations before congestion is reached.
  - **Strategic environmental impact assessment** analytics is used to study the environmental impact and the effect of highways on adjacent flora, fauna, air, soil, water, humans, landscape, cultural heritage, etc. based on historical and real-time analysis. Passive pollution monitoring involves collecting data about the diffusion of air pollutants, e.g. emission estimates based on traffic counting. Passive pollution monitoring has been used to determine trends in long-term pollution levels. Road traffic pollution monitoring and visualization requires the integration of high volumes of (historical) traffic data with other parameters such as vehicle

---

[10] http://www.pupin.rs/en/products-services/traffic-control-systems/pay-toll/.

emission factors, background pollution data, meteorology data, and road topography.

Here, we have pointed to just one mode of transport and traffic management, i.e. the control of highways and motorways. However, nowadays, an increasing number of cities around the world struggle with traffic congestion, optimizing public transport, planning parking spaces, and planning cycling routes. These issues call for new approaches for studying human mobility by exploiting machine learning techniques [406], forecasting models or through the application of complex event processing tools [135].

8   Conclusions

This chapter presents the author's vision of a *Big data ecosystem*. It serves as an introductory chapter to point to a number of aspects that are relevant for this book. Over the last two decades, advances in hardware and software technologies, such as the Internet of Things, mobile technologies, data storage and cloud computing, and parallel machine learning algorithms have resulted in the ability to easily acquire, analyze and store large amounts of data from different kinds of quantitative and qualitative domain-specific data sources. The monitored and collected data presents opportunities and challenges that, as well as focusing on the three main characteristics of volume, variety, and velocity, require research of other characteristics such as validity, value and vulnerability. In order to automate and speed up the processing, interoperable data infrastructure is needed and standardization of data-related technologies, including developing metadata standards for big data management. One approach to achieve interoperability among datasets and services is to adopt data vocabularies and standards as defined in the W3C Data on the Web Best Practices, which are also applied in the tools presented in this book (see Chaps. 4, 5, 6, 7, 8 and 9).

In order to elaborate the challenges and point to the potential of big data, a case study from the traffic sector is presented and discussed in this chapter, while more big data case studies are set out in Chap. 9 and Chap. 10.

Chapter 2
Knowledge Graphs: The Layered Perspective

Luigi Bellomarini[1], Emanuel Sallinger[2,3]([✉]) [ID], and Sahar Vahdati[3] [ID]

[1] Banca d'Italia, Rome, Italy
[2] TU Wien, Vienna, Austria
sallinger@dbai.tuwien.ac.at
[3] University of Oxford, Oxford, UK

Abstract. Knowledge Graphs (KGs) are one of the key trends among the next wave of technologies. Many definitions exist of what a Knowledge Graph is, and in this chapter, we are going to take the position that precisely in the multitude of definitions lies one of the strengths of the area. We will choose a particular perspective, which we will call the layered perspective, and three views on Knowledge Graphs.

1 Introduction

Knowledge Graphs (KGs) are one of the key trends among the next wave of technologies [340]. Despite the highlighted role in practice as well as research, and the variety of definitions of the notion, there is still no common understanding of what a Knowledge Graph *is*. In this introduction, we are *not* going to choose one definition of Knowledge Graphs. Many great introductions exist to particular definitions, and we will refer to some of them in this chapter. Instead, we are going to take the position that precisely in the *multitude of definitions* lies one of the *strengths* of the area.

At the same time, our aim is not towards a fully exhaustive, historical account of the evolution of Knowledge Graphs both regarding the term and the concept. Again, excellent historical and exhaustive accounts already exist, and we will refer to some of them in this chapter. Instead, we will choose a particular perspective, which we will call the *layered perspective*, and *three views* on Knowledge Graphs.

Views on Knowledge Graphs. While many ways of classifying types of Knowledge Graphs used in literature are possible, here we concentrate on the following three views:

- **knowledge representation tools:** where the focus is on how a Knowledge Graph is used to represent some form of knowledge.
- **knowledge management systems:** where the focus is the system managing the Knowledge Graph, similar to how database management systems play this role for databases.

V. Janev et al. (Eds.): Knowledge Graphs and Big Data Processing, LNCS 12072, pp. 20–34, 2020.
https://doi.org/10.1007/978-3-030-53199-7_2

– **knowledge application services:** where the focus is on providing a layer
of applications on top of a Knowledge Graph.

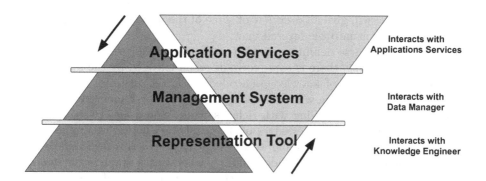

Fig. 1. Ordered pyramids of views on KGs.

The Layered Perspective. While these three views certainly have independent
value, they are most interesting when put *together as layers*: on the first layer
is the **representation** of knowledge, on the middle layer is the **management**
system for this knowledge, and on the top layer the **application** that it solves.
This is illustrated in Fig. 1. There are three additional factors at play here:

– There are generally two ways of looking at the order of these layers. Some
  communities tend to see it **top-down** with the *application* that the KG solves
  as the focus, others tend to see it as **bottom-up**, with the *representation* of
  knowledge as the focus. Interestingly, there is even another one, as the data
  management community often sees the *management* system in the middle as
  the focus.
– The **borders** between these layers are fuzzy. Many academic and industrial
  systems cover two or three of these layers. In some cases, representation tools
  partly fulfill some of the characteristics of management systems. The same
  applies for application platforms.
– The central aspect of **reasoning** poses vastly different requirements to the
  three layers. Chapter 6 will be fully dedicated to this aspect.

Of course, it is clear that to achieve a great overall system, all layers and their
interactions have to be taken into account; it is hardly possibly to provide a good
knowledge application platform if the knowledge representation layer is not fit
for the purpose.

Organization. The first three sections cover the three views we introduce above.
In Sect. 2, we consider the view of KGs as knowledge representations tools; in
Sect. 3, we consider the view of KGs a knowledge management systems; and in
Sect. 4, we consider the view of KGs as knowledge application platforms. We will
conclude with a section on challenges and opportunities.

2   KGs as Knowledge Representation Tools

One of the most common views on Knowledge Graphs, which covers most of the given definitions, is to primarily view them as knowledge representation tools. In this section, we will give an overview of some of the notions with a particular focus on how they fit into the layered view.

Common to all these definitions is that, somewhat unsurprisingly given the term *Knowledge Graph*, there is *some* form of graph encoded by the formalism, and there is *some* form of knowledge encoded in it. Yet, in terms of **graphs**, what they widely differ is in whether a simple graph is the primary structure or whether we are actually dealing with richer settings where e.g., the graph has attributes associated to nodes or edges of the graph, or whether we are actually dealing with a hyper-graph (similar to full relational structures). Similarly, in terms of **knowledge**, what they widely differ is whether the graph *is* the knowledge, or the knowledge actually *generates* the entirety or parts of the graph. In some of the particular communities of computer science, Knowledge Graphs are explicitly considered as collections of facts about entities, typically derived from structured data sources such as Babelnet, OpenCyc, DBpedia, Yago, Wikidata, NELL and their shared features FreeBase [377]. In this way, a collection of facts represented in different languages but in the same structure is called a KG.

Critically though, forming a bridge to what we discussed in the introduction, in many cases these differences are only at the surface, and are often a question of representation, rather than fundamental. For example, it is clear that an arbitrary relational structure – or, in fact, an arbitrary data structure – can be encoded as a graph, and vice versa. Similarly, it is in many cases not a fundamental difference whether technically knowledge is encoded into the graph, into a separate knowledge representation language, or provided via other AI and ML frameworks. Still, fundamental differences do remain between different notions of Knowledge Graphs, and as we mentioned in the beginning, it is our position that these multifaceted definitions are one of the strengths of the field. In this section, we will explore such different definitions of Knowledge Graphs, highlighting both their commonalities and differences.

Views on KGs as Representation Tools for Data. The following definitions are pointing to the data structure in the representation. They mostly take a graph representation as a baseline and provide different explanations of how the graph structure helps with mapping real world information.

A Mathematical Structure. This is often considered to be the first recorded appearance [399] of the term "knowledge graph" – though not necessarily the concept of "knowledge graph". Here, capturing knowledge from the real world as a teaching-leaning process is considered a way of building a graph of knowledge. In this work, prerequisites of learning are a necessary set of knowledge units that should usually be taught to the learner (human or machine) before. In this paper, a knowledge graph is essentially defined as:

A mathematical structure with vertices as knowledge units connected by edges that represent the prerequisite relation. – Marchi and Miquel, 1974 [298]

Although this definition has been given in the context of interactive learning between students and teachers, the concept can very well be adjusted for current machine learning and machine teaching [488] approaches where Knowledge Graphs are considered as the base of intelligence. In this definition, the degree of abstraction is hidden in the mathematical representation of knowledge in nodes as knowledge units and edges as connectors. Obviously, a specific language or data structure is not discussed due to its different context – so in our layer of *knowledge representation tools*, it is certainly a very abstract form of representation. It is roughly mentioned that knowledge units of a course for students to learn are represented as nodes of a graph in a game-theoretic way. And the links between the modes connect the knowledge units where the students can follow learning paths. In this way, the idea of representing common knowledge in a graph-based structure works in a similar way between this definition and today's KGs. Similar to this view is also represented quite at the same time [387] where the teacher or the student can be replaced by a computer. It is argued that the directed graph in which the knowledge is represented in nodes and labeled links can influence the learning process for data analysis purposes.

A Set of Justified True Beliefs. In a tutorial by Microsoft, Yuqing Gao [146] follows Plato's tripartite definition of knowledge as a subset of "Justified true beliefs" such that knowledge contains a truth condition, a belief condition and an inference of the former two that leads to justification of that. As example of such a "Justified true belief" is: *A is True. B knows A. B is justified in knowing A.* Knowledge in KGs is represented as triples of *(Subject, Predicate, Object)*, where Subject and Object are pointing to entities and Predicate represents the relation. A graph constructed from such triples contains nodes and edges where the nodes are pointing to entities as subject and object and the edges are for relations as predicates. There is extra information such as the metadata of each entity, which are shown as attributes. Following this, a set of key concepts for Knowledge Graphs as knowledge representation tools are introduced as:

- **Entity:** as real world entities
- **Edge:** relations of entities in a schema
- **Attribute:** metadata about an entity
- **Ontology:** definition of possible entities, relations and attributes
– Yuqing Gao, 2018 [146]

In this definition, two components of attribute and ontology are the concepts considered extra than other graph-based views. In fact, considering these components for knowledge representations adds on the characteristics of KGs. Entities and relations usually capture information stored in a Knowledge Base (KB).

An Unambiguous Graph. As seen before, most of the attempts in defining Knowledge Graphs have a focus on defining KGs as representing knowledge in a graph structure. Therefore, the KGs are often represented by the main components of a graph, namely nodes and edges. This graph is often considered as a directed and labeled graph, without which the structure of the graph cannot encode any significant meaning. When the nodes and edges are unambiguously unidentifiable, the graph is considered to be an unambiguous graph. With this foundation, a Knowledge Graph can be defined as:

> "An Unambiguous Graph with a limited set of relations used to label the edges that encodes the provenance, especially justification and attribution, of the assertions." – McCusker et al., 2018 [304]

This definition tried to go beyond representing KGs only as nodes and relations. In order to fulfills this definition, all the knowledge units of a KG including relations and nodes should be globally identifiable. In addition, the meaning of limited set of relations is followed from [440] meaning a core set of essential classes and relations that are true regardless of context. This level of abstraction is similar to data representation in triple format with unique resource identifiers.

World Knowledge Graphs and Metadata. At a basic level of observation, data represents elements as raw values collected from real-world domains of knowledge. Metadata represent information about the underlying data in a second abstract level. In order to represent knowledge from real world:

1. the real world objects need to be observed at least once and represented as data,
2. previous representation of such data is required to be captured as metadata and
3. all of these meta-level definitions on top of the abstractions of the objects of prime interest need to be connected.

At the formal and technical level, a formal and mathematical data structure, degree of abstraction, and a syntactic and semantic language are needed. Thus, characteristics of Knowledge Graphs lead the majority of the community to see and define them as tools for representing world knowledge in a graph model, where entities are represented as nodes and relations among entities are represented as directional edges. More formally, let $\mathcal{E} = \{e_1, \cdots, e_{N_e}\}$ be the set of entities, $\mathcal{R} = \{r_1, \cdots, r_{N_r}\}$ be the set of relations connecting two entities, $\mathcal{D} = \{d_1, \cdots, d_{N_d}\}$ be the set of relations connecting an entity and a literal, i.e., the data relations, and $\mathcal{L}$ be the set of all literal values. Then:

> "a knowledge graph $\mathcal{KG}$ is a subset of $(\mathcal{E} \times \mathcal{R} \times \mathcal{E}) \cup (\mathcal{E} \times \mathcal{D} \times \mathcal{L})$ representing the facts that are assumed to hold." – Wang et al., 2014 [462].

However, there are different attempts in defining the concept of KGs that we will present in the following parts of this section.

Views on KGs as a Representation Tool for Knowledge. The following definitions are pointing to a view where the structure of the graph representation is not the only advantage but also includes ontological aspects of knowledge.

The actual knowledge lies in the power of ontologies represented in the graph alongside the data level. In this way, the representation is enriched to handle the complexity of real world (not yet complete in coverage) and to empower learning, reasoning and inference abilities.

A Particular Kind of Semantic Network. The more intensive use of the term Knowledge Graphs starts from the early 1980s where the concept of Semantic Networks was introduced [13, 410, 482]. Later it was continued as a project by two universities from the Netherlands named Knowledge Graph [333, 449]. Following the definition of semantic networks as a specific structure of representing knowledge by labelled nodes and links between these nodes, KGs are defined as follows:

> A knowledge graph is a kind of semantic network representing some scientific theory. – Popping, 2003 [357]

In this view, representation of explicit knowledge is considered by way of its formulation (logical or structured) [372]. While knowledge can be represented in multi modals such as text, image etc., this definition is applicable only on text extraction and analysis. Semantic networks are a way of structural formalism used for knowledge representation in nodes and edges. Such networks are mainly used in expert systems with a rule base language, a knowledge base sitting in the background, and an inference engine. Knowledge represented and reasoned by semantic networks are called author graphs with points as concept units representing meaning and labeled links between concepts. One essential difference between other views on Knowledge Graphs (in a broader sense) and the one derived from semantic networks is the explicit choice of only a few types of relations [219, 440].

Representation of Human Knowledge. Although many of the definitions for Knowledge Graph represent the concept as an formation representing tool, some views see KGs as a lingua franca of humans and machines. KGs contain information that is consumable by AI approaches in order to provide applications such as semantic search, question answering, entity resolution, and representation learning.

> "A graph-theoretic representation of human knowledge such that it can be ingested with semantics by a machine; a set of triples, with each triple intuitively representing an assertion." – Kejriwal, 2019 [237]

Knowledge Represented with a Multi-relational Graph. A large volume of human knowledge can be represented with a multi-relational graph. Binary relationships encode facts that can be represented in the form of RDF-type triples (head; predicate; tail), where head and tail are entities and predicate is the relation type. The combination of all triples forms a multi-relational graph, where nodes represent entities and directed edges represent relationships. The resulting multi-relational graph is often referred to as a Knowledge Graph. Knowledge

Graphs (KGs) provide ways to efficiently organize, manage and retrieve this type of information, and are increasingly used as an external source of knowledge for problems like recommender systems, language modeling [2], question answering or image classification.

One critical point to emphasize is that while many of the KGs we see today contain as their *knowledge* mostly simple ground *data*, more and more applications need an *actionable knowledge* representation. To a certain extent, this is already the case of existing Knowledge Base Management Systems, backed by ontologies for which reasoning tasks are of different computational complexity and expressive power. The importance of supporting implicit knowledge becomes central for KGs as well, especially when they are a component of an Enterprise AI applications, to the point that intensional knowledge should be considered part of the KG itself. Consequently, reasoning, i.e., turning intensional into derived ground knowledge, becomes inherently part of the KG definition.

For example, in a financial Enterprise AI application, the body of regulatory knowledge and the functioning rules of the specific financial domain are of the essence. As another example, in a logistics setting, the knowledge of how particular steps in a supply chain interact is often more important than the pure data underlying the supply chain. Many more such examples could be given.

In total, it is clear that in modern KG-based systems a rich knowledge representation must be considered and properly handled in order to balance the increased complexity with many other relevant properties including usability, scalability, performance, and soundness of the KG application. We conclude with a relatively structured, concrete definition accounting for these aspects:

> "A semi-structured datamodel characterized by three components: (i) a ground extensional component, that is, a set of relational constructs for schema and data (which can be effectively modeled as graphs or generalizations thereof); (ii) an intensional component, that is, a set of inference rules over the constructs of the ground extensional component; (iii) a derived extensional component that can be produced as the result of the application of the inference rules over the ground extensional component (with the so-called "reasoning" process)." – Bellomarini et al., 2019 – [40].

Here we focus on the knowledge representation aspects covered in this view and in further layers we will discuss how this definition also sees KGs as management systems and application platforms.

3   KGs as Knowledge Management Systems

In this section, we present the view of Knowledge Graphs as knowledge management systems. The clear analogy to see here is what a database management system is for databases: A system to create, manipulate and retrieve data. What this adds to the previous section's view of KGs as knowledge representation tools is the *service* that a KG as a knowledge management system has to offer. In particular, it has to provide support for the user to (i) add knowledge to a KG (ii) derive new knowledge using existing knowledge, and (iii) retrieve data through a form of general-purpose query language. In both (ii) and (iii), the aspect of *reasoning* with and about knowledge becomes essential, which we will discuss in detail in Chap. 6.

A Network of All Kinds of Things. One of the early attempts after the appearance KGs in 2012, was a work clarifying the meaning of taxonomy, thesaurus, ontology and Knowledge Graph [54]. These concepts have been used by scholars mostly without specific borderlines. In some cases, they even utilized interchangeably. Starting from the Simple Knowledge Organization System (SKOS) as a standard for building an abstract model, taxonomies are introduced as controlled vocabularies to classify concepts and thesauri to express associations and relations between concepts and their labels including synonyms. Ontologies are considered as complex and more detailed versions of those domain conceptualizations when the dependencies between concepts and relations get more specific. There are also rules and constraints defined for representing knowledge which refer to ontologies as explicit and systematic specification of conceptualization for any kind of existence. By this, in building an abstract model of the world or a domain, the meaning of all concepts must be formally defined that can be interpreted correctly by machines. There must also be consensus about the definition of the concepts such as the meaning in transferred correctly. In AI-based approaches, the existence of things is defined when they can be represented [172]. Following these concepts, finally Knowledge Graphs are introduced as enriched models around the aforementioned concepts more precisely:

> "Knowledge Graphs could be envisaged as a network of all kinds of things which are relevant to a specific domain or to an organization. They are not limited to abstract concepts and relations but can also contain instances of things like documents and datasets." – Blumauer, 2014 [54].

The motivation behind having KGs is expressed in posing complex queries over a broader set of integrated information from different source for knowledge discovery, and in-depth analyses. Knowledge Graphs being the networks of all kinds of information, the industry-scale of such integration, together with the inclusion of Taxonomy, Thesaurus and Ontology is seen as Enterprise Knowledge Graphs (EKGs). Since this definition is mostly using semantic web technologies, the specific querying language that suits this definition is suggested to be SPARQL, and Resource Description Framework (RDF) is used as the data and ontology representation model.

A Graph-based Representation of Knowledge. In a similar way, Knowledge Graphs are considered to be any kind of graph-based representations of general information from the world [348]. This includes consideration of other graph-based data models such as the RDF standard pushed by Semantic Web or any knowledge representation languages such as description logic (DL). A simple triple of such a graph representation could be seen as two nodes representing entities which are connected by a relation. There are also predefined structural relations such as *is a* relation which denotes the type of entities, or relations denoting class hierarchies. As discussed before, such relations are usually represented as ontologies. In a universally unified level, this allows interlinking of different datasets, which leads to big data in graph representations, or so called Knowledge Graphs. Overall, this view mostly follows the basics of semantic representation of knowledge bases on the Web. The community has never come up with a formal definition but generally, on a technical level, the overlapping concepts have been coined together and built up a general understanding of the concept connections. Following this view, a structured list of four characteristics has been listed such that "a Knowledge Graph:

1. mainly describes real world entities and their interrelations, organized in a graph,
2. defines possible classes and relations of entities in a schema,
3. allows for potentially interrelating arbitrary entities with each other,
4. covers various topical domains." – Pullheim, 2017 [348]

Basically, the first characteristic refers to the terminological knowledge about concepts of a domain, and is represented as *TBox* in description logic. The second characteristic points to the assertions knowledge about individual entities as *ABox*. By such a definition, a DL knowledge base can be constructed, on top of which inference of new knowledge from the existence knowledge can be applied. More in common language, the ontologies without instances and the datasets without ontologies are not considered as a KG. As this way of knowledge representation involves logical rules and ontologies, the KG created by this has reasoning abilities. Complex queries are made possible with the power of data representation and the existence of ontologies. Thus, this definition also falls into the category of a KG being a management system.

A Finite Set of Ground Atoms. Looking at KGs as a graph of nodes and links, assuming $\mathcal{R}$ as a set of relations and $\mathcal{C}$ a set of entities, the following formal definition is given:

"A Knowledge Graph $\mathcal{G}$ is a finite set of ground atoms of the form $p(s, o)$ and $c(s)$ over $\mathcal{R} \cup \mathcal{C}$. With $\Sigma_g = \langle \mathcal{R}, \mathcal{C} \rangle$, the signature of g, we denote elements of $\mathcal{R} \cup \mathcal{C}$ that occur in g." – Stepanova, 2018 [413]

This adopts first-order logic (FOL), seeing a set of correct facts as a KG. These facts are represented as unary and binary triples. In addition to the reasoning and querying power that comes from this definition, the power of explainability is also addressed here. Such features are a must now for KGs as management systems for AI-based downstream tasks.

A Graph of Data with the Intent to Compose Knowledge. In one of the attempts in (re)defining Knowledge Graphs [55], datasets are seen in graph representations with nodes representing entities and links denoting their relations. Example graph representation can be considered as:

- directed edge-labelled graphs as labelled edges between entities as nodes,
- property graphs as additional annotations on the edges,
- name graph as a collection of data represented in directed edge-labelled.

In a succinct view, the definition of KGs is then summarized as:

"A graph of data with the intent to compose knowledge." – Hogan et al., 2019 [55]

This definition brings another management action into the picture, namely *composing knowledge*. This is not only about knowledge representation in a graph structure but also using that graph for a dedicated purpose. Construction of a KG under this definition means facilitating complex management steps.

An Open-World Probabilistic Database [58]. Probabilistic databases, often abbreviated PDBs, as the state of the art of processing large volumes of uncertain data in a complete platform which is a combination of methods from information extraction, natural language processing to relational learning [212].

"Knowledge Graphs are addressed as open-world Probabilistic databases (OpenPDBs)." – Borgwardt, 2017 – [58].

A Knowledge Graph Management System [42]. The authors pose a number of requirements or desiderata for a *Knowledge Graph Management System* (KGMS) in terms of the main system capabilities:

– *simple modular syntax:* easy to add and remove facts and rules
– *high expressive power:* at least as expressive as Datalog (i.e., full recursion)
– *numeric computation and aggregation:* real-world required features
– *ontological reasoning:* at least as expressive as SPARQL and OWL 2 QL
– *probabilistic reasoning:* should support a form of probabilistic reasoning
– *low complexity:* the core language should be tractable in data complexity
– *rule repository, management and ontology editor:* management facilities
– *dynamic orchestration:* allow orchestration of complex, real-world workflows

They also formulate a number of access/integration requirements, some of which are what we consider core capabilities in this section, some of which we will include in the following section on *application services*. The ones of core relevance for management systems are:

– *big data access:* must be able to consume Big Data sources and interface with such systems
– *database and data warehouse access:* must seamlessly integrate with relational databases, graph stores, RDF stores, etc.
– *ontology-based data access (OBDA):* allow queries on top of ontologies
– *multi-query support:* allow multiple queries executed in parallel to benefit from each other
– *procedural code support:* allow easy integration of procedural code

They subsequently presented the Vadalog system [38] in more technical detail, focusing on algorithms and data structures to meet the requirement on high expressive power, ontological reasoning and low complexity at the same time. Subsequent papers discuss highly parallelizable fragments [44, 45, 49], how to achieve maintainability [64] and other related topics, including more fundamental aspects [43, 162].

4   KGs as Knowledge Application Services

While not usually providing quotable definitions of Knowledge Graphs, there is a huge body of work that does not primarily treat KGs as representation tools or management systems, but as a platform to provide a large number of crucial applications. So instead of a KG being used to *represent* information or *manage* information, it is rather the capability of the KG to natively or easily support certain applications that define what a KG is.

For example, [116] introduces KGs not only as the graph containing all of the Amazon product data, but as a graph that has the special capability of natively supporting entity resolution (i.e., knowing when two products are the same) and entity linking (i.e., knowing when two products or other entities are related). Similar considerations can be found in many KG-related fields. It could even be argued that the amount of work in KG completion, etc., makes this application-oriented view of KG the most important one.

Clearly, the border between the two views of management and application is debatable, and we *invite* the reader to critically think of what one *should* consider as an essential general-purpose service of a knowledge management system, and what should be part of an application service. We shall explore this aspect in this section, and in particular in Chap. 6. For example, while *question answering* in our opinion would typically be considered as an application service, as would be offering *recommender system* capabilities, it is less clear for relatively general-purpose application services such as *entity resolution* and *link prediction*, which could be seen as a requirement of a *general purporse* knowledge management system. Here, we will consider all of four of these as application services as they clearly offer a *well-defined* application compared to a management system offering a query language that supports such applications.

Knowledge Organization System. This view is from the domain of libraries and humanities where KGs are sees as knowledge organization systems. Even in a further vision, KGs are seen to integrate the insights derived from analysis in large-scale domains. This vision is already in practice by reasoning systems considered as a part of the KG concept.

> "Knowledge Graphs represent concepts (e.g., people, places, events) and their semantic relationships. As a data structure, they underpin a digital information system, support users in resource discovery and retrieval, and are useful for navigation and visualization purposes." – Haslhofer, 2018 [188]

Scholarly communication artifacts, such as bibliographic metadata about scientific publications, research datasets, citations, description of projects,and profile information of researchers, has recently gained a lot of attention with KG technologies. With the help of Linked Data technologies, interlinking of semantically represented metadata has been made possible. Discovering and providing links between the metadata of scholarly artifacts is important in scholarly communities. This definition has a particular view of KGs for such purposes. The links are generated retrospectively by devising similarity metrics over sets of attributes of the artifact descriptions. Interlinking of such metadata provides shareable, extensible, and easily re-usable metadata in the form of KGs. We also address the scholarly domain as one of the example applications.

Rule Mining and Reasoners. One of the early attempts in systematic definitions of KGs goes beyond seeing them as only a representation tool but more as a management system close to database management systems.

> "A Knowledge Graph acquires and integrates information into an ontology and applies a reasoner to derive new knowledge." – Ehrlinger, 2016 – [121].

This is one of the early attempts in defining KGs in a systematic way with a different view. Similarly, the following definitions sees KGs as a specific data model. There are several rule mining reasoners around which are purely designed to consume the ontology and mine relational patterns out of the KG. One example of this category is AMIE [144]. We categorize it under this view because it is more than just a representation tool and performs some data management steps. It has RDF as the data model for representing the facts and rules and uses its own internal functions for rule mining.

Data Application Platform. The VADA project [257] saw many application services built on top of its Knowledge Graph Management System (KGMS) Vadalog [164]. Before going into concrete examples, let us inspect the application service requirements given in [42]:

- *data cleaning, exchange, integration:* often summarized as "data wrangling"
- *web data extraction, interaction and IoT:* to interact with the outside world
- *machine learning, text mining, NLP, data analytics:* providing and interfacing with external such services. An interesting side-note is that the authors here invert the perspective: it is not always the knowledge graph system providing the application service, but sometimes also using it.
- *data visualization:* for providing data consumable by an end-user or analyst

Let us now proceed to concrete examples of these abstract requirements. Prime among them is:

- *Data Wrangling*, i.e., the whole process of bringing raw data into an integrated format amenable to Big Data Analytics [141, 257, 258]. Further services seen as key were at the data acquisition phase the application service
- *Data Extraction* [132, 262, 308]. Further key application services are those of
- *Recommender Systems* [82], including services for downstream machine-learning applications which need feature engineering. A connected but independent application platform requirement is that of
- *Social Choice* [89, 90] where the application requirement is to choose among a number of different users' preferences the best joint solution. A further one, for which it is somewhat debatable whether it is a management system requirement or an application service is that of

- *Machine Learning* [41] service integration - bridging typical KGMS services and machine learning services. Another interesting case is that of a vertical application service collection, namely that of
- *Company Knowledge Graphs* [24,39], especially important for the COVID-19 perspective raised in one of the works on the economic impact of the pandemic.

5   KGs in Practice: Challenges and Opportunities

The initial release of KGs was started on an industry scale by Google and further continued with the publication of other large-scale KGs such as Facebook, Microsoft, Amazon, DBpedia, Wikidata and many more. As an influence of the increasing hype in KG and advanced AI-based services, every individual company or organization is adapting to KG. The KG technology has immediately reached industry, and big companies have started to build their own graphs such as the industrial Knowledge Graph at Siemens [206]. In a joint work [331] for sharing ideas from large-scale industrial Knowledge Graphs, namely Microsoft, Google, Facebook, eBay and IMB, authors stated a broad range of challenges ahead of research and industry involving KGs. Despite the content-wise difference and similarities of those Knowledge Graphs, the discussions involve data acquisition and provenance problems due to source heterogeneity and scalability of the underlying managements system. Here we introduce the Enterprise Knowledge Graph of Italian companies for the Central Bank of Italy.

5.1   Integrated Ownership and Company Control

The database at our disposal contains data from 2005 to 2018, regarding unlisted companies and their shareholders (companies or persons). If we see the database as a graph, where companies and persons are nodes and shareholding is represented by edges, on average, for each year the graph has 4.059M nodes and 3.960M edges. There are 4.058M Strongly Connected Components (SCC), composed on average of one node, and more than 600K Weakly Connected Components (WCC), composed on average of 6 nodes, resulting in an high level of fragmentation. Interestingly, the largest SCC has only 15 nodes, while the largest WCC has more than one million nodes. The average in- and out-degree of each node is ≈ 1 and the average clustering coefficient is ≈ 0.0084, which is very low compared to the number of nodes and edges. Furthermore, it is interesting to observe that the maximum in-degree of a node is more than 5K and the maximum out-degree is more than 28K nodes. We also observe a high number of self-loops, almost 3K, i.e. companies that directly own shares of themselves in order to subtract them from the market. The resulting graph shows a scale-free network structure, as most real-world networks [148]: the degree distribution follows a power-law and there are several nodes in the network that act as hubs.

The Register of Intermediaries and Affiliates (RIAD), the ownership network of European financial companies run by the European Central Bank, is a good example of the company control topology at the European level. It has one large SCC containing 88 nodes, and all the others with less than 10 nodes; there is one huge WCC, with 57% of the nodes, with the others scattered around small WCCs with 11.968 nodes on average and (apart from the largest one), none with more than 472 nodes.

5.2   Large-Scale Scholarly Knowledge Graphs

The complexity of scholarly data fully follows the *6 Vs* of Big Data characteristics towards building Scholarly Knowledge Graphs [405]. The term Big Scholarly Data (BSD) [474] is coined to represent the vast amount of information about scholarly networks including stakeholders and artifacts such as authors, organizers, papers, citations, figures. The heterogeneity and complexity of data and their associated metadata distributed on the Web perfectly qualifies this domain for Big Data challenges towards building Scholarly KGs:

- Volume refers to the ability to ingest and store very large datasets; in the context of scholarly metadata, at least over 114 million scholarly documents [240] were recorded in 2014 as being available in PDF format. In computer science, the total number of publications of the different types is reaching 4 million [423]. Different types of publication in different formats are being published every day in other scientific disciplines.
- Velocity denotes the growth rate generating such data; the average growth rate of scientific publishing is measured as 8 to 9% [61].
- Variety indicates multiple data formats and models; the domain of scholarly communication is a complex domain [29] including many different types of entities with complex interrelationships among them.
- Value concerns the impact of high quality analytics over data; certain facts play enormously important roles in the reputation and basic life of research stakeholders. Providing precise and comprehensive statistics supports researchers with already existing success measurement tools such as number of citations. In additions, deep and mined knowledge with flexible analytics can provide new insights about artifacts and people involved in the scholarly communication domain.
- Veracity refers to the biases, ambiguities, and noise in data; this characteristic is especially applicable in the context of the scholarly communication domain due to deduplication problems [296] and the ambiguity problem for various scholarly artifacts as well as person names.
- Variability of the meaning of the metadata [474].

Discovering high quality and relevant research-related information has a certain influence on the life of researchers and other stakeholders of the communication system [109]. For examples, scholars search for quality in the meaning of fitness for use in questions such as "the venues should a researcher participate" or "the papers should be cited". There are already attempts to assist researchers in this task, however, resulting in recommendations often being rather superficial and the underlying process neglecting the different aspects that are important for authors [439]. Providing recommendation services to researchers and a comprehensive list of criteria while they are searching for relevant information. Furthermore, having access to the networks of a paper's authors and their organizations, and taking into account the events in which people participate, enables new indicators for measuring the quality and relevance of research that are not just based on counting citations [438]. Thus each of the Vs of Big Data needs careful management to provide such services for scholarly communities.

6 Conclusion

In this chapter, we introduced Knowledge Graphs in a layered perspective: Knowledge Graphs as (1) knowledge representations tools, (2) knowledge management systems, and (3) knowledge application services. We did not focus on a single definition here but presented a multitude of definitions, putting them into the context of this layered perspective. We deliberately stopped short of the chapter being an exhaustive historical overview as excellent overviews have already been written.

We also pointed toward aspects of particular concern: The different ways that particular communities see KGs (top-down or bottom-up, or even middle-layer in focus). We concluded with the practical challenges of KGs by providing typical industrial and academic applications. Throughout the chapter, we discussed the aspect of *reasoning* being a natural counterpart to this "bigger picture" focus section, and we shall consider reasoning in greater detail in Chap. 6.

Acknowledgements. E. Sallinger acknowledges the support of the Vienna Science and Technology (WWTF) grant VRG18-013 and the EPSRC programme grant EP/M025268/1.

Chapter 3
Big Data Outlook, Tools, and Architectures

Hajira Jabeen$^{(\boxtimes)}$ (iD)

CEPLAS, Botanical Institute, University of Cologne, Cologne, Germany
hajira.jabeen@uni-koeln.de

Abstract. Big data is a persistent phenomena, the data is being generated and processed in a myriad of digitised scenarios. This chapter covers the history of 'big data' and aims to provide an overview of the existing terms and enablers related to big data. Furthermore, the chapter covers prominent technologies, tools, and architectures developed to handle this large data at scale. At the end, the chapter reviews knowledge graphs that address the challenges (e.g. heterogeneity, interoperability, variety) of big data through their specialised representation. After reading this chapter, the reader can develop an understanding of the broad spectrum of big data ranging from important terms, challenges, handling technologies, and their connection with large scale knowledge graphs.

1 Introduction

The digital transformation has impacted almost all aspects of modern society. The past decade has seen tremendous advancements in the areas of automation, mobility, the internet, IoT, health, and similar areas. This growth has led to enormous data-generation facilities, and data-capturing capabilities.

In the first section "Outlook", we review the definitions and descriptions of big data and discuss the drivers behind big data generation, the characteristics exhibited by big data, the challenges offered by big data, and the handling of this data by creating data value chains. In the section "Tools and Architectures", we cover the software solutions and architectures used to realise the big data value chains. We further cover characteristics and challenges relating to big data. The section "Harnessing the Big Data as Knowledge Graphs" connects knowledge graphs and big data, outlining the rationale and existing tools to handle large-scale knowledge graphs.

2 Big Data: Outlook

Today, big data is widespread across and beyond every aspect of everyday life. This trend of increasing data was first envisioned and defined years ago. Notably, the first evidence of the term big data comes from a paper [87] published in 1997,

© The Author(s) 2020
V. Janev et al. (Eds.): Knowledge Graphs and Big Data Processing, LNCS 12072, pp. 35–55, 2020.
https://doi.org/10.1007/978-3-030-53199-7_3

where the authors described the problem as *BigData* when the data do not fit in the main memory (core) of a computing system, or on the local disk. According to the Oxford English Dictionary (OED), big data is defined as: "data of a very large size, typically to the extent that its manipulation and management present significant logistical challenges." Later, when the terms velocity, variety, and volume were associated as characteristics of big data, the newer definitions of the term 'big data' came to cover these characteristics, as listed below:

1. "Big data is high volume, high velocity, and/or high variety information assets that require new forms of processing to enable enhanced decision making, insight discovery and process optimization," [271, 297].
2. "When the size of the data itself becomes part of the problem and traditional techniques for working with data run out of steam," [288].
3. Big Data is "data whose size forces us to look beyond the tried-and-true methods that are prevalent at that time," [217].
4. "Big Data technologies are a new generation of technologies and architectures designed to extract value economically from very large volumes of a wide variety of data by enabling high-velocity capture, discovery, and/or analysis," [470].
5. "Big data is high-volume, high-velocity and high-variety information assets that demand cost-effective innovative forms of information processing for enhanced insight and decision making," [271].
6. "Big Data is a term encompassing the use of techniques to capture, process, analyse and visualize potentially large datasets in a reasonable timeframe not accessible to standard IT technologies." By extension, the platform, tools and software used for this purpose are collectively called "Big Data technologies," [98].
7. "Big data can mean big volume, big velocity, or big variety," [414].
8. "The term is used for a collection of datasets so large and complex that it becomes difficult to process using on-hand database management tools or traditional data processing applications"[1].
9. "Big data represents the information assets characterized by such a high volume, velocity and variety to require specific technology and analytical methods for its transformation into value"[2].

Regardless of the defining text, big data is a persistent phenomenon and is here to stay. We take a brief overview of the key enabling technologies that made big data possible in the following section.

2.1 Key Technologies and Business Drivers

As recently as the year 2000, digital information only constituted about one quarter of all the stored information worldwide[3]. Other information was mainly

---

[1] http://en.wikipedia.org/.

[2] http://en.wikipedia.org/.

[3] https://www.foreignaffairs.com/articles/2013-04-03/rise-big-data.

stored on paper, film, or other analogue media. Today, by contrast, less than two percent of all stored information is non-digital. The key enablers of the big digital data revolution are the advancements in technologies, be it increased internet speed, the availability of low-cost handheld mobile devices, or the myriad of applications ranging from social media to personal banking. At present, organizations view the acquisition and possession of data as significant assets. A report by the World Economic Forum [315], "Big Data, Big Impact," declared 'data' an asset akin to currency or gold. This fact has led to significant changes in business models. Besides, aggressive acquisition and retention of data have become more popular among organizations. Prominent examples are internet companies such as Google, Yahoo, Amazon, or Facebook, which are driven by new business models. Technology proliferation is one of the major enablers of big data acquisition. Cheaper and accessible technology is being used in almost all parts of modern society, be it smart devices, mobile devices, wearable devices, or resources to store data on the cloud, enabling customers to make purchases and book vacations among other functions. In the following section, we will cover a few of the prominent big data enabling technologies and key drivers.

Internet. The advancements in internet bandwidth and streaming have enabled fast and efficient data transfer between physically distant devices. People around the globe are accessing the internet via their mobile devices and the number of connected devices is constantly increasing. The number of internet users increased from 4.021 billion to 4.39 billion from 2018 to 2019. Almost 4.48 billion people were active internet users as of October 2019, encompassing 58% of the global population [83]. In the age of digital society, there is a need for a powerful wireless network that can rapidly transfer large volumes of data. Presently, we are moving from 4G LTE to 5G NR, which will enable entirely new applications and data-collection scenarios. 5G not only comes with better bandwidth and faster speed but also lower latency. The low latency of 5G was demonstrated by "Orchestrating the Orchestra"[4] – an event that enabled musicians across different locations to perform at the Bristol 5G Smart Tourism event. Violinist Anneka Sutcliffe was playing in Bristol, Professor Mischa Dohler was playing the piano in The Guildhall, London, and vocalist Noa Dohler and violinist Rita Fernandes were at Digital Catapult in Euston, London. These developments have made it possible to share and curate large amounts of data at high speeds.

Automation and Digitization. Digital automation is a relatively broad term and it covers tasks that can be done automatically with minimal human assistance, increasing the speed and accuracy as a result. Businesses are more and more favouring the use of automatization tools to achieve more throughput. For example, advancements in automatic tools like scanning systems no longer require manual entry, easing and speeding up the process at the cost of more and reliable data capture. Similarly, in terms of digital data, cameras and photos are

---

[4] https://www.bristol.ac.uk/news/2019/march/orchestrating-the-orchestra.html.

another example. The number of digital photos taken in 2017 was estimated to be 1.2 trillion[5], which is roughly 160 pictures for every one of the roughly 7.5 billion people inhabiting planet earth. With more and more devices being digitized, more data is being created and stored in machine-readable form. Industries and businesses must harness this data and use it to their advantage.

Commodity Computing. Commodity hardware, also known as off-the-shelf, non-proprietary hardware, refers to low-cost devices that are widely available. These devices can be easily replaced with a similar device, avoiding vendor lock-in challenges. 'Commodity cluster computing' is the preference of using more of average-performing, low-cost hardware to work in parallel (scalar computing), rather than having a few high-performance, high-cost items of hardware. Hence, commodity computing enables the use of a large number of already existing computing resources for parallel and cluster computing without needing to buy expensive supercomputers. Commodity computing is supported by the fact that software solutions can be used to build multiple points of redundancy in the cluster, making sure that the cluster remains functional in case of hardware failures. Low-cost cluster computing resources have made it possible to build proprietary data centres on-premises and to reap the benefits of in-house big data handling and processing.

Mobile Computing. Handheld smart devices are becoming more and more common due to increased affordability, relevance, and digital literacy. There were 5.11 billion unique mobile users in 2018 and 5.135 billion in 2019, accounting for 67% of the global population, and it is estimated [83] that by 2020, almost 75% of the global population will be connected by mobile. Use of mobile computing has enabled almost everyone to access and generate data, playing a key role in big data generation and sharing.

Mobile Applications. Mobile devices are playing a key role in the present data explosion. Mobile phones are no longer only being used for voice calls. Currently, 56% of web access worldwide is generated by mobile devices. At the moment, more than 57% of the global population use the internet and more than 52% of the global population use mobile devices [83]. Businesses are developing mobile applications to not only assist users in ubiquitous computing but also to generate and capture data of interest. The mobile application development industry is creating mobile apps for almost all fields, and existing mobile applications cover a range of tasks like online banking, online purchases, social interactions, travelling, eating, studying, or entertainment. All of these applications not only assist in automated data collection related to tasks (e.g. orders) but also assist in generating additional data that was not easily possible before (e.g. correlating a new order with previous purchases).

---

[5] https://www.statista.com/statistics/617136/digital-population-worldwide/.

Ubiquitous Devices (IoT). The internet of things (IoT) enables scenarios where network connectivity and computing capability extends to objects, sensors and everyday items not normally considered computers, allowing these devices to generate, exchange and consume data with minimal human intervention. These devices are not only increasing in number to cover different facets of life but are also increasing their sensitivity. According to a GSMA report [16], between 2018 and 2025, the number of global IoT connections will triple to 25 billion. In an estimate by CGI [2], the total volume of data generated by IoT will reach 600 ZB per year by 2020.

Cloud Infrastructure. Cloud computing is the term used for storing, accessing and processing data over the internet from a remote server. This ability to store and manipulate data on the cloud using services like AWS [50], Google Cloud Platform [264], Cloudera [378], etc. has made it possible to store and analyse data on-demand with a pay-per-use model. Cloud computing saves costs, offers better performance, reliability, unlimited capacity, and quick deployment possibilities. Cloud computing has assisted organizations with providing the data centre management and efficient data-handling facilities.

2.2   Characteristics of Big Data

Driven by digital transformation, big data is identified by several key attributes. Interestingly, they all start with the letter 'V', and therefore are also called the V's of big data. The number of characteristic attributes is constantly increasing with advancements in technologies and underlying business requirements. In this section, we cover a few of the main V's used to describe big data.

Three Vs of Big Data [271, 489]

1. Volume: The size of data is increasing at unprecedented rates. It includes data generated in all fields including science, education, business, technology and governance. If we take the social media giant Facebook (FB) as an example, it has been reported that FB generates approximately 4 petabytes of data in 24 h with 100 million hours of video watch-time. FB users create 4 million likes per minute, and more than 250 billion photos have been uploaded to Facebook since its creation, which equates to 350 million photos per day. Apart from the applications, a vast amount of data is being generated by web, IoT and many other automation tools continuously. All of this data must be captured, stored, processed and displayed.

2. Velocity: The speed at which the data is being generated has increased rapidly over the years. The high rate and speed is contributed by the increase in the use of portable devices to allow data generation and ever-increasing bandwidth that allows fast data transfer. In addition, the rate of data generation (from the Internet of Things, social media, etc.) is increasing as well. Google, for example, receives over 63,000 searches per second on any given day. And 15% of all searches have never been searched before on Google. Therefore,

it is critical to manage and analyse the data at the same rate at which it is being generated and stored in the system.

3. Variety: The data comes from a variety of data sources and is generated in different forms. It can be structured or unstructured data. Data comes in the form of text (emails, tweets), logs, signals, records, photos, videos, etc. This data cannot be stored and queried via traditional structured database management systems. It is important to develop new solutions that are able to store and query diverse data; *4 Vs of Big Data* [106].

4. Veracity: This is the quality, truthfulness or reliability of data. Data might contain biases, noise, or abnormalities. It is important to be aware of whether data being used can be trusted for use in making important decisions, or if the data is meaningful to the problem being analysed. The data is to be used to make decisions that can bring strategic competitive advantages to the business; *10 Vs of Big Data* [60].

5. Variability: This is the dynamic and evolving nature of data. The data flow is not constant or consistent. The speed, density, structure, or format of data can change over time and several factors influence the consistency of data that changes the pattern, e.g. more shoppers near Christmas, more traffic in peak hours etc.

6. Value: This refers to the worth of the data being extracted. For an organization, it is important to understand the cost and associated benefits of collection and analysis of data. It is important to know that the data can be turned into value by analysis, and that it follows set standards of data quality, sparsity or relatedness.

7. Visualization is often thought of as the only way in which customers can interact with models. It is important to visualize the reports and results that can be communicated and extracted from data in order to understand underlying patterns and behaviours.

In addition to the characteristics mentioned above, some researchers have gone as far as to introduce 42 [395], or even 51 [243] different Vs to characterise big data.

2.3   Challenges of Big Data

The characteristics of data combined with targeted business goals pose plenty of challenges while dealing with big data. In this section, we briefly cover the main challenges involved in using big data.

Heterogeneity. Heterogeneity is one of the major features of big data, also characterised as the variety. It is data of different types and formats. The heterogeneous data introduces the problems of data integration in big data analytics, making it difficult to obtain the desired value. The major cause of data heterogeneity is disparate sources of data that generate data in different forms. The data can be text data coming from emails, tweets or replies; log-data coming from web activities, sensing and event data coming from IoT; and other forms.

It is an important challenge to integrate this data for value-added analytics and positive decision making.

Uncertainty of Data. The data gathered from heterogeneous sources like sensors, social media, web activities, and internal-records is inherently uncertain due to noise, incompleteness and inconsistency (e.g., there are 80% - 90% missing links in social networks and over 90% missing attribute values for a doctor diagnosis in clinic and health fields). Efficient analysis to discover value from these huge amounts of data demands tremendous effort and resources. However, as the volume, variety and velocity of the data increases, the uncertainty inherent in the data also increases, leading to doubtful confidence in the resulting analytics and predicted decisions.

Scalability. The volume of data is drastically increasing and therefore an important challenge is to deal with the scalability of the data. It is also important to develop efficient analytics solutions and architectures that can scale up with the increasing data without compromising the accuracy or efficiency. Most of the existing learning algorithms cannot adapt themselves to the new big-data paradigms like dealing with missing data, working with partial data access or dealing with heterogeneous data sources. While the problem complexity of big data is increasing at a very fast rate, the computational ability and the solution capability is not increasing at a similar pace, posing a vital challenge.

Timeliness. When looking for added business values, timing is of prime importance. It is related to capturing data, execution of analytics and making decisions at the right time. In a dynamic and rapidly evolving world, a slight delay (sometimes microseconds) could lead to incorrect analytics and predictions. In an example case of a bogus online bank transaction, the transaction must be disapproved in a timely manner to avoid possible money loss.

Data Security. Data storage and exchange in organizations has created challenges in data security and privacy. With the increasing sizes of data, it is important to protect e.g. transaction logs and data, real-time data, access control data, communication and encryption data. Also, it is important to keep track of data provenance, perform granular auditing of logs, and access control data to determine any misuse of data. Besides, the difference between legitimate use of data and customer privacy must be respected by organizations and they must have the right mechanisms in place to protect that data.

2.4   Big Data Value Chain

The ability to handle and process big data is vital to any organization. The previous sections have discussed data generation abilities, and the characteristics and challenges of dealing with big data. This section covers the required activities and actions to handle such data to achieve business goals and objectives. The term value chain [358] is used to define the chain of activities that an organization performs to deliver a product for decision support management and services. A value chain is composed of a sequence of interconnected sub-services, each with its own inputs, transformation processes, and outputs. The noteworthy services are described below.

Data Acquisition. This is the process of gathering data, filtering, and cleaning the data for storage and data analysis. Data acquisition is critical, as the infrastructure required for the acquisition of big data must bear low, predictable latency for capturing data as well as answering queries. It should be able to handle very high transaction volumes in a distributed scalable environment, and be able to support flexible and dynamic heterogeneous data.

Data Analysis. Interpreting the raw data and extraction of information from the data, such that it can be used in informed decision making, is called data analysis. There could be multiple domain-specific analysis based on the source and use of data. The analysis includes filtering, exploring, and transforming data to extract useful and often hidden information and patterns. The analysis is further classified as business intelligence, data mining, or machine learning.

Data Curation. This is the active and continuous management of data through its life cycle [350]. It includes the organization and integration of data from multiple sources and to ascertain that the data meets given quality requirements for its usage. Curation covers tasks related to controlled data creation, maintenance and management e.g. content creation, selection, validation or preservation.

Data Storage. This is persistent, scalable data management that can satisfy the needs of applications requesting frequent data access and querying. RDBMS have remained a de facto standard for organizational data management for decades; however, its ability to handle data of limited capacity and well-defined structure (ACID properties, Atomicity, Consistency, Isolation, and Durability) has made it less suitable to handle big data that has variety, in addition to volume and velocity. Novel technologies are being designed to focus on scalability and cope with a range of solutions handling numerous data models.

Data Usage. This is the analysis of data covering the business activities assisting in business decision making. The analysis is made possible through the use of specialised tools for data integration or querying.

3   Tools and Architectures

3.1   Big Data Architectures

Several reference architectures have been proposed to support the design of big data systems. Big data architecture is the conceptual model that defines the structure and behaviour of the system used to ingest and process "big data" for business purposes. The architecture can be considered a blueprint to handle the ingestion, processing, and analysis of data that is too large or complex for traditional database systems. The aim is to design a solution based on the business needs of the organization. Based on the requirements, the proposed solution must be able to handle different types of workloads like batch processing or real-time processing. Additionally, it should be able to perform analytics and mining on this large-scale data.

Good architecture design can help organizations to reduce costs, assist in making faster and better decisions, and predict future needs or recommend new solutions. However, the creation of such a system is not straightforward and certain challenges exist in designing an optimal architecture.

Data Quality: This is one of the important challenges in all domains of data handling. The data could be noisy, incomplete or simply missing. Substantial processing is desired to make sure that the resulting data is of the desired quality. It is a widely known fact that "data preparation accounts for about 80% of the work of data scientists".

Data Integration: The architecture must be able to handle the integration of heterogeneous data coming from disparate sources. It is challenging to handle and integrate data of multiple sizes and forms coming at different speeds from multiple sources. Finally, the system should be able to carry out meaningful analytics on the data to gain valuable insights.

Data Scale: It is important to design a system that works at an optimal scale without over-reserving the resources. At the same time, it should be able to scale up as needed without compromising performance.

In order to comply with the data value chain, any big data architecture comprises of the components that can allow to perform desired operations.

Data Sources: The data of an organization might be originating from databases, real-time sources like web-logs, activity data, IoT devices and many others. There should be data ingestion and integration components embedded in the architecture to deal with these data sources.

Data Ingestion: If the data is coming from the real-time sources, the architecture must support the real-time data ingestion mechanism.

Data Storage: Depending upon the number and types of data sources, efficient data storage is important for big data architecture. In the case of multiple types of data sources, a no-SQL "data lake" is usually built.

Data Processing: The data in the system needs to be queried and analysed, therefore it is important to develop efficient data-querying solutions, or data-processing tools that can process the data at scale. These processing solutions can either be real-time or batch, depending upon the originating data and organizational needs.

Data Analysis: Specialised tools to analyse data for business intelligence are needed to extract meaningful insights from the data.

Data Reporting, and Visualisation: These are the tools used to make reports from the analysed data and to present the results in visual form.

Process Automation: Moving the data across the big data architecture pipeline requires automated orchestration. The ingestion and transformation of the data, moving it for processing, storage, and deriving insights and reporting must be done in a repeatable workflow to continuously gain insights from the data.

Depending upon the type of data and the individual requirements of the organizations, the selected tasks must be handled by choosing corresponding services. To support the tasks and selected services, the overall architecture to realise the data value chain is designed. The big data architectures are mainly divided into three main types as below:

Lambda Architecture. The lambda architecture, first proposed by Nathan [99], addresses the issue of slow queries results on batch data, while real-time data requires fast query results. Lambda architecture combines the real-time (fast) query results with the queries (slow) from batch analysis of older data. Lambda architecture creates two paths for the data flow. All data coming into the system goes through these two paths. Batch Layer: also known as the cold path, stores all the incoming data in its raw form and performs batch processing on the data. This offers a convenient way to handle reprocessing. This layer executes long-living batch-processes to do analyses on larger amounts of historical data. Speed Layer: also known as the hot path, analyses the data in real-time. This layer is designed for low latency. This layer executes small/mini batch-processes on data according to the selected time window (e.g. 1 s) to do analyses on the latest data. Serving Layer: This layer combines the results from the batch and speed processing layer to enable fast interactive analyses by users.

Kappa Architecture. Kappa architecture was proposed by Jay Kreps [263] as an alternative to lambda architecture. Like Lambda architecture, all data in Kappa architecture flows through the system, but uses a single path, i.e. a stream processing system. Kappa architecture focuses only on data stream processing, real-time processing, or processing of live discrete events. Examples are IoT events, social networks, log files or transaction processing systems. The architecture assumes that: The events are ordered and logged to a distributed file system, from where they can be read on demand. The platform can repeatedly request the logs for reprocessing in case of code updates. The system can handle online machine learning algorithms.

Microservices-Based Architecture. "Microservice Architecture" has emerged over the last few years to describe a particular way of designing software applications as suites of independently deployable services [283]. Microservices architecture makes use of loosely coupled services which can be developed, deployed and maintained independently. These services can be built for business capability, automated deployment, intelligence in the endpoints, and decentralized control of languages and data.

Microservices-based architecture is enabled by a multitude of technology advancements like the implementation of applications as services, emergence of software containers for service deployment, orchestration of containers, development of object stores for storing data beyond container lifecycle, requirement for continuous integration, automated testing, and code analysis to improve software quality. Microservices-based architecture allows fast delivery of individual services independently. In this architecture, all the components of big data architecture are treated as services, deployable on a cluster.

3.2 Tools to Handle Big Data

In order to deal with big data, a variety of specialised tools have been created. This section provides an overview of the existing tools based on their functionalities. A distributed platform handling big data is made up of components needed for the following tasks. We will cover the tools developed to perform these specific tasks in the preceding sections (Fig. 1).

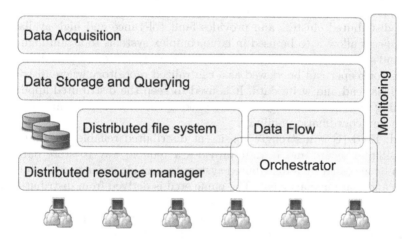

Fig. 1. Classification of tools to handle big data

Resource Orchestration. Distributed coordination and consensus is the backbone of distributed systems. Distributed coordination deals with tasks like telling each node about the other nodes in the cluster and facilitating communication and high availability. High availability guarantees the presence of the mediator node and avoids a single point of failure by replication resulting in a fault-tolerant system. In a distributed setting, the nodes must share common configurations and runtime variables and may need to store configuration data in a distributed key-value store. The distributed coordination manages the sharing of the locks, shared-variables, realtime-configurations at runtime among the nodes.

In addition, fault-tolerant distributed systems contain methods to deal with the consensus problem, i.e. the servers or mediators in the distributed system perform agreement on certain values or variables, e.g. there can be a consensus that the cluster with 7 servers can continue to operate if 4 servers get down, i.e. with only 3 servers running successfully. The popular orchestration tools are Apache zookeeper and etcd. The systems are consistent and provide primitives to be used within complex distributed systems. Such distributed orchestrators ease the development of distributed applications and make them more generic and fault resilient.

Apache Zookeeper: Apache Zookeeper [209] is an open-source project that originated from the Hadoop ecosystem and is being used in many top-level projects including Ambari, Mesos, Yarn, Kafka, Storm, Solr, and many more (discussed in later sections). Zookeeper is a centralised service for managing cluster configuration information, naming and distributed synchronization and coordination. It is a distributed key-value store that allows the coordination of distributed processes through a shared hierarchical name space of data registers (znodes), like a file system. Zookeeper provides high throughput, low latency, high availability and strictly ordered access to the znodes. Zookeeper is used in large distributed clusters and provides fault tolerance and high availability. These aspects allow it to be used in large complex systems to attain high availability and synchronization for resilient operations. In these complex distributed systems, Zookeeper can be viewed as a centralized repository where distributed applications read and write data. It is used to keep the distributed application functioning together as a single unit by making use of its synchronization, serialization and coordination abilities.

Etcd: Etcd [1] is a strongly consistent distributed reliable key-value store that is simple, secure and fast. It provides a reliable way to store data that needs to be accessed by a distributed system to provide consistent cluster coordination and state management. The name etcd is derived from distributing the Unix "/etc" directory used for global configurations. It gracefully handles leader elections and can tolerate machine failure, even in the leader node. The leaders in etcd handle all client requests needing consensus. Requests like reading can be handled by any cluster node. The leader accepts, replicates and commits the new changes after the followers verify the receipt.

Etcd uses the raft protocol to maintain the logs of state-changing events. It uses full replication, i.e. the entire data is available on every node, making it highly available. This also makes it possible that any node can act as a leader. The applications can read and write data to etcd and it can be used for storing database connection details, or feature flags. These values can be watched and allow the applications to reconfigure themselves when values change. In addition, etcd consistency is used to implement leader election or distributed locking. etcd is used as the coordinating mechanism for Kubernetes and Cloud Foundry. It is also used in production environments by AWS, Google Cloud Platform and Azure.

Resource Management. The big data platform works on top of a set of distributed computing and memory resources. The resource manager performs the task of resource allocation in terms of CPU time and memory usage. In a cluster, multiple applications are usually deployed at one time, e.g. it is common to have a distributed application like Apache Spark running in parallel to a distributed database for storage like Apache Hbase in the same cluster. A resource manager is an authority that arbitrates resources among all the applications in the system. In addition, the resource manager is also responsible for job scheduling with the help of a scheduler, or an application master.

YARN: Yet another resource manager (YARN) [444] is an important integral part of the Hadoop ecosystem and mainly supports Hadoop workloads. In YARN, the application-level resource manager is a dedicated scheduler that runs on the master daemon and assigns resources to the requesting applications. It keeps a global view of all resources in the cluster and handles the resource requests by scheduling the request and assigning the resources to the requesting application. It is a critical component in the Hadoop cluster and runs on a dedicated master node. The resource manager has two components: a scheduler and an application manager. The application manager receives the job-submissions, looks for the container to execute the ApplicationMaster and helps in restarting the ApplicationMaster on another node in case of failure. The ApplicationMaster is created for each application and it is responsible for the allocation of appropriate resources from the scheduler, tracking their status and monitoring their progress. ApplicationMaster works together with the Node Manager. The Node manager runs on slave daemon and is responsible for the execution of tasks on each node. It monitors their resource usage and reports it to the ResourceManager. The focus of YARN on one aspect at a time enables YARN to be scalable, generic and makes it able to support multi-tenant cluster. The High available version of Yarn uses Zookeeper to establish automatic failover.

Mesos: Apache Mesos is an open-source cluster manager [233] that handles workloads in a distributed environment through dynamic resource sharing and isolation. It is also called a distributed systems kernel. Mesos works between the application layer and the operating system and makes it easier to manage and deploy applications in large distributed clusters by doing resource management. It turns a cluster into a single large pool of resources by leveraging the features of modern kernels of resource isolation, prioritization, limiting, and accounting, at a higher level of abstraction. Mesos also uses zookeeper to achieve high availability and recovery from master failure. Mesos carries out microscale resource management as it works as a microkernel.

Data Flow: Message Passing. Message passing is crucial to distributed big data applications that must deal with real-time data. This data could be event logs, user activities, sensor signals, stock exchanges, bank transactions, among many others. Efficient and fault free ingestion of this real-time data is critical for real-time applications. Message passing solutions are needed for real-time streaming applications and data flows.

Message passing tools, as the name suggests, assist in communication between the software components of a big data processing pipeline. The systems usually decouple the sender and receiver by using a message broker that hides the implementation details like the operating system or network interface from the application interfaces. This creates a common platform for messaging that is also easy to develop for the developers. The applications of message passing pipelines are website activity monitoring, metrics collection, log aggregation etc. Below we briefly discuss Apache Kafka, which is frequently used in real-time big data applications.

Apache Kafka: Apache Kafka [147] is a distributed messaging system that uses the publish-subscribe mechanism. It was developed to support continuous and resilient messaging with high throughput at LinkedIn. Kafka is a fast, scalable, durable, and fault-tolerant system. It maintains feeds of messages in categories called topics. These topics are used to store messages from the producers and deliver them to the consumers who have subscribed to that topic.

Kafka is a durable, high volume message broker that enables applications to process, persist and re-process streaming data. Kafka has a straightforward routing approach that uses a routing key to send messages to a topic. Kafka offers much higher performance than message brokers like RabbitMQ. Its boosted performance makes it suitable to achieve high throughput (millions of messages per second) with limited resources.

Data Handling. The data handling and acquisition assists in collecting, selecting, filtering and cleaning the data being received and generated. This data can be later stored in a data warehouse, or another storage solution, where further processing can be performed for gaining the insights.

Apache Flume: Apache Flume [198] is a framework to collect massive amounts of streaming event data from multiple sources, aggregate it, and move it into HDFS. It is used for collecting, aggregating, and moving large amounts of streaming data such as log files, events from various sources like network traffic, social media, email messages etc. to HDFS. Flume provides reliable message delivery. The transactions in Flume are channel-based where two transactions (one sender and one receiver) are maintained for each message. If the read rate exceeds the write rate, Flume provides a steady flow of data between read and write operations. Flume allows ingestion of data from multiple servers (and sources) into Hadoop.

Apache Sqoop: Most of the older companies have stored their data on RDBMS, but with the increase in data sizes beyond terabytes, it is important to switch to HDFS. Apache Sqoop [428] is a tool designed to transfer bulk data between structured data stores such as RDBMS and Hadoop in an efficient manner. Sqoop imports data from external datastores into HDFS and vice versa. It can also be used to populate tables in Hive and HBase. Sqoop uses a connector-based architecture which supports plugins providing smooth connectivity to the external systems.

Data Processing. Data-flow processing technologies are mainly categorised into batch (historical data) processing systems and stream (real-time) processing systems.

Batch processing systems are high throughput systems for processing high volumes of data collected over some time. The data is collected, entered, processed and then the batch results generated resulting in high latency systems.

Stream processing systems are high throughput i.e. the system continuously receives data that is under constant change (e.g. traffic control, sensor data, social media), low latency stream processing systems. The data is processed on the fly and produces real-time insights. There are three main methods for streaming: At least once, At most once, and Exactly once.

Until a few years ago, a clear distinction between these two processing systems existed. However, recent technologies such as Apache Spark and Apache Flink can handle both kinds of processing, diminishing this distinction. We will discuss some of the key technologies in the following sections.

Hadoop MapReduce: Hadoop is a platform for distributed storage and analysis of very large data sets. It has four main modules: Hadoop Common, HDFS, MapReduce and YARN [153]. MapReduce is the distributed data processing engine of Hadoop. It is a programming model and provides a software framework to write the applications for distributed processing of very large amounts of data in parallel. MapReduce processes the data in two phases: The map phase and the reduce phase. In the map phase, the framework reads data from HDFS. Each dataset is called an input record and split into independent chunks that are processed by the map tasks in parallel. In the reduce phase, the results from the map phase are processed and stored. The storage target can either be a database or back HDFS or something else. Working with MapReduce requires a low level and specialised design thinking and programming models, making it challenging for developers to create generic applications. As a result, many tools have been developed around Hadoop MapReduce to address these limitations. These tools include:

Apache Pig: This provides a high-level language for expressing data analysis programs that can be executed in MapReduce [150]. The platform was developed by Yahoo. The developers can write programs for data manipulation and transformation as data flow sequences using Pig Latin language. These programs are easy to write, understand, and maintain. In addition, Apache Pig offers an infrastructure to evaluate and optimize these programs automatically. This allows developers to focus more on semantics and productivity. Apache Pig can execute its jobs in Apache Tez, or Apache Spark (covered in the following sections).

Apache Hive: This offers a higher-level API to facilitate reading, writing, and managing large datasets [203] residing in distributed storage (e.g. HDFS) using SQL-like queries in a custom query language, called HiveQL. Implicitly, each query is translated into MapReduce commands.

Apache Mahout: This is a machine learning library [337] developed to be used with MapReduce. It provides an API for distributed or scalable machine learning algorithms mostly focusing on linear algebra. It provides algorithms like classification, likelihood estimation, and clustering. All algorithms are implicitly transformed into MapReduce jobs.

Apache Spark: Apache Spark is a generic, in-memory data processing engine [480]. It provides high-level APIs in Java, Python and Scala. Apache Spark has simplified the programming complexity by introducing the abstraction of Resilient Distributed Datasets (RDD), i.e. a logical collection of data partitioned across machines. The rich API for RDDs manipulation follows the models for processing local collections of data, making it easier to develop complex programs. Spark provides higher-level constructs and libraries to further facilitate users in writing distributed applications. At the time of writing, Apache Spark provides four libraries:

Spark SQL - Offers support for SQL querying of data stored in RDDs, or an external data source. It allows structured data processing using high-level collections named dataset and data frame. A Dataset is a distributed collection of data and a DataFrame is a Dataset organized into named columns. It is conceptually similar to a table in a relational database. The DataFrames can be constructed in numerous different ways like reading from structured data files, tables in Hive, external databases, or existing RDDs.

Spark streaming - Spark implements stream processing by ingesting data in minibatches. Spark streaming makes it easy to build scalable fault-tolerant real-time applications. The data can be ingested from a variety of streaming sources like Kafka, Flume (covered in earlier sections). This data can be processed using complex real-time algorithms using a high-level API.

MLlib Machine Learning Library - Provides scalable machine learning algorithms. It provides common algorithms for classification, regression, clustering, algorithms for feature extraction, feature selection and dimensionality reduction, high-level API for machine learning pipelines, saving and loading algorithms, and utilities for linear algebra and statistics.

GraphX - Provides a distributed graph processing using graph-parallel computation. GraphX extends the Spark RDD by introducing "Graph": a directed multigraph with properties attached to each vertex and edge. GraphX comes with a variety of graph operators like subgraph, joinVertices, or algorithms like pageRank, ConnectedComponents, and several graph builders that allow building a graph from a collection of vertices and edges from RDD or other data sources.

Apache Flink: Apache Flink is a true distributed streaming data-flow engine [69] and offers a unified stream and batch processing. It treats batch processing as a special case of streaming with bounded data. The APIs offered by Flink are similar but the implementation is different. Flink executes arbitrary dataflow programs in a data-parallel and pipelined manner. It offers a complete software stack of libraries using building blocks, exposed as abstract data types, for streams (DataStream API), for finite sets (DataSet API) and for relational data processing (relational APIs - the Table API and SQL). The high-level libraries offered by Apache Flink are:

Gelly: Flink Graph - provides methods and utilities to simplify the development of graph analysis applications in Flink. The graphs can be transformed and modified using high-level functions similar to the ones provided by the batch processing API. Gelly provides graph algorithms like pageRank, communityDetection, connectedComponents, or shortestPath finding.

Machine Learning: FlinkML is a machine learning library aimed to provide a list of machine learning algorithms. At the moment, it has been temporarily deprecated in Apache Flink 1.9.0 for the sake of developing ML core and ML pipeline interfaces using high-level APIs.

FlinkCEP: Complex event processing for Flink - Allows detection of event patterns in the incoming stream.

State Processor API - provides functionality to read, write, and modify save points and checkpoints using DataSet API. It also allows using relational Table API or SQL queries to analyze and process state data.

Data Storage: Distributed File Systems. Distributed file systems allow access to the files from multiple hosts, in addition to distributing the storage of large files over multiple machines. Such systems mostly provide the interfaces and semantics, similar to the existing local files systems, while the distributed file system handles the network communication, data movement and distributed directories seamlessly.

Hadoop Distributed File System (HDFS): HDFS, the main component of the Hadoop ecosystem, has become the de facto standard for distributed file systems [62]. It is known as the most reliable storage system. HDFS is designed to run on commodity hardware, making it more popular for its cost-effectiveness. In addition to working with the conventional file management commands (e.g. ls, rm, mkdir, tail, copy, etc), HDFS also works with a REST API that complies with the FileSystem/FileContext interface for HDFS. HDFS architecture is designed to store very large files and does not suit models with large numbers of small files. The files are split into blocks which are then distributed and replicated across the nodes for fault-tolerance. HDFS stores data reliably, even in the case of hardware failure. HDFS provides parallel access to data, resulting in high throughput access to application data.

Data Storage and Querying. RDBMS and SQL have remained the main choice for data storage and management for organizations for years. Gradually, the main strength of RDBMS technology (the fixed schema design) has turned into its fundamental weakness in the era of big and heterogeneous data. Today's data appears in structured and unstructured forms and originates from a variety of sources such as emails, log files, social media, sensor events etc. Besides, high volumes of data are being generated and are subject to high rates of change. On the other hand, one of the key characteristics of big data applications is that they demand real-time responses, i.e. data needs to be stored, such that it can be accessed quickly when required. The non-conventional, relatively new NoSQL (not only SQL) stores are designed to efficiently and effectively tackle these big data requirements. Not only do these stores support dynamic schema design but they also offer increased flexibility, scalability and customization compared to relational databases. These stores are built to support distributed environments, with the ability to scale horizontally by adding new nodes as demand increases. Consistent with the CAP theorem (which states that distributed systems can only guarantee at most two properties from Consistency, Availability and Partition tolerance), NoSQL stores compromise consistency in favour of high availability and scalability. Generally, NoSQL stores support flexible data models, provide simple interfaces and use weak consistency models by abandoning the ACID (Atomicity, Consistency, Isolation, and Durability) transactions in favour of BASE (Basically Available, Soft state, Eventually Consistent) transaction models. Based on the data models supported by these systems, NoSQL databases can be categorised into four groups, i.e. key-value stores, document stores, column-oriented stores and graph databases. The following section describes these NoSQL database models in further detail and lists a few examples of the technologies per model.

Key-Value Stores: Key-value stores can be categorised as the simplest NoSQL databases. These stores are designed for storing schema-free data as Key-Value pairs. The keys are the unique IDs for the data, and they can also work as indexes for accessing the data. The Values contain the actual data in the form of attributes or complex objects. All the values may not share the same structure.

Examples: Redis, Riak KV, Amazon DynamoDB, Memcached, Microsoft Azure Cosmos DB, and etcd.

Document Stores: Document stores are built upon the idea of key-value stores. They pair each key with a complex data structure described as a document. These documents may contain different key-value pairs, key-array pairs or even nested documents. The document stores are designed for storing, retrieving and managing document-oriented information, also known as semi-structured data. There is no schema that all documents must adhere to as in the case for records in relational databases. Each document is assigned a unique key, which is used to retrieve the document. However, it is possible to access documents by querying their internal structure, e.g searching for a field with the specified value. The capability of the query interface is typically dependent on the encoding format like XML or JSON.

Examples: CouchDB, MongoDB

Column-Oriented Stores: Column-oriented stores are also known as widecolumn stores and extensible record stores. They store each column continuously, i.e. on disk or in-memory each column is stored in sequential blocks. Instead of storing data in rows, these databases are designed for storing data tables as sections of columns of data. Therefore, these stores enable faster column-based analytics compared to traditional row-oriented databases.

Examples: Apache HBase, Cassandra

4 Harnessing Big Data as Knowledge Graphs

Today, the term big data is potentially misleading as the size is only one of many important aspects of the data. The word big promotes the misconception that more data means good data and stronger insights. However, it is important to realise that data volume alone is not sufficient to get good answers. The ways we distribute, organize, integrate, and represent the data matters as much as, if not more than, the size of the data. In this section, we briefly cover the variety or the heterogeneity of the data and the possibility of organizing this data as a graph. Organizing the data as a graph has several advantages compared to alternatives like database models. Graphs provide a more intuitive and succinct abstraction for the knowledge in most of the domains. Graphs encode the entities as nodes, and their relationships as edges between entities. For example, in social inter-actions the edges could represent friendship, co-authorship, co-worker-ship, or other types of relations, whereas people are represented as the nodes. Graphs have the ability to encode flexible, incomplete, schema-agnostic information that is typically not possible in the relational scenario. Many graph query languages cannot only support standard operations like joins but also support specialised operators like arbitrary path-finding. At the same time, formal knowledge repre-sentation (based on Ontologies) formats could also be used to create Graphs in a semantically coherent and structured representation (RDF, RDFS). The term knowledge graph was popularised in 2012 by Google with the slogan "things not strings" with an argument that the strings can be ambiguous but in the Knowledge Graphs, the entities (the nodes in a Knowledge Graph) can be dis-ambiguated more easily by exploiting their relationships (edges/properties) with other entities. Numerous definitions of Knowledge Graphs have been proposed in the literature, and a recent and generic definition portrays the "knowledge graph as a graph of data intended to accumulate and convey knowledge of the real world, whose nodes represent entities of interest and whose edges represent relations between these entities" [199]. A high number of public, open, cross-domain knowledge graphs have been created and published online. Examples include DBPedia, Wikidata or YAGO, which are either created by the commu-nity or extract knowledge from Wikipedia. Domain dependent open knowledge graphs have also been published covering areas like geography, life sciences, and tourism. At the same time, numerous enterprise knowledge graphs (mostly in-house) are created by e.g. IBM, Amazon, Facebook, LinkedIn and many others. The creation of these knowledge graphs mainly involves three methods.

Manual Curation e.g. Cyc, Wikidata, Freebase etc.
Creation using Semi-structured sources e.g. Wikipedia (from Wikipedia infoboxes), YAGO (WordNet, Wikipedia etc.) BableNet etc.
Creation from Unstructured Sources e.g. NELL (free text), WebIsA (free text)

As briefly discussed above, such graphs could be created schema-agnostically, as well as using a formal ontology that defines the set of concepts and categories in a given domain alongside their properties and the relations. The knowledge contained in the knowledge graphs can be characterized around two main dimensions: a) Coverage of a single domain, which can be defined by the number of Instances. The instances depict the details covered in a given knowledge graph in a particular area, and more instances mean more details. Coverage could further be defined by the number of assertions, i.e. the relationships contained in the graph. Also, the link degree (average, median) can also assist in estimation of the coverage of the graph. For b) Knowledge Coverage (multiple domains), one can consider the number of classes in the schema, the number of relations, the class hierarchy (depth and width), or the complexity of schema can help in assessing the breadth and depth of the knowledge covered by a given knowledge graph. In practice, the graphs can differ in their sizes in orders of magnitude, but the complexity (linkage) of smaller graphs could still be higher. Similarly, the underlying schema could either be simple or rather deep and detailed. The number of instances per class could vary; on the contrary, there could be fewer instances per class, covering more classes in total. In conclusion, the knowledge graphs differ strongly in size, coverage, and level of detail.

4.1   Graph Stores

In order to handle large sizes of this relatively new-hyped knowledge representation format, several tools have been created which can be categorised into two types, one more general and simple, like graphs, and other relatively formal for RDF data named as Triple Stores.

Graph Databases. Graph databases are based on graph theory and store data in graph structures using nodes and edges connecting each other through relations. These databases are designed for data containing elements which are interconnected, with an undetermined number of relations between them. Graph databases usually provide index-free adjacency, i.e. every element contains a direct pointer to its adjacent elements and no index lookups are necessary. Examples: Neo4J, FlockDB, HyperGraphDB.

Triple Stores. Triple stores are database management systems for the data modelled using RDF. RDF data can be thought of as a directed labelled graph wherein the arcs start with subject URIs, are labelled with predicate URIs, and end up pointing to object URIs or scalar values. This RDF data can be queried using SPARQL query language. Triple stores can be classified into three categories: Native triple stores - Triple stores implemented from scratch exploiting the RDF data model to efficiently store and access the RDF data. Examples: Stardog, Sesame, OWLIM RDBMS-backed triple stores - Triple stores built by adding an RDF specific layer to an existing RDBMS. Example: OpenLink Virtuoso NoSQL triple stores - Triple stores built by adding an RDF specific layer to existing NoSQL databases. Example: CumulusRDF (built on top of Cassandra).

Efficient handling of large-scale knowledge graphs requires the use of distributed file systems, distributed data stores, and partitioning strategies. Apart for several centralised systems, many recent graph processing systems have been built using existing distributed frameworks, e.g. Jena-HBase [241] and H2RDF [341], H2RDF+ [342] make use of HBase, Rya [363] makes use of Accumulo, D-SPARQ [320] works using MongoDB. S2RDF [385], S2X [384], SPARQLGX [168] and SparkRDF [78] handle RDF data using Apache Spark. The main idea behind representing data as a graph is not only querying the data, but also efficient knowledge retrieval including reasoning, knowledge base completion, enrichment (from other sources), entity linking and disambiguation, path mining, and many other forms of analytics. It can be seen from many recent surveys [192, 235, 473] that several systems have been proposed in the literature to deal with one or a few of the many aspects of large-scale knowledge graph processing. It is important to realize this gap and the need for a scalable framework that caters for different tasks for large-scale knowledge graphs.

5   Conclusion

This chapter connects the term big data and knowledge graphs. The first section of this chapter provides an overview of big data, its major enabling technologies, the key characteristics of big data, the challenges that it poses, and the necessary activities to create a big data value chain. In the second section, we cover the big data architectures and provide a taxonomy of big data processing engines. In the last section, we connect the big data with large-scale knowledge graphs covered in Chap. 1 and Chap. 2 of this book. We discuss a few key technologies and cover the possibilities and key challenges to harness large-scale knowledge graphs.

Architecture

Chapter 4
Creation of Knowledge Graphs

Anastasia Dimou[✉][iD]

Department of Electronics and Information Systems,
Ghent University, Ghent, Belgium
anastasia.dimou@ugent.be

Abstract. This chapter introduces how Knowledge Graphs are generated. The goal is to gain an overview of different approaches that were
proposed and find out more details about the current prevalent ones.
After reading this chapter, the reader should have an understanding
of the different solutions available to generate Knowledge Graphs and
should be able to choose the mapping language that best suits a certain
use case.

1 Introduction

The real power of the Semantic Web will be realized once a significant number of
software agents requiring information from different heterogeneous data sources
become available. However, human and machine agents still have limited ability
to interact with heterogeneous data as most data is not available in the form
of knowledge graphs, which are the fundamental cornerstone of the Semantic
Web. They have *different structures* (e.g., tabular, hierarchical), appear in *heterogeneous formats* (e.g., CSV, XML, JSON) and are accessed via *heterogeneous
interfaces* (e.g., database interfaces or Web APIs).

Therefore, different approaches were proposed to generate knowledge graphs
from existing data. In the beginning, custom implementations were proposed
[67,292] and they remain prevalent today [71,177]; however, more generic
approaches emerged as well. Such approaches were originally focused on
data with specific formats, namely dedicated approaches for, e.g., relational
databases [93], data in Excel (e.g. [274]), or in XML format (e.g. [272]). However, data owners who hold data in different formats need to learn and maintain
several tools [111].

To deal with this, different approaches were proposed for integrating heterogeneous data sources while generating knowledge graphs. Those approaches
follow different directions, but detaching the rules definition from their execution
prevailed, because they render the rules interoperable between implementations,
whilst the systems that process those rules are use-case independent. To generate
knowledge graphs, on the one hand, *dedicated mapping languages* were proposed,
e.g., RML [111], and, on the other hand, existing languages for other tasks were
repurposed as mapping languages, e.g., SPARQL-Generate [278].

V. Janev et al. (Eds.): Knowledge Graphs and Big Data Processing, LNCS 12072, pp. 59–72, 2020.
https://doi.org/10.1007/978-3-030-53199-7_4

We focus on *dedicated mapping languages*. The most prevalent dedicated mapping languages are extensions of R2RML [97], the W3C recommendation on knowledge graph generation from relational databases. RML was the first language proposed as an extension of R2RML, but there are more alternative approaches and extensions beyond the originally proposed language. For instance, xR2RML [305], for generating knowledge graphs from heterogeneous databases, and KR2RML [407], for generating knowledge graphs from heterogeneous data.

In the remainder of this chapter, we introduce the Relational to RDF Mapping Language (R2RML) [97] and the RDF Mapping Language (RML) [111] which was the first mapping language extending R2RML to support other heterogeneous formats. Then we discuss other mapping languages which extended or complemented R2RML and RML, or their combination.

2   R2RML

The Relational to RDF Mapping Language (R2RML) [97] is the W3C recommendation to express customized mapping rules from data in relational databases to generate knowledge graphs represented using the Resource Description Framework (RDF) [94]. R2RML considers any custom target semantic schema which might be a combination of vocabularies. The R2RML vocabulary namespace is http://www.w3.org/ns/r2rml# and the preferred prefix is `r2rml`.

In R2RML, RDF triples are generated from the original data in the relational database based on one or more *Triples Maps* (`rr:TriplesMap`, Listing 4.1, line 3). Each *Triples Map* refers to a *Logical Table* (`rr:LogicalTable`, line 4), specified by its *table name* (`rr:tableName`). A *Logical Table* (`rr:LogicalTable`) is either a SQL base table or view, or an R2RML view. An R2RML view is a logical table whose contents are the result of executing a SQL query against the input database. The SQL query result is used to generate the RDF triples (Table 1).

Table 1. Results of female pole vault for 2019 world championship

Rank	Name	Nationality	Mark	Notes
1	Anzhelika Sidorova	Authorized Neutral Athlete	4.95	WL,PB
2	Sandi Morris	United States (USA)	4.90	SB
3	Katerina Stefanidi	Greece	4.85	SB
4	Holly Bradshaw	Great Britain	4.80	
5	Alysha Newman	Canada	4.80	
6	Angelica Bengtsson	Sweden	4.80	NR

```
1   @prefix rr: <http://www.w3.org/ns/r2rml#>.
2
3   <#FemalePoleVault>    rr:logicalTable <#PoleVaultersDBtable> .
4   <#PoleVaultersDBtable> rr:tableName "femalePoleVaulters" .
```

Listing 4.1. A Triples Map refers to a Logical Table specified by its name

A *Triples Map* defines how an RDF triple is generated. It consists of three parts: (i) one *Logical Table* (`rr:LogicalTable`, Listing 4.1), (ii) one *Subject Map* (`rr:SubjectMap`, Listing 4.2, line 2), and (iii) zero or more *Predicate-Object Maps* (`rr:PredicateObjectMap`, Listing 4.2, lines 3 and 4).

```
1  # Triples Map
2  <#FemalePoleVault>  rr:subjectMap          <#Person_SM> ;
3                      rr:predicateObjectMap <#Mark_POM> ;
4                      rr:predicateObjectMap <#Nationality_POM> .
```

Listing 4.2. A Triples Map consists of one Logical Table one Subject Map and zero or more Predicate Object Maps

The *Subject Map* (`rr:SubjectMap`, Listing 4.3, line 2) defines how unique identifiers, using IRIs [118] or blank nodes, are generated. The RDF term generated from the *Subject Map* constitutes the subject of all RDF triples generated from the *Triples Map* that the *Subject Map* is related to.

A *Predicate-Object Map* (`rr:PredicateObjectMap`, Listing 4.3, lines 5 and 10) consists of (i) one or more *Predicate Maps* (`rr:PredicateMap`, line 5), and (ii) one or more *Object Maps* (`rr:ObjectMap`, line 6) or *Referencing Object Maps* (`rr:ReferencingObjectMap`, line 11).

```
1   # Subject Map
2   <#Person_SM>.     rr:template          "http://ex.com/person/{name}"
3
4   # Predicate Object Map with Object Map
5   <#Mark_POM>       rr:predicate         ex:score ;
6                     rr:objectMap         [ rr:column "Mark" ;
7                                            rr:language "en" ] .
8
9   # Predicate Object Map with Referencing Object Map
10  <#Nationality_POM> rr:predicateMap     <#Country_PM> ;
11                     rr:objectMap        <#Country_ROM> ;
```

Listing 4.3. A Predicate Object Map consists of one or more Predicate Maps and one or more Object Maps or Referencing Object Maps

A *Predicate Map* (`rr:PredicateMap`, Listing 4.3, lines 5 and 10) is a *Term Map* (`rr:TermMap`) defining how a triple's predicate is generated. An *Object Map* (`rr:ObjectMap`, line 6) or *Referencing Object Map* (`rr:ReferencingObjectMap`, Listing 4.4, line 11) defines how a triple's object is generated.

A *Referencing Object Map* defines how the object is generated based on the *Subject Map* of another *Triples Map*. If the *Triples Maps* refer to different *Logical Tables*, a join between the *Logical Tables* is required. The *join condition* (`rr:joinCondition`, Listing 4.4, line 3) performs joins as joins are executed in SQL. The join condition consists of a reference to a column name that exists in the *Logical Table* of the *Triples Map* that contains the *Referencing Object Map* (`rr:child`, line 4) and a reference to a column name that exists in the *Logical Table* of the *Referencing Object Map*'s *Parent Triples Map* (`rr:parent`, line 5).

```
1   # Referencing Object Map
2   <#Country_ROM>   rr:parentTriplesMap <#Country_TM> ;
3                    rr:join [
4                                 rr:cild "nationality" ;
5                                 rr:parent "country_name"] .
6
7   <#Country_TM>    rr:logicalTable [ rr:tableName "country" ];
8                    rr:subjectMap   rr:template "http://ex.com/country/{country_name}" .
```

Listing 4.4. A Referencing Object Map generates an object based on the Subject Map of another Triples Map

A *Term Map* (`rr:TermMap`) defines how an RDF term (an IRI, a blank node, or a literal) is generated and it can be constant-, column- or template-valued.

A *constant-valued Term Map* (`rr:constant`, Listing 4.3, line 5) always generates the same RDF term which is by default an IRI.

A *column-valued term map* (`rr:column`, Listing 4.3, line 6) generates a literal by default that is a column in a given *Logical Table*'s row. The language (`rr:language`, line 7) and datatype (`rr:datatype`) may be optionally defined.

A *template-valued* Term Map (`rr:template`, Listing 4.3, line 8) is a valid string template containing referenced columns and generates an IRI by default. If the default termtype is desired to be changed, the term type (`rr:termType`) needs to be defined explicitly (`rr:IRI`, `rr:Literal`, `rr:BlankNode`).

3 RML

The RDF Mapping Language (RML) [110,111] expresses customized mapping rules from heterogeneous data structures, formats and serializations to RDF. RML is a superset of R2RML, aiming to extend its applicability and broaden its scope, adding support for heterogeneous data. RML keeps the mapping rules as in R2RML but excludes its database-specific references from the core model. This way, the input data that is limited to a certain database in R2RML (because each R2RML processor may be associated to only one database), becomes a broad set of one or more input data sources in RML.

RML provides a generic way of defining mapping rules referring to different data structures, combined with case-specific extensions, but remains backwards compatible with R2RML, as relational databases form such a specific case. RML enables mapping rules defining how a knowledge graph is generated from a set of sources that altogether describe a certain domain, can be defined in a combined and uniform way. The mapping rules may be re-used across different sources describing the same domain to incrementally form well-integrated datasets.

The RML vocabulary namespace is http://semweb.mmlab.be/ns/rml# and the preferred prefix is `rml`.

In the remainder of this subsection, we will talk in more details about data retrieval and transformations in RML, as well as other representations of RML.

3.1 Data Retrieval

Data can originally (i) reside on **diverse locations**, e.g., files or databases on the local network, or published on the Web; (ii) be accessed using **different**

interfaces, e.g., raw files, database connectivity for databases, or different interfaces from the Web such as Web APIs; and (iii) have **heterogeneous structures and formats**, e.g., tabular, such as databases or CSV files, hierarchical, such as XML or JSON format, or semi-structured, such as HTML.

In this section, we explain how RML performs the retrieval and extraction steps required to obtain the data whose semantic representation is desired.

Logical Source. RML's *Logical Source* (`rml:LogicalSource`, Listing 4.5) extends R2RML's *Logical Table* and determines the data source with the data to generate the knowledge graph. The R2RML *Logical Table* definition determines a database table, using the *Table Name* (`rr:tableName`). In the case of RML, a broader reference to any input source is required. Thus, the *Logical Source* (`rml:source`) is introduced to specify the source with the original data.

For instance, if the data about countries were in an XML file, instead of a *Logical Table*, we would have a *Logical Source* `<#PoleVaultersXML>` (Listing 4.5, line 3):

```
1  @prefix rml: <http://semweb.mmlab.be/ns/rml#>.
2
3  <#Countries> rml:logicalSource <#CountriesXML> ;
4  <#CountriesXML> rml:source <http://rml.io/data/lambda/countries.xml> .
```

Listing 4.5. A Triples Map refers to a Logical Source whose data is in XML format

The countries data can then be in XML format as below:

```
1   <countries>
2     <country continent="Europe">
3       <country_abb>GR</country_abb>
4       <country_name country_language="en">Greece</country_name>
5       <country_name country_language="nl">Griekenland</country_name>
6     </country>
7     <country continent="Europe">
8       <country_abb>UK</country_abb>
9       <country_name country_language="en">United Kingdom</country_name>
10      <country_name country_language="nl">Verenigd Koninkrijk</country_name>
11    </country>
12    <country continent="America">
13      <country_abb>CA</country_abb>
14      <country_name country_language="en">Canada</country_name>
15      <country_name country_language="nl">Canada</country_name>
16    </country>
17    ...
18  </countries>
```

Listing 4.6. Country data in XML format

Reference Formulation. RML deals with different data serialisations which use different ways to refer to data fractions. Thus, a dedicated way of referring to the data's fractions is considered, while the mapping definitions that define how the RDF terms and triples are generated remain generic. RML considers that any reference to the *Logical Source* should be defined in a form relevant to the input data, e.g. XPath for XML data or JSONPath for JSON data. To this end, the *Reference Formulation* (rml:referenceFormulation) declaration is introduced (Listing 4.7, line 4), indicating the formulation (for instance, a standard, query language or grammar) used to refer to its data.

```
1    @prefix rml: <http://semweb.mmlab.be/ns/rml#>.
2
3    <#Countries>        rml:logicalSource <#CountriesXML> .
4    <#CountriesXML>     rml:referenceFormulation ql:XPath .
5    <#CountriesXML>     rml:iterator "/countries/country" .
```

Listing 4.7. A Logical Source specifies its Reference Formulation and iterator

Iterator. While in R2RML it is already known that a per-row iteration occurs, as RML remains generic, the iteration pattern, if any, cannot always be implicitly assumed, but it needs to be determined. Thereafter, the *iterator* (`rml:iterator`) is introduced (Listing 4.7, line 5). The *iterator* determines the iteration pattern over the data source and specifies the extract of the data during each iteration. The *iterator* is not required to be explicitly mentioned in the case of tabular data sources, as the default per-row iteration is implied.

Source. Data can originally reside on diverse, distributed locations and be accessed using different access interfaces [112]. Data can reside locally, e.g., in files or in a database at the local network, or can be published on the Web. Data can be accessed using diverse interfaces. For instance, metadata may describe how to access the data, such as dataset's metadata descriptions in the case of data catalogues, or dedicated access interfaces might be needed to retrieve data from a repository, such as database connectivity for databases, or different Web interfaces, such as Web APIs.

RML considers an original data source, but the way this input is retrieved remains out of scope, in the same way it remains out of scope for R2RML how the SQL connection is established. Corresponding vocabularies can describe how to access the data, for instance the dataset's metadata (Listing 4.8), hypermedia-driven Web APIs or services, SPARQL services, and database connectivity frameworks (Listing 4.9) [112].

```
1    <#FemalePoleVault>   rr:logicalTable   <#PoleVaultersCSVtable> ;
2    <#PoleVaultersCSVtable> rml:source <#CSVW_source> .
3
4    <#CSVW_source> a csvw:Table;
5              csvw:url "femalePoleVaulters.csv" ;
6              csvw:dialect [ a csvw:Dialect; csvw:delimiter ";" ] .
```

Listing 4.8. A CSV file on the Web as RML Data Source

```
1    <#FemalePoleVault>   rr:logicalTable   <#PoleVaultersDBtable> ;
2    <#PoleVaultersDBtable> rml:source <#DB_source>;
3                     rr:sqlVersion rr:SQL2008;
4                     rr:tableName "femalePoleVaulters" .
5
6    <#DB_source> a d2rq:Database;
7              d2rq:jdbcDSN "CONNECTIONDSN";
8              d2rq:jdbcDriver "com.mysql.cj.jdbc.Driver";
9              d2rq:username "root";
10             d2rq:password "" .
```

Listing 4.9. A table as RML Data Source

Logical Reference. According to R2RML, a *column-valued* or *template-valued term map* is defined as referring to a column name. In the case of RML, a more generic notion is introduced, the logical reference. Its value must be a valid reference to the data of the input dataset according to the specified reference formulation. Thus, the reference's value should be a valid expression according to the *Reference Formulation* defined at the *Logical Source*.

```
1    # Predicate Object Map with Object Map
2    <#CountryName_POM>    rr:predicate ex:name ;
3                          rr:objectMap [
4                              rml:reference "country_name" ;
5                              rml:languageMap [ rml:reference "@country_language"] ] .
```

Listing 4.10. An Object Map in RML with a reference to data according to the Reference Formulation and a language Map to define the language.

RDF Term Maps are instantiated with data fractions referred to using a reference formulation relevant to the corresponding data format. Those fractions are derived from data extracted at a certain iteration from a *Logical Source*. Such a *Logical Source* is formed by data retrieved from a repository accessed as defined by the corresponding dataset or service description vocabulary.

Language Map. RML introduces a new *Term Map* for defining the language, the *Language Map* (rml:LanguageMap, Listing 4.10, line 5), which extends R2RML's language tag (rr:language). The *Language Map* allows not only constant values for language but also references derived from the input data. rr:language is considered then an abbreviation for the rml:languageMap, as rr:predicate is for the rr:predicateMap.

3.2   Data Transformations: FnO

Mapping rules involve (re-)modeling the original data, describing how objects are related by specifying correspondences between data in different schemas [126], and deciding which vocabularies and ontologies to use. *Data transformations*, as opposed to *schema transformations* that the mapping rules represent, are needed to support any changes in the structure, representation or content of data [367], for instance, performing string transformations or computations.

The *Function Ontology* (FnO) [102,104] describes functions uniformly, unambiguously, and independently of the technology that implements them. As RML extends R2RML with respect to *schema transformations*, the combination of RML with FnO extends R2RML with respect to *data transformations*.

A *function* (fno:Function) is an activity which has input parameters, output, and implements certain algorithm(s) (Listing 4.11, line 1). A *parameter* (fno:Parameter) is a function's input value (Listing 4.11, line 4). An *output* (fno:Output) is the function's output value (Listing 4.11, 5). An *execution* (fno:Execution) assigns values to the parameters of a function for a certain execution. An *implementation* (fno:Implementation) defines the internal workings of one or more functions.

```
1  grel:string_split a fno:Function;
2      fno:name "split";
3      dcterms:description "split";
4      fno:expects (grel:string_s grel:string_sep);
5      fno:returns (grel:output_array).
```

Listing 4.11. A function described in FnO that splits a string

The *Function Map* (`fnml:FunctionMap`) is another *Term Map*, introduced as an extension of RML, to facilitate the alignment of the two, RML and FnO. A *Function Map* is generated by executing a function instead of using a constant or a reference to the raw data values. Once the function is executed, its output value is the term generated by this *Function Map*. The `fnml:functionValue` property indicates which instance of a function needs to be executed to generate an output and considering which values.

```
1  <#FemalePoleVault> rr:predicateObjectMap [
2      rr:predicate ex:record;
3      rr:objectMap [
4        fnml:functionValue [
5          rr:predicateObjectMap [
6                rr:predicate fno:executes ;
7                rr:objectMap [ rr:constant grel:split ] ] ;
8          rr:predicateObjectMap [
9                rr:predicate grel:string_s ;
10               rr:objectMap [ rml:reference "notes" ] ] ;
11         rr:predicateObjectMap [
12               rr:predicate grel:string_sep ;
13               rr:objectMap [ rr:constant "," ] ] ] ].
```

Listing 4.12. A Function Map aligns FnO with RML

3.3   Other Representations: YARRRML

YARRRML [103,196] is a human readable text-based representation for mapping rules. It is expressed in YAML [46], a widely used human-friendly data serialization language. YARRRML can be used with both R2RML and RML.

A *mapping* (Listing 4.13, line 1) contains all definitions that state how subjects, predicates, and objects are generated. Each mapping definition is a key-value pair. The key *sources* (line 3) defines the set of data sources that are used to generate the entities. Each source is added to this collection via a key-value pair. The value is a collection with three keys: (i) the key *access* defines the local or remote location of the data source; (ii) the key *reference formulation* defines the reference formulation used to access the data source; and (iii) the key *iterator* (conditionally required) defines the path to the different records over which to iterate. The key *subjects* (line 5) defines how the subjects are generated. The key *predicateobjects* (line 6) defines how combinations of predicates and objects are generated. Below the countries example (Listing 4.6) is shown in YARRRML:

```
1   mappings:
2     country:
3       sources:
4         - ['countries.xml~xpath', '/countries/country']
5       s: http://ex.com/$(country_abb)
6       po:
7         - [ex:name, $(country_name)]
8         - [ex:abbreviation, $(country_abb)]
```

Listing 4.13. A YARRRML set of mapping rules

4 [R2]RML Extensions and Alternatives

Other languages were proposed based on differentiation on (i) data retrieval and (ii) data transformations. The table below (Table 2) summarizes the mapping languages extensions, their prefixes and URIs. xR2RML [306] and KR2RML [407] are the two most prominent solutions that showcase extensions and alternatives respectively for data retrieval. On the one hand, xR2RML extends R2RML following the RML paradigm to support heterogeneous data from non-relational databases. On the other hand, KR2RML extends R2RML relying on the Nested Relational Model (NRM) [455] as an intermediate form to represent data originally stored in relational databases. KR2RML also provided an alternative for data transformations, but FunUL is the most prominent alternative to FnO.

Table 2. [R2]RML extensions, their URIs and prefixes

Language	Prefix	URI
R2RML	rr	http://www.w3.org/ns/r2rml#
RML	rml	http://semweb.mmlab.be/ns/rml#
xR2RML	xrr	http://www.i3s.unice.fr/ns/xr2rml#
FnO+RML	fnml	http://semweb.mmlab.be/ns/fnml#
FnO	fno	https://w3id.org/function/ontology#

4.1 XR2RML

xR2RML [306] was proposed in 2014 in the intersection of R2RML and RML. xR2RML extends R2RML beyond relational databases and RML to include non-relational databases. xR2RML extends R2RML following the RML paradigm but is specialized for non-relational databases and, in particular, NoSQL and XML databases. NoSQL systems have heterogeneous data models (e.g., key-value, document, extensible column, or graph store), as opposed to relational databases. xR2RML assumes, as R2RML does, that a processor executing the rules is connected to a certain database. How the connection or authentication is established against the database is out of the language's scope, as in R2RML.

The xR2RML vocabulary preferred prefix is **xrr** and the namespace is the following: http://www.i3s.unice.fr/ns/xr2rml#.

Data Source. Similarly to RML, an xR2RML Triples Map refers to a Logical Source (`xrr:logicalSource`, Listing 4.14, line 3), but similarly to R2RML, this Logical Source can be either an xR2RML base table (`xrr:sourceName`, for databases where tables exist) or an xR2RML view representing the results of executing a query against the input database (`xrr:query`, line 4).

```
1  @prefix xrr: <http://www.i3s.unice.fr/ns/xr2rml#> .
2
3  <#CountriesXML> xrr:logicalSource [
4      xrr:query """for $i in ///countries/country return $i; """;
5      rml:iterator "//countries/country";];
6  <#CountryName_POM>    rr:predicate ex:name ;
7                        rr:objectMap [ xrr:reference "country_name"] .
```

Listing 4.14. xR2RML logical source over an XML database supporting XQuery

Iterator. xR2RML originally introduced the `xrr:iterator`, according to the `rml:iterator`, to iterate over the results. In a later version, xR2RML converged using the `rml:iterator` (Listing 4.14, line 5).

Format or Reference Formulation. In contrast to RML that considers a formulation (`rml:referenceFormulation`) to refer to its input data, xR2RML originally specified explicitly the format of data retrieved from the database using the property `xrr:format` (Listing 4.15, line 2). For instance, RML considers XPath or XQuery or any other formulation to refer to data in XML format, xR2RML would refer to the format, e.g. `xrr:XML`. While RML allows for other kinds of query languages to be introduced, xR2RML decides exactly which query language to use. In an effort to converge with RML, xR2RML considers optionally a reference formulation.

```
1  <#FemalePoleVault>    xrr:logicalSource    <#PoleVaultersCSVtable> ;
2  <#PoleVaultersCSVtable> xrr:format xrr:Row .
```

Listing 4.15. A CSV file on the Web as xR2RML Logical Source

Reference. Similar to RML, xR2RML uses a reference (`xrr:reference`) to refer to the data elements (Listing 4.14, line 7). xR2RML extends RML's reference to refer to data elements in data with mixed formats. xR2RML considers cases where different formats are nested; for instance, a JSON extract is embedded in a cell of a tabular structure. A path with mixed syntax consists of the concatenation of several path expressions separated by the slash '/' character.

Collections and Containers. Several RDF terms can be generated by a *Term Map* during an iteration if multiple values are returned. This can normally generate several triples, but it can also generate hierarchical values in the form of RDF collections or containers. To achieve the latter, xR2RML extends R2RML by introducing corresponding datatypes to support the generation of containers. xR2RML introduces new *term types* (`rr:termType`): `xrr:RdfList` for an `rdf:List`, `xrr:RdfBag` for `rdf:Bag`, `xrr:RdfSeq` for `rdf:Seq` and `xrr:RdfAlt` for `rdf:Alt`. All *RDF terms* produced by the *Object Map* during one triples map iteration step are then grouped as members of one term. To achieve this, two more constructs are introduced: *Nested Term Maps* and *Push Downs*.

```
1   <#Countries> rr:predicateObjectMap [
2       rr:predicate ex:name;
3       rr:objectMap [
4         xrr:reference "country_name";
5         rr:termType xrr:RdfList;
6         xrr:pushDown [ xrr:reference "@continent"; xrr:as "continent" ];
7         xrr:nestedTermMap [
8           rr:template "{continent}: {country_name}" ;
9           rr:termType rr:Literal ;
10          rr:dataType xsd:string ] ].
```

Listing 4.16. An xrr:RdfList in xR2RML

Nested Term Map. A *Nested Term Map* (`xrr:NestedTermMap`, Listing 4.16, line 7) accepts the same properties as a *Term Map* and can be used to specify a term type, a language tag or a data type for the members of the generated RDF collection or container.

Push Down. Within an iteration, it may be needed to access data elements higher in the hierarchical documents in the context of hierarchical data formats, such as XML or JSON. To deal with this, xR2RML introduces the `xrr:pushDown` property (Listing 4.16, line 6).

4.2   KR2RML

KR2RML [407] extends R2RML in a different way than xR2RML. KR2RML relies on the Nested Relational Model (NRM) as an intermediate form to represent data. The data is mapped into tables by translating it into tables and rows where a column in a table can be either a scalar value or a nested table. Besides the data retrieval part, KR2RML extends R2RML with data transformations using User Defined Functions (UDFs) written in Python.

Data Source. Mapping *tabular data* (e.g., CSV) into the Nested Relational Model is straightforward. The model has a one-to-one mapping of tables, rows, and columns, unless a transformation like splitting on a column occurs, which will create a new column that contains a nested table.

Mapping *hierarchical data* (e.g., JSON, XML) into the Nested Relational Model requires a translation algorithm for each data format next to the mapping language. Such an algorithm is considered for data in XML and JSON format. If the data is in JSON, an object maps to a single row table in NRM with a column for each field. Each column is populated with the value of the appropriate field. Fields with scalar values do not need translation, but fields with array values are translated to their own nested tables: if the array contains scalar or object values, each array element becomes a row in the nested table. If the elements are scalar values like strings as in the tags field, a default column name "values" is provided. If a JSON document contains a JSON array at the top level, each element is treated like a row in a database table. If the data is in XML format, its elements are treated like JSON objects, and its attributes and repeated child elements as single-row nested table where each attribute is a column.

References. The *column-valued term map* is not limited to SQL identifiers as it occurs in R2RML to support mapping nested columns in the NRM. A JSON array is used to capture the column names that make up the path to a nested column from the document root. The *template-valued term map* is also extended to include columns that do not exist in the original input but are the result of the transformations applied by the processor.

Joins. Joins are not supported because they are considered to be impractical and require extensive planning and external support.

Execution Planning. A tag (`km-dev:hasWorksheetHistory`) is introduced to capture the cleaning, transformation and modeling steps.

Data Transformations. The Nested Transformation Model can also be used to embed transformation functions. A transformation function can create a new set of nested tables instead of transforming the data values.

4.3   FunUL

FunUL [232] is an alternative to FnO for data transformations. FunUL allows the definition of functions as part of the mapping language. In FunUL, functions have a name and a body. The name needs to be unique. The body defines the function using a standardized programming language. It has a return statement and a call refers to a function with an optional set of parameters.

The FunUL vocabulary namespace is http://kdeg.scss.tcd.ie/ns/rrf# and the preferred prefix is `rrf`.

The class `rrf:Function` defines a function (Listing 4.17, line 3). A function definition has two properties defining the name (`rrf:functionName`, line 4), and the function body (`rrf:functionBody`, line 5).

A function can be called using the property `rrf:functionCall` (Listing 4.17, line 13). This property refers to a `rrf:Function` with the property `rr:function` (line 14). Parameters are defined using `rrf:parameterBindings` (line 15).

```
1    @prefix rrf: <http://kdeg.scss.tcd.ie/ns/rrf#> .
2
3    <#SplitTransformation> a rrf:Function ;
4        rrf:functionName "splitTransformation" ;
5        rrf:functionBody
6            """function split(value, separator) {
7                str = value.split(separator).trim();
8                return str; ""; } """ ; .
9
10   <#FemalePoleVault> rr:predicateObjectMap [
11       rr:predicate ex:record;
12       rr:objectMap [
13         rrf:functionCall [
14           rrf:function <#SplitTransformation> ;
15           rrf:parameterBindings (
```

```
16          [ rml:reference "notes" ]
17          [ rml:reference "," ] ); ];
```

Listing 4.17. A Function Call aligns FunUL with RML

5 Conclusions

A lack of in-depth understanding of the complexity of generating knowledge
graphs and the many degrees of freedom in modeling and representing knowledge
prevents human and software agents from profiting of the Semantic Web potential. This chapter identified the different approaches that were proposed in recent
years for generating knowledge graphs from heterogeneous data sources. Then,
the chapter focused on approaches that distinguish mapping rules definition
from their execution. Two types of mapping languages prevailed, *dedicated mapping languages* and *repurposed mapping languages*. The chapter further focused
on *dedicated mapping languages* because they follow the W3C-recommended
R2RML.

This chapter presents the author's view on knowledge graph generation. It
serves as an introductory chapter to knowledge graphs, which are considered in
greater detail in the following chapters. The next two chapters will explain how
to perform federated querying and reasoning over knowledge graphs (Table 3).

Table 3. Mapping Languages comparison with respect to data retrieval

	R2RML	RML	xR2RML	KR2RML
Extends	–	R2RML	R2RML & RML	R2RML
Data source	rr:LogicalTable	rml:LogicalSource	xrr:LogicalSource	rr:LogicalTable
Data references	–	Reference formulation	xrr:format	–
Reference	rr:column rr:template	rml:reference rr:template	xrr:reference rr:template	rr:column rr:template
Reference formulation	SQL	SQL/XPath/ JSONPath acc. Reference formulation	SQL/XPath/ JSONPath acc. xrr:format	SQL/XPath/ JSONPath
Join	rr:join	rr:join (extended)	rr:join (extended)	Not supported
Declarative iterator	No	Yes	Yes	No
Iterator	–	rml:iterator	xrr:iterator	–
Query	rr:sqlQuery	rml:query	xrr:query	rr:sqlQuery
Lists	–	–	xrr:RdfList	–

Chapter 5
Federated Query Processing

Kemele M. Endris[1,2]([envelope])[iD], Maria-Esther Vidal[1][iD], and Damien Graux[3][iD]

[1] TIB Leibniz Information Centre For Science and Technology, Hannover, Germany
[2] L3S Research Center, Hannover, Germany
endris@L3S.de
[3] ADAPT SFI Research Centre, Trinity College, Dublin, Ireland

Abstract. Big data plays a relevant role in promoting both manufacturing and scientific development through industrial digitization and emerging interdisciplinary research. Semantic web technologies have also experienced great progress, and scientific communities and practitioners have contributed to the problem of big data management with ontological models, controlled vocabularies, linked datasets, data models, query languages, as well as tools for transforming big data into knowledge from which decisions can be made. Despite the significant impact of big data and semantic web technologies, we are entering into a new era where domains like genomics are projected to grow very rapidly in the next decade. In this next era, integrating big data demands novel and scalable tools for enabling not only big data ingestion and curation but also efficient large-scale exploration and discovery. Federated query processing techniques provide a solution to scale up to large volumes of data distributed across multiple data sources. Federated query processing techniques resort to source descriptions to identify relevant data sources for a query, as well as to find efficient execution plans that minimize the total execution time of a query and maximize the completeness of the answers. This chapter summarizes the main characteristics of a federated query engine, reviews the current state of the field, and outlines the problems that still remain open and represent grand challenges for the area.

1 Introduction

The number and variety of data collections have grown exponentially over recent decades and a similar growth rate is expected in the coming years. In order to transform the enormous amount of disparate data into knowledge from where actions can be taken, fundamental problems, such as data integration and query processing, must be solved. Data integration requires the effective identification of entities that, albeit described differently, correspond to the same real-world entity. Moreover, data is usually ingested in myriad unstructured formats and may suffer reduced quality due to biases, ambiguities, and noise. These issues impact on the complexity of the solutions for data integration. Semantic integration of big data entails variety by enabling the resolution of several interoperability conflicts

V. Janev et al. (Eds.): Knowledge Graphs and Big Data Processing, LNCS 12072, pp. 73–86, 2020.
https://doi.org/10.1007/978-3-030-53199-7_5

[159, 446], e.g., structuredness, schematic, representation, completeness, granularity, and entity matching conflicts. Conflicts arise because data sources may have different data models or none, follow various schemes for data representation, and contain complementary information. Furthermore, a real-world entity may be represented using diverse properties or at various levels of detail. Thus, techniques able to solve interoperability issues while addressing data complexity challenges imposed by big data characteristics are required [402].

Existing solutions to the problem of query processing over heterogeneous datasets rely on a unified interface for overcoming interoperability issues, usually based on metamodels [224]. Different approaches have been proposed, mainly with a focus on data ingestion and metadata extraction and management. Exemplary approaches include GEMMS [365], PolyWeb [244], BigDAWG [119], Ontario [125], and Constance [179]. These systems collect metadata about the main characteristics of the heterogeneous data collections, e.g., formats and query capabilities. Additionally, they resort to a global ontology to describe contextual information and relationships among data sets. Rich descriptions of the properties and capabilities of the data have shown to be crucial for enabling these systems to effectively perform query processing.

In the context of the Semantic Web, the problem of federated query processing has also been actively studied. As a result, diverse federated SPARQL query engines have been defined that enable users to execute queries over a federation of SPARQL endpoints. State-of-the-art techniques include FedX [389], ANAPSID [6], and MULDER [124]. FedX implements adaptive techniques to identify relevant sources to evaluate a query. It is able to contact SPARQL endpoints on the fly to decide the subqueries of the original query that can be executed over the endpoints of the federation. ANAPSID makes use of metadata about the vocabularies used on the RDF datasets to perform source selection. Based on the selected sources, ANAPSID decomposes original queries and finds efficient plans to collect the answers incrementally. Finally, MULDER resorts to description of the RDF datasets based on the classes and relations of the dataset vocabularies. MULDER proposes the concept of the RDF Molecule Templates (RDF-MTs) to describe the datasets and efficiently perform source selection and query planning. The rich repertoire of federated query engines just reveals the importance of query processing against the RDF dataset, as well as the attention that the problem has received from the database and semantic web communities.

The contributions of the work are summarized as follows:

- A description of the concept of the data integration system and an analysis of the different parameters that impact on the complexity of a system.
- A characterization of the challenges addressed by federated query engines and analysis of the current state of the federated query processing field.
- A discussion of the analysis of the grand challenges in this area and future directions.

The remainder of the chapter is structured as follows: Sect. 2 presents an overview of the data integration system and the roles that they play in the problem of accessing and processing queries over heterogeneous data sources.

Section 3 describes the problem of federated query processing, the main challenges to be addressed by a federated query engine, and the state of the art. Finally, grand challenges and future directions are outlined in Sect. 4.

2 Data Integration Systems

An enormous amount of data is being published on the web [379]. In addition, different data sources are being generated and stored within enterprises as well due to technological advances in data collection, generation, and storage. These data sources are created independently of each other and might belong to different administrative entities. Hence, they have different data representation formats as well as access interfaces. Such properties of the data sources hinder the usage of the information available in them. Data integration is the process of providing uniform access to a set of distributed (or decentralised), autonomous, and heterogeneous data sources [114]. Data integration systems provide a global schema (also known as mediated schema) to provide a reconciled view of all data available in different data sources. Mapping between the global schema and source schema should be established to combine data residing in data sources considered in the integration process. Generally, data integration system is formally defined as follows [280]:

Definition 1 (Data Integration System). *A data integration system, $\mathbb{I}$, is defined as a triple $<G, S, M>$, where:*

- *G is the global schema, expressed in a language L_G over an alphabet A_G. The alphabet comprises a symbol for each element of G.*
- *S is the source schema, expressed in a language L_S over an alphabet A_S. The alphabet A_S includes a symbol for each element of the sources.*
- *M is the mapping between G and S, constituted by a set of assertions of the forms: $q_S \rightarrow q_G$, $q_G \rightarrow q_S$; where q_S and q_G are two queries of the same arity, respectively over the source schema S, and over the global schema G. An assertion specifies the connection between the elements of the global schema and those of the source schema.*

Defining schema mapping is one of the main tasks in a data integration system. Schema mapping is the specification of correspondences between the data at the sources and the global schema. The mappings determine how the queries posed by the user using the global schema are answered by translating to the schema of the source that stores the data. Two basic approaches for specifying such mappings have been proposed in the literature for data integration systems are *Global-as-View (GAV)* [140, 180] and *Local-as-View (LAV)* [282, 433].

Rules defined using the Global-as-View (GAV) approach define concepts in the global schema as a set of views over the data sources. Using the GAV approach, the mapping rules in M define the concepts of the schema in the sources, S, with each element in the global schema. A query posed over the global schema, G, needs to be reformulated by rewriting the query with the views defined in, M. Such rewriting is also known as *query unfolding* – the process of rewriting the query defined over global schema to a query that only refers to the source schema. Conceptually, GAV mappings specify directly how to compute tuples of the global schema relations from tuples in the sources. This characteristics of GAV mappings makes them easier for query unfolding strategy. However, adding and removing sources in the GAV approach may involve updating all the mappings in the global schema, which requires knowledge of all the sources. Mappings specified using the Local-as-View (LAV) approach describe the data sources as views over the global schema, contrary to the GAV approach that defines the global schema as views over the data sources. Using the LAV approach, the mapping rules in M associates a query defined over the global schema, G, to each elements of source schema, S. Adding and removing sources in LAV is easier than GAV, as data sources are described independently of each other. In addition, it allows for expressing incomplete information as the global schema represents a database whose tuples are unknown, i.e., the mapping M defined by LAV approach might not contain all the corresponding sources for all the elements in the global schema, G. As a result, query answering in LAV may consist of querying incomplete information, which is computationally more expensive [114].

In this chapter, we define a source description model, RDF Molecule Template (RDF-MT), an abstract description of entities that share the same characteristics, based on the GAV approach. The global schema is defined as a consolidation of RDF-MTs extracted from each data source in the federation. Rule-based mappings, such as RML, are used to define the GAV mappings of heterogeneous data sources. RDF-MTs are merged based on their semantic descriptions defined by the ontology, e.g., in RDFS.

2.1   Classification of Data Integration Systems

Data integration systems can be classified with respect to the following three dimensions: autonomy, distribution, and heterogeneity [338], Fig. 1. *Autonomy* dimension characterizes the degree to which the integration system allows each data source in the integration to operate independently. Data sources have autonomy over choice of their data model, schema, and evolution. Furthermore, sources

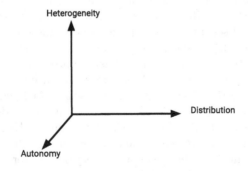

Fig. 1. Dimensions of data integration systems

also have autonomy to join or leave the integration system at any time as well as to select which fragments of data to be accessible by the integration system and its users. *Distribution* dimension specifies the data that is physically distributed across computer networks. Such distribution (or decentralization) can be achieved by controlled distribution or by the autonomous decision of the data providers. Finally, *heterogeneity* may occur due to the fact that autonomous development of systems yields different solutions, for reasons such as different understanding and modeling of the same real-world concepts, the technical environment, and particular requirements of the application [338]. Though there are different types of heterogeneity of data sources, the important ones with respect to data interoperability are related to data model, semantic, and interface heterogeneity. Data model heterogeneity captures the heterogeneity created by various modeling techniques such that each data model has different expressive power and limitations, e.g., relational tables, property graph, and RDF. Semantic heterogeneity concerns the semantics of data and schema in each source. The semantics of the data stored in each source are defined through the explicit definition of their meanings in the schema element. Finally, interface heterogeneity exists if data sources in the integration system are accessible via different query languages, e.g., SQL, Cypher, SPARQL, and API call.

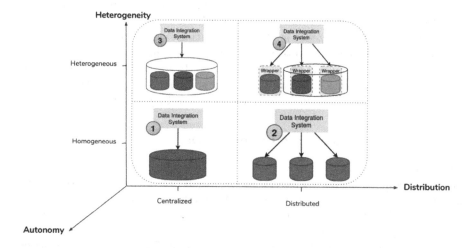

Fig. 2. Classification of data integration systems

Figure 2 shows different classifications of data integration systems with respect to distribution and heterogeneity dimensions. The first type of data integration systems, Fig. 2.(1), loads heterogeneous data from data sources to a centralized storage after transforming them to a common data representation format. The second type of data integration systems, Fig. 2.(2), supports data distributed across networks; however, they only support if the data sources in the system are homogeneous in terms of data model and access methods. The third type of data integration systems, Fig. 2.(3), supports data heterogeneity among data sources in the integration system. However, these data integration systems are managed in a centralized way and data is stored in a distributed file system (DFS), such as Hadoop[1]. Finally, the fourth type of data integration systems, Fig. 2.(4), supports data distributed across networks as well as heterogeneity of data sources. Such integration systems utilize special software components to extract data from the data sources using native query language and access mechanism. They can also transform data extracted from the sources to data representation defined by the integration system. Data sources in the integration system might also be autonomous. Such types of system are different from the third type by how data is distributed and stored. While the fourth type supports any storage management, including DFS, the third type of data integration systems supports only DFS in a centralized way. Mostly the distribution task is handled by the file system. For instance, data might be stored in a multi-modal data management system or in Data Lake storage based only on a distributed file system (DFS). In the third type of data integration system, data is loaded from the original source to the centralized storage for further processing. Federated query processing systems fall in the second and fourth type of integration system when the data sources are autonomous.

Data integration systems also have to make sure that data that is current (fresh) is accessed and integrated. Especially, for DFS-based Data Lakes, Fig. 2.(2), and the centralized, Fig. 2.(4), integration systems, updates of the original data sources should be propagated to guarantee the freshness of data. Furthermore, when accessing an original data source from the provider is restricted, or management of data in a local replica is preferred, integration systems Fig. 2.(1) and (3), need to guarantee data freshness by propagating changes.

2.2   Data Integration in the Era of Big Data

In the era of big data, a large amount of structured, semi-structured, and unstructured data is being generated at a faster rate than ever before. Big data systems that integrate different data sources need to handle such characteristics of data efficiently and effectively. Generally, big data is defined as data whose volume, acquisition speed, data representation, veracity, and potential value overcome the capacity of traditional data management systems [77]. Big data is characterized by the 5Vs model: *Volume* denotes that generation and collection of data are produced at increasingly big scales. *Velocity* represents that data is generated and collected rapidly. *Variety* indicates heterogeneity in data types, formats, structuredness, and data generation scale. Veracity refers to noise and quality issues in the data. Finally, *Value* denotes the benefit and usefulness that can be obtained from processing and mining big data.

---

[1] https://hadoop.apache.org/.

There are two data access strategies for data integration: *schema-on-write* and *schema-on-read*. In the schema-on-write strategy, data is cleansed, organized, and transformed according to a pre-defined schema before loading to the repository. In schema-on-read strategy, raw data is loaded to the repository as-is and schema is defined only when the data is needed for processing [27]. Data warehouses provide a common schema and require data cleansing, aggregation, and transformation in advance, hence, following the schema-on-write strategy. To provide scalable and flexible data discovery, analysis, and reporting, *Data Lakes* have been proposed. Unlike data warehouses, where data is loaded to the repository after it is transformed to a target schema and data representation, Data Lakes store data in its original format, i.e., the schema-on-read strategy. Data Lakes provide a central repository for raw data that is made available to the user immediately and defer any aggregation or transformation tasks to the data analysis phase, thus addressing the problem of disconnected information silos, which is the result of non-integrated heterogeneous data sources in isolated repositories with diverse schema and query languages. Such a central repository may include different data management systems, such as distributed file systems, relational database management systems, graph data management systems, as well as triple stores for specialized data model and storage.

3 Federated Query Processing

A federated query processing system[2], provides a unified access interface to a set of autonomous, distributed, and heterogeneous data sources. While distributed query processing systems have control over each dataset, federated query processing engines have no control over datasets in the federation and data providers can join or leave the federation at any time and modify their datasets independently. Query processing in the context of data sources in a federation is more difficult than in centralized systems because of the different parameters involved that affect the performance of the query processing engine [114]. Data sources in a federation might contain fragments of data about an entity, have different processing capabilities, support different access patterns, access methods, and operators. The role of a federated query engine is to transform a query expressed in terms of the global schema, i.e., the federated query, into an equivalent query expressed in the schema of the data sources, i.e., local query. The local query represents the actual execution plan of the federated query by the data sources of the federation. The transformation of the federated query to a local query needs to be both effective and efficient. Query transformations are effective if the generated query is equivalent to the original one, i.e., both the original and the transformed queries produce same results. On the other hand, query transformations are efficient if the execution strategy of the transformed query makes use of minimum computational resources and communication cost. Producing

---

[2] We use the terms *federated query processing system, federated query engine,* and *federated query processing system* interchangeably.

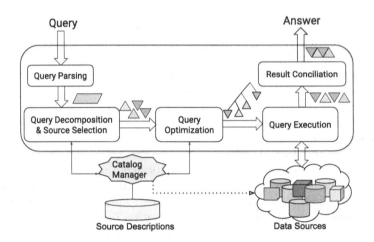

Fig. 3. Federated query processing basic components

an efficient execution strategy is difficult as many equivalent and correct transformations can be produced and each equivalent execution strategy leads to
different consumption of resources [338]. The main objective of federated query
processing is to transform a query posed on a federation of data sources into a
query composed of the union of subqueries over individual data sources of the
federation. Further, a query plan is generated in order to speed up the processing
of each individual subquery over the selected sources, as well as the gathering of
the results into the query answer. An important part of query processing in the
context of federated data sources is query optimization as many execution plans
are correct transformations of the same federated query. The one that optimizes
(minimizes) resource consumption should be retained. Query processing performance can be measured by the total cost that will be used in query processing
and the response time of the query, i.e., time elapsed for executing the query.

As an RDF data model continues gaining popularity, publicly available RDF
datasets are growing in number and size. One of the challenges emerging from
this trend is how to efficiently and effectively execute queries over a set of
autonomous RDF datasets. Saleem et al. [380] study federated RDF query
engines with web access interfaces. Based on their survey results, the authors
divide federation approaches into three main categories: *Query Federation over
SPARQL endpoints*, *Query Federation over Linked Data (via URI lookups)*, and
Query Federation on top of Distributed Hash Tables. Moreover, Acosta et al. [5]
classified federated RDF query processing engines based on the type of data
sources they support into three categories: *Federation of SPARQL endpoints*,
Federation of RDF Documents, and *Federation of Triple Pattern Fragments*.

Conceptually, federated query processing involves four main sub-problems
(components): (i) *data source description*, (ii) *query decomposition and source
selection*, (iii) *query planning and optimization*, and (iv) *query execution*. Federated query engines also include two additional sub-problems: *query parsing* and

result conciliation. Query parsing and result conciliation sub-problems deal with syntactic issues of the given query and formatting the results returned from the query execution, respectively. Below we provide an overview of the data source description, query decomposition and source selection, query planning and optimization as well as query execution sub-problems.

3.1   Data Source Description

The data source description sub-problem deals with describing the data available in data sources and managing catalogs about data sources that are participating in the federation. Data source descriptions encode information about available data sources in the federation, types of data in each data source, access method of data sources, and privacy and access policies of these data sources [114]. The specification of what data exist in data sources and how the terms used in data sources are related to the global schema are specified by the schema mapping. Schema mappings also represent privacy and access control restrictions as well as statistics on the available data in each data source. Federated query engines rely on the description of data sources in the federation to select relevant sources that may contribute to answer a query. Data source descriptions are utilized by source selection, query decomposition, and query optimization sub-problems.

A catalog of data source descriptions can be collected offline or during query running-time. Based on the employed catalog of source descriptions, SPARQL federation approaches can be divided into three categories [380]: *pre-computed catalog assisted, on-the-fly catalog assisted, and hybrid (uses both pre-computed and on-the-fly)* solutions. Pre-computed catalog-assisted federated SPARQL query engines use three types of catalogs: service descriptions, VoID (*Vocabulary of Interlinked Datasets*) description, and list of predicates [335]. The first two catalogs are computed and published by the data source providers that contains descriptions about the set of vocabularies used, a list of classes and predicates, as well as some statistics about the instances such as number of triples per predicate, or class. Specifically in VoID descriptions, there is information about external linksets that indicate the existence of *owl:sameAs* and other linking properties. The third type of catalog, i.e., a list of predicates, is generated by contacting the data source endpoints and issuing SPARQL queries and extracting predicates from the other two types of catalog.

FedX [389] does not require a catalog of source descriptions computed beforehand but uses triple pattern-wise ASK queries sent to data sources at query time. Triple pattern-wise ASK queries are SPARQL ASK queries which contain only one triple pattern in the graph expression of the given query. Lusail [4], like FedX, uses an on-the-fly catalog solution for source selection and decomposition. Unlike FedX, Lusail takes an additional step to check if pairs of triple patterns can be evaluated as one subquery over a specific endpoint; this knowledge is exploited by Lusail during query decomposition and optimization. Posting too many SPARQL ASK queries can be a burden for data sources that have limited compute resources, which may result in DoS. Pre-computed catalog of data source descriptions can be used to reduce the number of requests sent to the data sources. ANAPSID [6] is a federated query processing engine that employs a hybrid solution and collects a list of RDF predicates of the triple patterns that can be answered by the data sources and sends ASK queries when required during query time. Publicly available dataset metadata are utilized by some federated query processing engines as catalogs of source descriptions. SPLENDID [160] relies on instance-level metadata available as *Vocabulary of Interlinked Datasets* (VoID) [10] for describing the sources in a federation. SPLENDID provides a hybrid solution by combining VoID descriptions for data source selection along with SPARQL ASK queries submitted to each dataset at run-time for verification. Statistical information for each predicate and types in the dataset are organized as inverted indices, which will be used for data source selection and join order optimization. Similarly, Semagrow [75] implements a hybrid solution, like SPLENDID, and triple pattern-wise source selection method which uses VoID descriptions (if available) and SPARQL ASK queries.

MULDER [124] and Ontario [125] federated query engine employs source description computed based on the concept of RDF molecules; a set of triples that share the same subject values are called *RDF Molecules*. RDF Molecule Templates (RDF-MTs) encode an abstract description of a set of RDF molecules that share similar characteristics such as semantic type of entities. RDF Molecule Template-based source descriptions leverage the semantics encoded in data sources. It is composed of a semantic concept shared by RDF molecules, a set of mapping rules, a list of properties that a molecule can have, and a list of intra- and inter-connections between other RDF molecule templates. Such description models provide a holistic view over the set of entities and their relationships within the data sources in the federation. For instance, Fig. 4 shows RDF-MT based descriptions of the FedBench benchmark composed on 10 RDF data sources.

3.2   Query Decomposition and Source Selection

Selecting the relevant data sources for a given query is one of the sub-problems in federated query processing. Given a federated query parsed with no syntactic problems, the query is first checked if it is semantically correct with respect to the global schema. This step eliminates an incorrect query that yields no results early on. The query is then simplified by, for example, removing redundant predicates. The task of source selection is to select the actual implementation of subqueries in the federation at specific data sources. The sources schema and global schema are given by the data source descriptions as input to this sub-problem. The query decomposition and source selection sub-problem decomposes the federated query into subqueries associated with data sources in the federation that are selected for executing the subqueries. The number of data sources considered for selection are bounded by the data source description given to the federated query processing engine. Each sub-query may be associated to zero or more data source, thus, if the query contains at least one sub-query without data source(s) associated with it, then the global query can be rejected. Source selection task is a critical part of query optimization. Failure to select correct data sources might

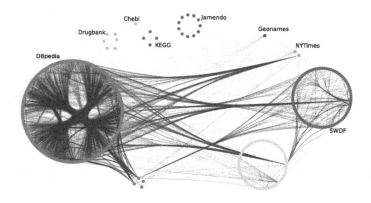

Fig. 4. RDF-MT-based description of FedBench. The graph comprises 387 RDF-MTs and $6,317$ intra- and inter-dataset links. The dots in each circle represent RDF-MTs. A line between dots in the same circle shows intra-dataset links, while a line between dots in different circles corresponds to inter-dataset links. In numbers, there is only one RDF-MT in ChEBI, 234 in DBpedia, six in Drugbank, one in Geonames, 11 in Jamendo, four in KEGG, 53 in LinkedMDB, two in NYTimes, and 80 in SWDF dataset. Four of these RDF-MTs belong to at least two FedBench datasets, modeled as separate circular dots.

lead to incomplete answers as well as high response time and resource consumption. The output of this component is a decomposed query into subqueries that are associated with the selected data sources in the federation. Identifying the relevant sources of a query not only leads to a complete answer but also faster execution time.

3.3 Query Planning and Optimization

The goal of query planning is to generate an execution plan that represent the steps on how the query is executed and which algorithms (operators) are used. The task of query plan generation produces query execution plans, e.g., a tree-based plan where the leaf of the tree corresponds to the sub-queries to be executed in selected data sources and the internal nodes corresponds to the physical (algebraic) operators, such as join, union, project, and filter, that perform algebraic operations by the federated query processing engine. Many semantically equivalent execution plans can be found by permuting the order of operators and subqueries. However, the cost of executing different ordering of a query is not always the same. In a federated setting, the number of intermediate results as well as the communication costs impacts the performance of query execution. Federated query processing engines should use an optimization techniques to select an optimal execution plan that reduces execution time and resource usage, such as memory, communication, etc. Optimization of the query execution plan starts from selecting only relevant sources, decomposition and finally

making decisions on the selection of appropriate implementation of join operations. These optimization techniques include making decisions on selection of
the join methods, ordering, and adapting to the condition of the sources. The
objective of the planning and optimization sub-problem is to find an execution
plan that minimizes the cost of processing the given query, i.e., finding the "best"
ordering of operators in the query, which is close to optimal solution. Finding
an optimal solution is computationally intractable [210]. Assuming a simplified
cost function, it is proven that the minimization of this cost function for a query
with many joins is NP-Complete. To select the ordering of operators, it is necessary to estimate execution costs of alternative candidate orderings. There are
two type of query optimization in the literature: cost-based and heuristics-based
query optimization. In cost-based optimization techniques, estimating the cost
of the generated plans, i.e., candidate orderings, requires collecting statistics on
each of the data sources either before query executions, *static optimization* or
during query execution, *dynamic optimization*. In federated settings, where data
sources are autonomous, collecting such statistics might not always be possible.
Cost-based approaches are often not possible because the data source descriptions do not have the needed statistics. Heuristic-based optimization techniques
can be used to estimate the execution cost using minimum information collected
from sources as well as the properties of the operators in the query, such as type
of predicates, operators, etc. The output of the query planning and optimization
is an optimized query, i.e., query execution plan, with operations (join, union)
between subqueries.

3.4   Query Execution

Query execution is performed by data sources that are involved in answering
sub-query(s) of the given query. Each sub-query executed in each data source is
then optimized using the local schema and index (if available) of the data source
and executed. The physical operator (and algorithms) to perform the relational
operators (join, union, filter) may be chosen. Five different join methods are used
in federated query engines: nested loop join, bound-join, hash join, symmetric
join, and multiple join [335]. In nested-loop join (NLJ) the inner sub-query is
executed for every binding of the intermediate results from the outer sub-query of
the join. The bindings that satisfy the join condition are then included in the join
results. Bound-join, like NLJ, executes inner sub-query for the set of bindings,
unlike NLJ which executes the inner sub-query for every single binding of the
intermediate results from the outer sub-query. This set of bindings can be sent as
a UNION or FILTER SPARQL operators can be used to send multiple bindings
to the inner sub-query. In the hash-join method, each sub-query (operands of the
join operation) is executed in parallel and the join is performed locally using a
single hash table at the query engine. The fourth type of join method, symmetric

(hash) join, is a non-blocking hash-based join that pipelines parallel execution of the operands and generates output of the join operation as early as possible. Several extended versions of this method are available, such as XJoin [436], agjoin [6], and adjoin [6]. Finally, the multiple (hash) join method uses multiple hash tables to join more than two sub-queries running at the same time.

4   Grand Challenges and Future Work

In this section, we analyze the grand challenges to be addressed in the definition and implementation of federated query engines against distributed sources of big data. These challenges can be summarized as follows:

- Definition of formal models able to describe not only the properties and relationships among data sources, but also represent and explain causality relations, bias, and trustworthiness.
- Adaptive query processing techniques able to adjust query processing schedules according to the availability of the data, as well as to the validity and trustworthiness of the published data.
- Machine learning models able to predict the cost of integrating different sources, and the benefits that the fusion of new data sources adds to the accuracy, validity, and trustworthiness of query processing.
- Hybrid approaches that combine computational methods with human knowledge with the aim to enhance, certify, and explain the outcomes of the main data-driven tasks, e.g., schema matching, and data curation and integration.
- Query processing able to interoperate during query execution. Furthermore, data quality assessment and bias detection methods are required in order to produce answers that ensure validity and trustworthiness.
- Methods capable of tracing data consumed from the selected sources, and explainable federated systems able to justify all the decisions made to produce the answer of a query over a federation of data sources.

The diversity of the problems that remain open presents enormous opportunities both in research and development. Advancement in this area will contribute not only more efficient tools but also solutions that users can trust and understand. As a result, we expect a paradigm shift in the area of big data integration and processing towards explainability and trustworthiness – issues that have thus far prevented global adoption of data-driven tools.

Chapter 6
Reasoning in Knowledge Graphs:
An Embeddings Spotlight

Luigi Bellomarini[1], Emanuel Sallinger[2,3](✉) ⓘ, and Sahar Vahdati[3] ⓘ

[1] Banca d'Italia, Rome, Italy
[2] TU Wien, Vienna, Austria
`sallinger@dbai.tuwien.ac.at`
[3] University of Oxford, Oxford, UK

Abstract. In this chapter we introduce the aspect of reasoning in Knowledge Graphs. As in Chap. 2, we will give a broad overview focusing on the multitude of reasoning techniques: spanning logic-based reasoning, embedding-based reasoning, neural network-based reasoning, etc. In particular, we will discuss three dimensions of reasoning in Knowledge Graphs. Complementing these dimensions, we will structure our exploration based on a pragmatic view of reasoning tasks and families of reasoning tasks: reasoning for knowledge integration, knowledge discovery and application services.

1 Introduction

The notion of intelligence is closely intertwined with the ability to reason. In turn, this ability to reason plays a central role in AI algorithms. This is the case not only for the AI of today but for any form of knowledge representation, understanding and discovery, as stated by Leibniz in 1677: "It is obvious that if we could find characters or signs suited for expressing all our thoughts as clearly and as exactly as arithmetic expresses numbers or geometry expresses lines, we could do in all matters insofar as they are subject to reasoning all that we can do in arithmetic and geometry. For all investigations which depend on reasoning would be carried out by transposing these characters and by a species of calculus" [279].

Research in reasoning was carried out by mathematicians and logicians, and naturally adopted and also carried out by computer scientists later on. Concrete references of having knowledgeable machines date back to at least the 1940s – V. Bush talked about a machine able to think like a human in his influential essay in 1945 "As We May Think" [65]. Later in 1950, with Alan Turing's seminal work [432], the idea behind Artificial Intelligence and impressing thinking power to machines began with mathematically employed reasoning. The developments of symbolic reasoning continued towards providing mathematical semantics of logic

V. Janev et al. (Eds.): Knowledge Graphs and Big Data Processing, LNCS 12072, pp. 87–101, 2020.
https://doi.org/10.1007/978-3-030-53199-7_6

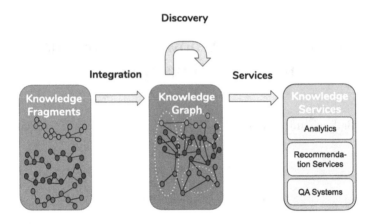

Fig. 1. A simplified life-cycle of Knowledge Graphs

programming languages [303,441] and new forms of efficient reasoning foundations [73,234]. Reasoning about facts of belief networks, as in today's Knowledge Graphs, is addressed in [349].

However, at the scale at which they were envisioned, all of these approaches were simply not possible in practice without large-scale data management, processing, inference and retrieval. The last decade witnessed a technology boost for AI-driven technologies with the emergence of Big Data. This has created an incredible number of industrial-scale applications of Machine Learning approaches over data represented and managed in Knowledge Graphs. The technology behind KGs created a practical platform for the envisioned AI machines.

Perspectives. In Chap. 2, we introduced the *layered perspective* of Knowledge Graphs, and noted that the aspect of *reasoning* will be considered particularly in this chapter. It is clear that the requirements on reasoning are different between the three layers introduced in Chap. 2:

- At the bottom-most layer (**representation**), reasoning is an important design consideration to achieve a good balance between expressive power and computational complexity.
- At the middle layer (**management**), similar to a relational database management system, providing a general-purpose reasoning (or in a RDBMS: querying) service is of utmost importance.
- At the top layer (**application**), the specific reasoning service required or exposed by the application becomes the focus.

Given both the history of use of reasoning methods in computer science, as well as their concrete use in the construction and use of Knowledge Graphs, it would be tempting to divide them according to their use in the life-cycle of KGs. This is illustrated in Fig. 1 where we see knowledge fragments being integrated into a Knowledge Graph, this KG being enriched using discovery, and finally services provided based on the Knowledge Graph:

- **Reasoning for Knowledge Integration:** where the focus is to use reasoning in order to deal with knowledge acquisition and integration from heterogeneous, interconnected and distributed data.
- **Reasoning for Knowledge Discovery:** where the focus is to use reasoning in order to identify new – and possible hidden – knowledge based on existing knowledge.
- **Reasoning for Application Services:** where the focus is to employ reasoning techniques to directly provide services at the application level of the Knowledge Graph.

The position that we will take in this chapter is that while these three phases of the life-cycle are clearly important, and many of the available reasoning techniques fall into one category or the other, many others as we shall see permeate these life-cycle phases. We thus refer to them rather as *dimensions*.

This chapter shall not be a survey of reasoning techniques, but for each of the three dimensions it shall give one or two prominent examples to give the reader an impression on the breadth and variation between reasoning techniques on Knowledge Graphs.

Organization. In Sect. 2, we will consider the dimension of integration; in Sect. 3, we consider the dimension of discovery; and in Sect. 4, we consider the dimension of application services. We will conclude with a summary.

2 Reasoning for Knowledge Integration

In recent years, a huge number of Knowledge Graphs has been built both in academia and industry. Knowledge Graph creation follows a set of steps for data acquisition and integration from heterogeneous resources. It requires a comprehensive domain conceptualization and a proper data representation model. In many cases, data transformation from the already existing formats formed the Knowledge Graph for many individual or enterprise agents. With post-processing stages, such Knowledge Graphs have been made usable by other approaches for further investigations.

Yet, considering the potential amount of information that could be mapped into such Knowledge Graphs from the real world, they are greatly incomplete. A number of manual and automated data curation, harvesting and integration techniques are being developed for data completion tasks already from decades ago. However, considering the characteristics of Knowledge Graphs, they became ideal for applying machine learning approaches to Knowledge Graph completion. Thus, KG completion tasks gain a new dimension meaning the coverage increase of knowledge. Therefore, new communities of research have been merged or revived such as knowledge embedding. Application of such models have been investigated with the objective of providing services for link predictions, resource classification and recommendation services.

Aforementioned representations are attempts to create a real world model where a lack of full coverage and information correctness problems will always be present. Thus, proposing embedding models for Knowledge Graphs gained a lot of attention by giant companies and received great hype in research in recent years. Such models are probabilistic-based approaches to predict missing relations in a graph. Although there have already been proposals of using ML and such probabilistic link prediction models on top of data modeled in triples from the early 2000s, the application of such models has been practiced with the emergence of KGs. Three conflicting dimensions of challenges in the construction of such a Knowledge Graph have been mentioned [146] namely *freshness*, *coverage* and *correctness*.

2.1   Schema/Ontology Matching

Ontology matching in the meaning of finding semantic relationships between entities of one or several Knowledge Graphs plays an important role in KG integration and construction. Due to the heterogeneity of KGs, the process of KG integration and mapping ontologies end with high complexities. Therefore scalability is one of the main focal points in this regard. The approaches for providing light weighted ontology matching tools includes ontology partitioning [130], use of data and ontology structure [230, 383]. There are two main categories of approaches: logic-based and graph-based [3]. In the early years of the Semantic Web community [166, 167], some logic-based reasoning approaches, which are used to partition the relationships of an ontology, have been discussed.

Another set of approaches are ontology-based data access (OBDA) [356] approaches, which are well-known where ontologies are used to encode the domain knowledge, which enables new fact deduction. In [58], a datalog-based approach is proposed for KG completion tasks. A datalog is an ontology-based approach that is applied in question answering [289].

The proposed approach is a partitioning model that incorporates the ontology graph and the distribution of extractions. In a related work, reasoning by using ontology-based approaches is used to query probabilistic knowledge bases [59, 74]. The application of such ontology-based reasoning in relation to other inference tasks such as maximum a posteriori (MAP) computations and most probable explanations (MPE) corresponds to identifying tuples that contribute the most to the satisfaction of an observed query. The concept of common sense is introduced as a type of knowledge in [59] with regard to closed world or open world assumptions. With a closed world assumption, question-answering systems that are built on top of knowledge bases fail to answer anything that requires intuitive or deductive reasoning.

A logic-based scalable ontology matching system is introduced in [228] named LogMap. The ontology obtained by integrating LogMap's output mappings with the input ontologies is consistent. Although it belongs to the period before KGs were introduced, its capability in terms of dealing with semantically rich ontologies makes it considerable for application in KGs as well. Logical reasoning is also used in other works over the union of the source ontologies, e.g. in the medical domain [229].

In general, Knowledge Graph identification (KGI) is used as a reasoning technique in Knowledge Graph construction. For example, [362] deals with challenges in automation of KG creation from noisy extractions. In order to handle the scaling problems, partitioning extractions is an approach that allows parallel reasoning in carving valid KG from a collection of noisy information. KGIs uses logical constraints and entity resolution and the results can be used in classification and link prediction tasks. In a series of works [359, 361, 362], probabilistic soft logic (PSL) is used for running reasoning jointly with extraction of knowledge from a noisy collection of information. The proposed solution is based on an ontology-aware technique that uses universally quantified logical rules. It performs efficient reasoning on KGs with rich representation of ontologies and statements in Web Ontology Language (OWL). In the reasoning process, frequent patterns, constraints or paths are used to infer new knowledge.

The rules are defined to relate the uncertain information discovered in the extraction process. The extracted triples are labeled to be a candidate relation or a candidate label and a value is assigned which shows the probable truth of the triple. The model combines the weights from several sources and retrieves a list of classifications or predicted links. Ontological information such as domain and range constraints are used to further enrich the reasoning. The joint reasoning means that logical rules as well as entity resolution are used in parallel such that a) logical rules relate the ontological knowledge about the predicates of the constructed Knowledge Graph and b) entity resolution are injected in prediction.

F-OWL is another ontology matching the engine proposed in [491], and was originally designed for knowledge bases. It is a rule-based reasoning engine which also considers entity resolution for extracting hidden knowledge. Pellet, an open source OWL-DL reasoner [403], employs an incremental reasoning mechanism. Thus semantic expressively of such formalism for representing and querying probabilistic knowledge has gained significant importance in recent years. Another application of KG integration is given in [117], which explains a chain of processes in which domain knowledge about Chinese Intangible cultural heritage (ICH) was extracted from textual sources using Natural Language Processing (NLP) technology. The extracted knowledge is shaped as a knowledge base using on domain ontology and instances.

2.2   Entity Resolution

One of the techniques required for combining multiple Knowledge Graphs is using entity resolution. In some cases, this task turns to a pair-wise matching task between the target KGs for integration. This can bring a set of challenges caused by different ontologies used by KGs and additional complexity. In [360], a unified model for entity resolution is provided for KG integration tasks.

Some of these reasoning techniques are used for Knowledge Graph refinement after data integration processes. Several researchers of the KG domain (e.g., Paulheim, Dong) have been using the KG "Refinement" notion to define a range of technology application with the purpose of KG enrichment including completion and error detection. In some other views, refinement has seen improvements in KGs by considering that ontology learning mainly deals with learning a concept-level description of a domain.

2.3 Data Exchange and Integration

While the focus of this chapter shall be on embedding-based reasoning, we do want to at least give a glimpse at the huge body of logic-based reasoning methods and techniques developed in the database and artificial intelligence area over basically the last decades, including large research organizations such as IBM research and others spearheading these kinds of developments.

Logical rules that play the role of knowledge in a Knowledge Graph, and are thus reasoned upon have been historically often called *schema mappings*. There exist countless papers in this area [18,52,127,251,434], a survey on reasoning about schema mappings can be found at [382]. Key formalisms in these area are *tuple-generating dependencies* (tgds), i.e., logical formulas of the form

$$\varphi(\bar{x}) \rightarrow \exists \bar{y}\, \psi(\bar{x}, \bar{y})$$

where φ and ψ are conjunctions of relational atoms and all free variables are universally quantified (which we will assume for all formulas presented in what follows by some abuse of notation), and *equality-generating dependencies* (egds), i.e., logical formulas of the form

$$\varphi(\bar{x}) \rightarrow x_i = x_j$$

These together can express a large amount of knowledge typically expressed in database constraints, and thus usable for data exchange and data integration, or simply as knowledge in Knowledge Graphs.

Research foci include the higher expressive power needed for particular reasoning tasks, including

- *second-order (SO) tgds* [128,133,134,161,163] for expressing ontological reasoning and composition, i.e., logical formulas that, in simplified form have the structure

$$\exists \bar{f}((\varphi_1 \rightarrow \psi_1) \wedge \ldots \wedge (\varphi_n \rightarrow \psi_n))$$

  where $\bar{f}$ are function symbols.
- *nested tgds* [142,252] for expressing reasoning on tree-like data, i.e., normal tgds of the form

$$\chi = \varphi(\bar{x}) \rightarrow \exists \bar{y}\, \psi(\bar{x}, \bar{y})$$

  but with the extension that each conjunct of ψ may in addition to a relational atom also be a formula of the form χ again, i.e., allow nesting.

A particularly important restriction is the study of reasoning with conjunctive queries (CQs), i.e., in the form of logical rules

$$\exists \bar{x}\, \varphi(\bar{x}, \bar{y}) \rightarrow Ans(\bar{y})$$

where *Ans* is an arbitrary predicate name representing the answer of a query. These CQs are at the core of almost all practical data processing systems, including of course databases and Knowledge Graph management systems that allow reasoning or querying of almost any level. Under the name of "projective views", reasoning on them has been studied intensively, for pointers see e.g. [173], but there are countless papers studying this formalism central to KGs.

While we will avoid making this section a full-blown survey on reasoning in data exchange and integration, we do want to give a (biased) selection of, in our opinion, particularly interesting reasoning problems in this area:

- *limits* [253]: like limits in the mathematical, it is particularly relevant for *approximating* data exchange and integration scenarios to also reason about limits in this context. Similarly to limits, other operators such as union and intersection are important [20,351].
- *equivalence* [355]: equivalence is a fundamental reasoning problem for all other services building upon it, such as optimization, approximation, etc.
- *inconsistency* [19,22,353]: reasoning in an inconsistent state of data or knowledge is the standard case for Knowledge Graphs, and needs delicate handling.
- *representability* [21]: how can knowledge be represented in different parts of a Knowledge Graph?

Many other topics could have been mentioned here – and many more references given – as this is a particularly rich area of reasoning on this important sub-area of Knowledge Graphs. Bridging the gap towards our main focus in this chapter, embedding-based reasoning, we conclude by mentioning that substantial parts of the logic-based reasoning formalisms presented in this section can be *injected* into embedding-based reasoning methods to make them perform far better than they could have if no such knowledge were present in the Knowledge Graph.

3   Reasoning for Knowledge Discovery

In this section, we structure reasoning approaches for task-based AI challenges. There is a long list of possible approaches that could go in this category; however, we will focus on embedding-based reasoning for link prediction. Examples of other approaches could be Statistical Relational Learning (SLRs) which are well covered in several review articles [330,487], Markov Logic Networks (MLN) [250,373], and Probabilistic Graphical Models [8,254,317].

3.1   Link Prediction

The power of specific knowledge representation in Knowledge Graphs facilitates information systems in dealing with challenges of Big Data and supports solving challenges of data heterogeneity. However, KGs suffer from incompleteness, inaccuracy and low data quality in terms of correctness [17,326]. This highly affects the performance of AL-based approaches, which are used on top of KGs in order to provide effective services. Therefore, graph completing methods gained a lot of interest to be applied on KGs. One of the most popular methods is Knowledge Graph Embedding models, which obtain the vector representation for entities and/or relations to be used in downstream tasks such as Knowledge Graph Completion tasks. KGEs are a type of deductive reasoning in the vector space through discovery of new links.

For a Knowledge Graph with a set of triples in the form of *(h, r, t)* representing (head, relation, tail), KG embeddings aim at mapping entities and relations into a low-dimensional vector space. Then, the KGE model defines a score and loss functions to further optimize the vectors through a specific embedding representation. The embedding of entities and relations is generally learned over existing positive samples inside the KGs. A set of negative samples are also usually injected into the model in order to optimize the learning phase and help the KGE model gain strength. In these ways, the score function is trained over both the positive and negative samples and assigns a high score for positive samples and a low score to negative samples. Each embedding model also has a loss function that optimizes the scoring. Here we will look into the existing embedding models from the lens of their reasoning power in knowledge discovery. Knowledge Graph embedding models can be roughly divided into three main categories:

– **Translational and Rotational Based Models.** A large number of KGE models are designed using mathematical transnational (plus) or rotational (Hadamard product). The score and loss function of these models optimize the vectors in a way that their plausibility is measured by the distance or degree of the entities with regard to the relation.
– **Semantic Matching Models.** Some of the embedding models are designed based on element-wise multiplication. In this case, the similarity of the vectors is evaluated to define the plausibility of the entities an relations.
– **Neural Network-Based Models.** A third category of the KGE models are the ones designed on top of neural networks. These models have two learning phases: one for calculating and creating the vectors and the second for evaluating the plausibility in a layer-based learning approach, which comes from NN.

Translational and Rotational Models. In this type of model, the plausibility of a triple is computed based on distance function (e.g. based on the Euclidean distance) [458]. In the following, we describe KGE models that are relevant in the context of this work; however, many others have been proposed.

TransE [57] is one of the early KGE models that is the base for several other families of models where the score function takes a relation r as the translation from the head entity h to the tail entity t:

$$h + r \approx t \tag{1}$$

To measure the plausibility of a triple, the following scoring function is defined:

$$f_r(h, t) = -\|h + r - t\| \tag{2}$$

The TransE model is extremely simple and computationally efficient. Therefore, it is one of the most common embedding models used on large-scale KGs with the purpose of reasoning for knowledge discovery. However, TransE is limited in modeling 1-N, N-1 and N-M relations. For this reason, several extensions have been proposed [458]. Due to this fact, encoding relations with reflexive and symmetric patterns becomes impossible, which is an important aspect in the inference of new knowledge. Therefore, several new models have tried to solve this problem, which will be discussed in the remainder of this section.

TransH [462] is en extension of TransE, which addresses the limitations of TransE in modeling N-M relations. It uses relation-specific entity representation to enable encoding of such relational patterns. This model uses an additional hyperplane to represent relations. Then, the translation from the head to the tail entity is performed in that relation-specific hyperplane. This method is called projecting head and tail entities into the relation-specific hyperplane. The formulation of this method is as follows:

$$h_\perp = h - w_r^\top h w_r \tag{3}$$

$$t_\perp = t - w_r^\top t w_r \tag{4}$$

where w_r is the normal vector of the hyperplane. The plausibility of the triple (h, r, t) is computed:

$$f_r(h, t) = -\|h_\perp + d_r - t_\perp\|_2^2 \tag{5}$$

where d_r is the relation-specific translation vector.

TransR is another KGE model that followed the basics from TranE as an extension of TransH with a difference that it encodes entities and relations in different vector spaces. This is a relation-specific solution in contrast to the hyperplanes of TransH where the translation happens in the specific space of each relation. Relations are in matrix representation of M_r which takes entities projected into the relational specific space:

$$h_r = h M_r \tag{6}$$

$$t_r = t M_r \tag{7}$$

Based on this representation, the score function is designed as following:

$$f_r(h, t) = -\|h_r + r - t_r\|_2^2 \tag{8}$$

This model is capable of handling complex relations as it uses different spaces; however its computation is highly costly due to the high number of required parameters.

TransD [225] is an attempt to improve TransR by reducing the number of required parameters by removing the need for matrix vector multiplications. The core of this model is to use two vectors for representation of entities and relations. Assuming that h, r, t encode the semantics, and h_p, r_p, t_p constructs projection, the projection of entities in relation-specific spaces is defined as follows:

$$M_{rh} = r_p h_p^T + I^{m \times n} \tag{9}$$

$$M_{rt} = r_p t_p^T + I^{m \times n}, \tag{10}$$

In this definition, I is a matrix where the values of the diagonal elements are 1 and 0 elsewhere. The head and tail entities are computed as:

$$h_\perp = M_{rh} h \tag{11}$$

$$t_\perp = M_{rt} t \tag{12}$$

The score of the triple (h,r,t) is then computed based on these projections:

$$f_r(h, t) = -\|h_\perp + r - t_\perp\|_2^2 \tag{13}$$

RotatE. [417] is one of the early models which uses rotation than translation. The model is mainly designed with the objective of reasoning relational patterns, which was not mainly addressed by other translational models. RotatE is designed to reason new knowledge based on the Euler formula $e^{i\theta} = \cos(\theta) + i \sin(\theta)$. Based on its score function, for every correct triple (h, r, t) there should be the relation of $h_j r_j = t_j$ which holds $\forall j \in \{0, \ldots, d\}$. h_j, r_j, t_j are the j-th elements of the embedding vectors of $\mathbf{h}, \mathbf{r}, \mathbf{t} \in \mathbb{C}^d$. Since it deals with complex space, r_i is set to 1 i.e. $|r_j| = \sqrt{Re(r_j)^2 + Im(r_j)^2} = 1$. The model performs a rotation of the j-th element h_j of the head vector $\mathbf{h}$ by the j-th element $r_j = e^{i\theta_{r_j}}$ of a relation vector $\mathbf{r}$ to get the j-th element t_j of the tail vector $\mathbf{t}$, where θ_{r_j} is the phase of the relation r. Therefore, the score function of RotatE is designed as a rotation using $\circ$ which is a Hadmard product of two vectors:

$$f_{h,t}^r = \|\mathbf{h} \circ \mathbf{r} - \mathbf{t}\|, \tag{14}$$

In this way, the RotatE model becomes capable of encoding symmetric, inverse, and composition relation patterns. Due to this capability, its performance is high and due to the high quality of the newly discovered links in the reasoning process, it outperforms all the previous models.

Semantic Matching Models. As discussed before, the second category of embedding models in reasoning over KGs determines the plausibility of a triple by comparing the similarity of the latent features of the entities and relations. A number of KGE models fall into this category; we will discuss a few of the best performing ones.

RESCAL [327] is an embedding-based reasoning model that represents each entity as a vector and each relation as a matrix, M_r to capture the latent semantics. The score of the triples is measured by the following formulation:

$$f_r(h,t) = h^T M_r t \qquad (15)$$

where M_r is a matrix associated with relations, which encodes pairwise interactions between the features of the head and tail entities.

DistMult is a model that focuses on capturing the relational semantics and the composition of relations as characterized by matrix multiplication [476]. This model considers learning representations of entities and relations within the underlying KG. DistMult [476] simplifies RESCAL by allowing only diagonal matrices as $diag(\mathbf{r})$. The score function of this model is designed in a way that triples are ranked through pair-wise interactions of the latent features:

$$f_r(h,t) = h^T diag(r) t \qquad (16)$$

where $r \in R^d$ and $M_r = diag(r)$. The restriction to diagonal matrices makes DistMult more computationally efficient than RESCAL but less expressive.

ComplEx ComplEx [430] is an extension of DistMult into the complex space. Considering the scoring function of DistMult, it can be observed that it has a limitation in representing anti-symmetric relations since $h^T diag(r) t$ is equivalent to $t^T diag(r) h$. Equation 16 can be written in terms of the Hadamard product of h, r, t: $<h, r, t> = \sum_{i=1}^{d} h_i * r_i * t_i$, where $h, r, t \in R^d$. The scoring function of ComplEx uses the Hadamard product in the complex space, i.e. $h, r, t \in C^d$:

$$f_r(h,t) = \Re(\sum_{i=1}^{d} h_i * r_i * \overline{t_i}) \qquad (17)$$

where $\Re(x)$ represents the real part of a complex number and $\overline{x}$ its conjugate. It is straightforward to show that $f_r(h,t) \neq f_r(t,h)$, i.e. ComplEx is capable of modeling anti-symmetric relations.

Neural Network-Based Models. As the last category of the embedding models that we will discuss here, we consider the ones which are built on top of Neural Networks. Such models inherit a second layer from NNs for the learning phase. This category is also known as Neural Link Predictors, which is in the downstream task level, the ultimate objective of such models. Such models contain a multi-layered learning approach with two main components: namely, encoding of the vectors and scoring of the vectors.

ConvE [107] is a multi-layer embedding model designed on top of the neural networks.

$$f(h,t) = g(\text{Vec}(g([\bar{\mathbf{h}}; \bar{\mathbf{r}}] * \omega)) W) \mathbf{t} \qquad (18)$$

Neural Tensor Network (NTN). [408] is one of the earlier methods which includes textual information in the embedding. It learns the word vectors from a corpus and initializes each entity by the average of vectors of words associated with the entity.

$$\vec{w}_r^T \tanh(\vec{h}^T W_r \vec{t} + W_r^{(1)} \vec{h} + W_r^{(2)} \vec{t} + \vec{b}_r) \tag{19}$$

LogicENN. [323] is an NN-based model which performs reasoning on top of a KG through jointly learning embeddings of entities $(\mathbf{h}, \mathbf{t})$ and relations $(\beta_\mathbf{r})$ of the KG and the weights/biases $(\mathbf{w}/b)$ of the NN. Given a triple of (h, r, t), the network passes the entity vectors $(\mathbf{h}, \mathbf{t})$ through a universally shared hidden layer with L nodes to obtain the joint feature mapping of the entities (h, t) i.e. $\Phi_{h,t}^T = [\phi_{h,t}(\mathbf{w}_1, b_1), \ldots, \phi_{h,t}(\mathbf{w}_L, b_L)] = [\phi(\langle \mathbf{w}_1, [\mathbf{h}, \mathbf{t}] + b_1 \rangle), \ldots, \phi(\langle \mathbf{w}_L, [\mathbf{h}, \mathbf{t}] + b_L \rangle)]$. The network considers the weights of the output nodes (i.e. $\beta_\mathbf{r}$) as the embedding of relation r. The score of the triple (h, r, t) is computed by the inner product of $\Phi_{h,t}$ and $\beta_\mathbf{r}$ as follows

$$f(h, r, t) = \sum_{i=1}^{L} \phi(\langle \mathbf{w}_i, [\mathbf{h}, \mathbf{t}] + b_i \rangle) \beta_i^r = \sum_{i=1}^{L} \phi_{h,t}(\mathbf{w}_i, b_i) \beta_i^r \tag{20}$$
$$= \Phi_{h,t}^T \beta^r.$$

Considering the formulation of the score function, the algebraic formulae (algebraic constraints) corresponding to each of the logical rules – namely symmetric, inverse, transitive, negation, implication, equivalence etc – are derived. The formulae are then used as penalty terms to be added to the loss function for optimization. This enables the injection of rules into the learning process of the network. Consequently, the performance of the model is improved.

Overall, the network has the following advantages:

- The model is proven to be capable of expressing any ground truth of a KG with n facts.
- The network separates the spaces of entities $(\phi_{h,t})$ and relation $\beta_\mathbf{r}$. Therefore, the score-based algebraic constraints corresponding to the symmetric, inverse, implication and equivalence rules do not need the grounding of entities. This feature enables the model to better inject rules with a lower computational cost due to lifted groundings.
- The model has been shown to obtain state-of-the-art performance on several standard datasets.

Summary. So far we have given a detailed description of some highlighted methods in embedding-based reasoning methods. More information can be found in [326, 459]. Despite the fact that most of embeddings only consider the relation and entities of a KG, there are several types of complementary knowledge (e.g., text, logical rules, ontology, complementary KG) from which embedding models can be improved. In [328], ontological knowledge is introduced as complementary knowledge, which can be used in the factorization process of embedding models. In some of the more focused work, ontological knowledge such as entity types is used as constraints [201, 265, 460, 475] which improves the performance of the embedding models. In recent years, logic-based reasoning and embedding-based reasoning have come together and attracted a great deal of academic attention. Some initial work is done using logical rules as a post-processing task after embedding [460, 465]. [375] optimizes the embeddings using first order logical rules to obtain entity pairs and relations. [202] provides a general framework to transfer information in logical rules to the weights of different types of neural networks.

4   Reasoning for Application Services

The ultimate goal of the aforementioned approaches is to provide better knowledge aware services such as smart analytics and recommendation and prediction services as well as to facilitate query answering. In many knowledge management tasks, learning and reasoning is an important component towards providing such services. There are also hybrid systems which integrate many such models consuming different learning representation and learning methods. Such methods are usually defined as high-level tasks where the purpose is to gain a certain practical step in KGs where it is ready for low-level tasks. This section includes some AI-driven applications with an underlying knowledge-aware learning and reasoning engine.

4.1   Recommendation Systems

In many of the high-level tasks related to Knowledge Graphs, learning and reasoning methods are considered to be well-suited to providing recommendation services. Recommendation services are typical applications of reasoning for knowledge discovery and link prediction approaches. Logic-based reasoning provides explainable recommendations while embedding-based reasoning mostly explores the interlinks within a knowledge graph. The learning phase in both of these approaches is mostly about analysis of the connectivity between entities and relations in order to discover possible news paths. This can be facilitated with rich and complementary information. These approaches reveal the semantics of entities and relations and facilitate recommendation services to comprehend ultimate user interests.

In the domain application level, such approaches can be applied for any graph-based scenario. For example, KGs of social networks [457] are one of the most interesting application domains on which learning frameworks are applied. Item recommendation in online shopping is a typical application for link prediction. Such problems are usually formulated as ML-based problems in KGs and employ link prediction approaches. Another typical example is link prediction between co-authors in scholarly Knowledge Graphs. The plausibility of such recommendations is prediction-based for the future and might not happen. Adding a temporal feature for such recommendations by making Knowledge Graphs time-aware makes such applications more interesting.

4.2   Question Answering

A number of reasoning-based applications for which intelligent systems are built goes under the umbrella of question answering systems (QA). In addition to normal search engines and query-based systems, into this category falls conversational AI systems, speech assistants, and chat-bots. Example of such systems are Apple's Siri, Microsoft's Cortana, and Amazon's Alexa, for which the source of knowledge is an underlying KG. Despite the huge success in building such systems, the possible incorrect answers as well as their limits in retrieving a certain level of knowledge queries is not avoidable. There are multiple reasons for this, such as KG incompleteness or other quality issues on the data side, which cause minimal semantic understanding. However, for the complete part of the data in practice, any simple question has the potential to require complex queries and thus complex reasoning over multiple computational steps [277]. Therefore, all of these systems are facilitated with reasoning and inference techniques in order to retrieve hidden information.

In recent years, one of the hyped applications of reasoning for question answering is on Knowledge Graphs with diverse modality of data. This is because, by nature, Knowledge Graphs contain different types of information ranging from images, text, numerical data or even videos and many more. The main challenge is that, on the application side, most of the learning approaches are mainly considered with one modal. While there has been a lot of progress from computer vision communities in audio and video processing, such multi-disciplinary research is still at an early stage. Such KGs are known as *Multi-modal Knowledge Graphs (MKGs)* and have fundamental differences with other visual-relational resources. There are recent works on construction of *Multi-Modal Knowledge Graphs* and application of ML-related models on top of such KGs. Visual QA systems are designated specifically for MKGs [66].

Due to the explainability power of rule-based reasoning techniques, they are an important part of QA systems as well. In the case of complex questions with a need for multiple steps, it is easier to provide explainable and certain statements. Multi-hop reasoning is a solution for such cases, which is elevated by end-to-end differentiable (deep learning) models [108,464].

5   Challenges and Opportunities

In this chapter, we considered reasoning in Knowledge Graphs in multiple dimensions: namely that of integration, discovery and application. For each of these, we picked some techniques that showcase some of the diversity of reasoning techniques encountered in Knowledge Graphs. As a grand challenge, we see the integration of multiple reasoning techniques, such as logic-based and embedding-based reasoning techniques, and similarly neural network-based reasoning and other reasoning techniques. Clearly, also each individual reasoning problem that we introduced in this chapter would allow for challenges and opportunities to be listed, but that would go beyond the scope of this chapter.

Acknowledgements. E. Sallinger acknowledges the support of the Vienna Science and Technology (WWTF) grant VRG18-013 and the EPSRC programme grant EP/M025268/1.

Methods and Solutions

Chapter 7
Scalable Knowledge Graph Processing Using SANSA

Hajira Jabeen[1]([✉]) [iD], Damien Graux[3] [iD], and Gezim Sejdiu[2,4] [iD]

[1] CEPLAS, Botanical Institute, University of Cologne, Cologne, Germany
hajira.jabeen@uni-koeln.de
[2] Smart Data Analytics, University of Bonn, Bonn, Germany
[3] ADAPT SFI Research Centre,
Trinity College, Dublin, Ireland
[4] Deutsche Post DHL Group, Bonn, Germany

Abstract. The size and number of knowledge graphs have increased tremendously in recent years. In the meantime, the distributed data processing technologies have also advanced to deal with big data and large scale knowledge graphs. This chapter introduces Scalable Semantic Analytics Stack (SANSA), that addresses the challenge of dealing with large scale RDF data and provides a unified framework for applications like link prediction, knowledge base completion, querying, and reasoning. We discuss the motivation, background and the architecture of SANSA. SANSA is built using general-purpose processing engines Apache Spark and Apache Flink. After reading this chapter, the reader should have an understanding of the different layers and corresponding APIs available to handle Knowledge Graphs at scale using SANSA.

1 Introduction

Over the past decade, vast amounts of machine-readable structured information have become available through the increasing popularity of semantic knowledge graphs using semantic technologies in a variety of application domains including general knowledge [25,448], life sciences [468], scholarly data [129], open source projects [266], patents [261] or even food recommendations [189]. These knowledge bases are becoming more prevalent and this trend can be expected to continue in future.

The size of knowledge graphs has reached the scale where centralised analytical approaches have become either infeasible or too expensive. Recent technological progress has enabled powerful distributed in-memory analytics that have been shown to work well on simple data structures. However, the application of such distributed analytics approaches on semantic knowledge graphs is lagging behind significantly. To advance both the scalability and accuracy of large-scale knowledge graph analytics to a new level, fundamental research on

© The Author(s) 2020
V. Janev et al. (Eds.): Knowledge Graphs and Big Data Processing, LNCS 12072, pp. 105–121, 2020.
https://doi.org/10.1007/978-3-030-53199-7_7

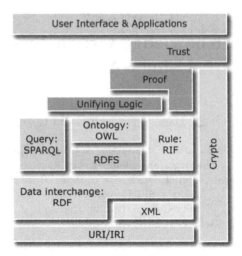

Fig. 1. W3C Semantic Web layer cake.

methods of leveraging distributed in-memory computing and semantic technologies in combination with advancements in analytics approaches is indispensable. In this chapter, we present the Scalable Semantic Analytics Stack (SANSA), which addresses the challenge of dealing with large scale RDF data and provides a unified framework for designing complex semantic applications.

2   Semantic Layer Cake

As presented in the previous chapters, there are many different types of data source available that are collecting and providing information structured *via* different formats. In addition, most of them are available on the Web and often share some information about the same concepts or entities; as a consequence, the need to allow alignments between sources has increased. This motivation fuelled the Semantic Web initiative where the main idea is to enable linkage between remote data entities so that several facets of information become available at once. The Semantic Web mainly relies on the dereferencing concept where identifiers (IRIs - Internationalised Resource Identifier) are used to represent entities and are therefore to navigate from one piece of information to another.

The Semantic Web has been mainly pushed by the World Wide Web Consortium (W3C), which proposed a set of standards to technically back up this movement. Practically, these standards are built following a "layer cake" structure where standards are constructed on top of other ones (see Fig. 1). In particular, the stack is completely built on top of the identifier concept, which serves as a basis then to represent data using the following RDF structure.

The Semantic Web does not limit its scope to only linking and representing data on the web; it also provides a range of specifications to help users enrich their knowledge. First of all, RDF comes with an associated query language (SPARQL) in order to extract data from sources. Moreover, several standards specify how to structure the data:

1. The RDF Schema (RDFS) lists a set of classes with certain properties using the RDF representation data model and provides basic elements for the description of ontologies.
2. The Web Ontology Language (OWL) is a family of knowledge representation languages for authoring ontologies which are a formal ways to describe taxonomies and classification networks, essentially defining the structure of knowledge for various domains.
3. The Shapes Constraint Language (SHACL) allows to design validations over graph-based data considering a set of conditions. Among others, it includes features to express conditions that constrain the number of values that a property may have, the type of such values, numeric ranges etc. ...

These specifications then allow users to specify several properties about Semantic Web data and therefore one can use them to extend one's own knowledge. Indeed, ontologies are the cornerstone of all the studies made around inferring data from a set of triples *e.g.* using the structure of the graph, it is possible to "materialize" additional statements and thereby to extend the general knowledge.

As a consequence, the W3C – *via* the diverse standards and recommendations it set up – allows users to structure pieces of information. However, the large majority of existing tools are focusing on one or two standards at once, meaning that they are usually not encompassing the full scope of what the Semantic Web is supposed to provide and enable. Indeed, designing such a "wide-scope" Semantic Web tool is challenging. Recently, such an initiative was created: SANSA [411]; in addition, SANSA also pays attention to the Big Data context of the Semantic Web and adopts a fully distributed strategy.

3   Processing Big Knowledge Graphs with SANSA

In a nutshell, SANSA[1] presents:

1. efficient data distribution techniques and semantics-aware computation of latent resource embeddings for knowledge graphs;
2. adaptive distributed querying;
3. efficient self-optimising inference execution plans; and
4. efficient distributed machine learning on semantic knowledge graphs of extremely large scale.

3.1   Knowledge Representation and Distribution

SANSA follows the modular architecture where each layer represents a unique component of functionality, which could be used by other layers of the SANSA framework. The Knowledge Representation and Distribution is the lowest layer

---

[1] http://sansa-stack.net/.

on top of the existing distributed computing framework (either Apache Spark[2] or Apache Flink[3]). Within this layer, SANSA provides the functionality to read and write native RDF or OWL data from HDFS or a local dive and represents it in native distributed data structures of the framework. Currently, it supports different RDF and OWL serializations/syntax formats. Furthermore, it provides a dedicated serialization mechanism for faster I/O. The layer also supports Jena and OWL API interfaces for processing RDF and OWL data, respectively. This particularly targets usability, as many users are already familiar with the corresponding libraries.

This layer also gives access to a mechanism for RDF data compression in order to lower the space and processing time when querying RDF data (c.f Sect. 3.2). It also provides different partitioning strategies in order to facilitate better maintenance and faster access to this scale of data. Partitioning the RDF data is the process of dividing datasets in a specific logical and/or physical representation in order to ease faster access and better maintenance. Often, this process is performed to improve the system availability, load balancing and query processing time. There are many different data partitioning techniques proposed in the literature. Within SANSA, we provide 1) semantic-based partitioning [392], 2) vertical-based partitioning [411], and 3) graph-based partitioning.

Semantic-based partitioning – A semantically partitioned fact is a tuple (S, R) containing pieces of information $R \in (P, O)$ about the same S where S is a unique subject on the RDF graph and R represents all its associated facts i.e predicates P and objects O. This partitioned technique was proposed in the SHARD [376] system. We have implemented this technique using the in-memory processing engine, Apache Spark, for better performance.

Vertical partitioning – The vertical partitioning approach in SANSA is designed to support extensible partitioning of RDF data. Instead of dealing with a single three-column table (s, p, o), data is partitioned into multiple tables based on the used RDF predicates, RDF term types and literal datatypes. The first column of these tables is always a string representing the subject. The second column always represents the literal value as a Scala/Java datatype. Tables for storing literals with language tags have an additional third string column for the language tag.

In addition, this layer of SANSA allows users to compute RDF statistics [391] and to apply quality assessment [393] in a distributed manner. More specifically, it provides a possibility to compute different RDF dataset statistics in a distributed manner via the so-called DistLODStats [392] software component. It describes the first distributed in-memory approach for computing 32 different statistical criteria for RDF datasets using Apache Spark. The computation of statistical criteria consists of three steps: (1) saving RDF data in scalable storage, (2) parsing and mapping the RDF data into the *main dataset* – an RDD data structure composed of three elements: *Subject*, *Property* and *Object*, and (3) performing statistical criteria evaluation on the *main dataset* and generating results.

---

[2] http://spark.apache.org/.
[3] https://flink.apache.org/.

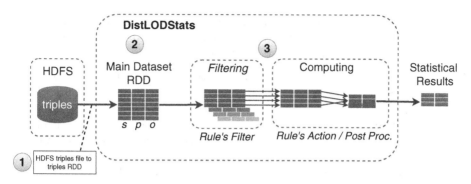

Fig. 2. Overview of DistLODStats's abstract architecture [392].

Fetching the RDF Data (Step 1): RDF data needs first to be loaded into a large-scale storage that Spark can efficiently read from. For this purpose, we use HDFS (Hadoop Distributed File-System). HDFS is able to accommodate any type of data in its raw format, horizontally scale to arbitrary number of nodes, and replicate data among the cluster nodes for fault tolerance. In such a distributed environment, Spark adopts different data locality strategies to try to perform computations as close to the needed data as possible in HDFS and thus avoid data transfer overhead.

Parsing and Mapping RDF into the Main Dataset (Step 2): In the course of Spark execution, data is parsed into triples and loaded into an RDD of the following format: *Triple<Subj,Pred,Obj>* (by using the Spark *map* transformation).

Statistical Criteria Evaluation (Step 3): For each criterion, Spark generates an execution plan, which is composed of one or more of the following Spark transformations: *map, filter, reduce* and *group-by*. *Filtering* operation apply the Rule's Filter and produce a new *filtered* RDD. The *filtered RDD* will serve as an input to the next step: *Computing* where the rule's action and/or post processing are effectively applied. The output of the *Computing* phase will be the statistical results represented in a human-readable format, e.g. VoID, or row data.

Often when designing and performing large-scale RDF processing tasks, the quality of the data is one of the key components to be considered. Existing solutions are not capable of dealing with such amounts of data, therefore a need for a distributed solution for a quality check arises. To address this, within SANSA we present DistQualityAssessment [393] – an open-source implementation of quality assessment of large RDF datasets that can scale out to a cluster of machines. This is the first distributed, in-memory approach for computing different quality metrics for large RDF datasets using Apache Spark. We also provide a quality assessment pattern that can be used to generate new scalable metrics that can be applied to big data. A more detailed overview of the approach is given below. The computation of the quality assessment using the Spark framework consists of four steps:

Defining Quality Metrics Parameters. The metric definitions are kept in a dedicated file, which contains most of the configurations needed for the system to evaluate quality metrics and gather result sets.

Retrieving the RDF Data. RDF data first needs to be loaded into a large-scale storage that Spark can efficiently read from. We use Hadoop Distributed File-System (HDFS). HDFS is able to fit and store any type of data in its Hadoop-native format and parallelize them across a cluster while replicating them for fault tolerance. In such a distributed environment, Spark automatically adopts different data locality strategies to perform computations as close to the needed data as possible in HDFS and thus avoids data transfer overhead.

Parsing and Mapping RDF into the Main Dataset. We first create a distributed dataset called *main dataset* that represent the HDFS file as a collection of triples. In Spark, this dataset is parsed and loaded into an RDD of triples having the format *Triple<(s,p,o)>*.

Quality Metric Evaluation. Considering the particular quality metric, Spark generates an execution plan, which is composed of one or more Spark transformations and actions. The numerical output of the final action is the quality of the input RDF corresponding to the given metric.

3.2 Query

As presented before, the Semantic Web designed several standards on top of RDF. Among them, one is to manipulate RDF data: SPARQL. In a nutshell, it constitutes the *de facto* querying language for RDF data and hereby provides a wide range of possibilities to either extract, create or display information.

The evaluation of SPARQL has been a deeply researched topic by the Semantic Web communities for approximately twenty years now; dozens of evaluators have been implemented, following as many different approaches to store and organise RDF data[4]. Recently, with the increase of cloud-based applications, a new range of evaluators have been proposed following the distributed paradigm which usually suits Big Data applications[5].

Distributed RDF Data. As part of the SANSA stack, a layer has been developed to handle SPARQL queries in a distributed manner and it offers several strategies in order to fit users' needs. Actually, following existing studies from the literature, the developers decided by default to rely on the Apache Spark SQL engine: in practice, the SPARQL queries asked by the users are automatically translated in SQL to retrieve information from the in-memory virtual tables (the Sparklify [411] approach) created from the RDF datasets. Such a method then allows SANSA to take advantage of the relational engine of Spark especially designed to deal with distributed Big Data. In parallel, other evaluation

---

[4] See [131] for a comprehensive survey of single-node RDF triplestores.
[5] See [235] or [169] for an extensive review of the cloud-based SPARQL evaluators.

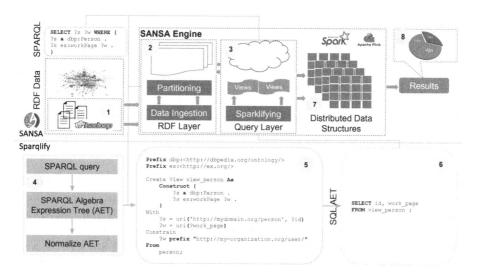

Fig. 3. SANSA's query layer architecture overview.

strategies are available to fit specific use-cases as they consist of different distribution strategies of the original RDF data in memory. While the default (vertical) partitioning scheme splits datasets into blocks based on common predicates, SANSA provides an implementation of the semantic partitioning [392] based on common subjects. It also has built-in features enabling compression on-the-fly, which allows it to handle bigger datasets.

The overall system architecture is shown in Fig. 3. It consists of four main components: Data Model, Mappings, Query Translator and Query Evaluator.

Data Ingestion (Step 1). RDF data first needs to be loaded into large-scale storage that Spark can efficiently read from.

We use the Hadoop Distributed File-System (HDFS) [62]. Spark employs different data locality schemes in order to accomplish computations nearest to the desired data in HDFS, as a result avoiding i/o overhead.

Data Partition (Step 2). The vertical partitioning approach in SANSA is designed to support extensible partitioning of RDF data. Instead of dealing with a single three-column table (s, p, o), data is partitioned into multiple tables based on the used RDF predicates, RDF term types and literal datatypes. The first column of these tables is always a string representing the subject. The second column always represents the literal value as a Scala/Java datatype. Tables for storing literals with language tags have an additional third string column for the language tag.

Mappings/Views. After the RDF data has been partitioned using the extensible VP (as it has been described on *step 2*), the relational-to-RDF mapping is performed. Sparqlify supports both the W3C standard R2RML sparqlification [412].

The main entities defined with SML are *view definitions*. See *step 5* in the Fig. 3 as an example. The actual view definition is declared by the *Create View ... As* in the first line. The remainder of the view contains these parts: (1) the *From* directive defines the logical table based on the partitioned table (see *step 2*). (2) an RDF template is defined in the *Construct* block containing, URI, blank node or literals constants (e.g. *ex:worksAt*) and variables (e.g. *?emp, ?institute*). The *With* block defines the variables used in the template by means of RDF term constructor expressions whose arguments refer to columns of the logical table.

Query Translation. This process generates a SQL query from the SPARQL query using the bindings determined in the mapping/view construction phases. It walks through the SPARQL query (*step 4*) using Jena ARQ[6] and generates the SPARQL Algebra Expression Tree (AET). Essentially, rewriting SPARQL basic graph patterns and filters over views yields AETs that are UNIONS of JOINS. Further, these AETs are normalized and pruned in order to remove UNION members that are known to yield empty results, such as joins based on IRIs with disjointed sets of known namespaces, or joins between different RDF term types (e.g. literal and IRI). Finally, the SQL is generated (*step 6*) using the bindings corresponding to the views (*step 5*).

Query Evaluation. Finally, the SQL query created as described in the previous section can now be evaluated directly into the Spark SQL engine. The result set of this SQL query is a distributed data structure of Spark (e.g. DataFrame) (*step 7*), which then is mapped into SPARQL bindings. The result set can be further used for analysis and visualization using the SANSA-Notebooks[7] (*step 8*).

DataLake. SANSA also has a DataLake component which allows it to query heterogeneous data sources ranging from different databases to large files stored in HDFS, to NoSQL stores, using SPARQL. SANSA DataLake currently supports CSV, Parquet files, Cassandra, MongoDB, Couchbase, ElasticSearch, and various JDBC sources e.g., MySQL, SQL Server. Technically, the given SPARQL queries are internally decomposed into subqueries, each extracting a subset of the results.

The DataLake layer consists of four main components (see numbered boxes in the Fig. 4). For the sake of clarity, we use here the generic ParSets and DEE concepts instead of the underlying equivalent concrete terms, which differ from engine to engine. ParSet, from Parallel dataSet, is a data structure that can be distributed and operated in parallel. It follows certain data models, like tables in tabular databases, graphs in graph databases, or documents in a document database. DEE, from Distributed Execution Environment, is the shared physical space where ParSets can be transformed, aggregated and joined together. The architecture accepts three user inputs:

---

[6] https://jena.apache.org/documentation/query/.
[7] https://github.com/SANSA-Stack/SANSA-Notebooks.

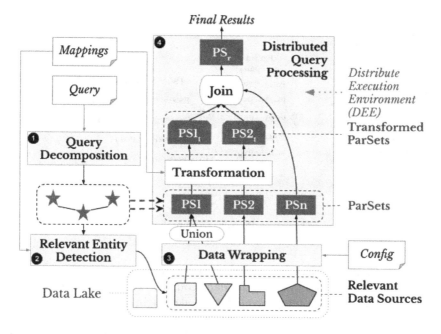

Fig. 4. SANSA's DataLake layer internal architecture [295].

- Mappings: it contains associations between data source entities[8] and attributes to ontology properties and classes.
- Config: it contains the access information needed to connect to the heterogeneous data sources, *e.g.*, username, password, or cluster setting, *e.g.*, hosts, ports, cluster name, etc.
- Query: a query in the SPARQL query language.

The fours components of the architecture are described as follows:

Query Decomposor. This component is commonly found in OBDA and query federation systems. It decomposes the query's Basic Graph Pattern (BGP, conjunctive set of triple patterns in the where clause) into a set of star-shaped sub-BGPs, where each sub-BGP contains all the triple patterns sharing the same subject variable. We refer to these sub-BGPs as stars for brevity (see below figure left; stars are shown in distinct colored boxes).

Relevant Entity Extractor. For every extracted star, this component looks in the Mappings for entities that have attributes mapping to each of the properties of the star. Such entities are relevant to the star.

---

[8] These entities can be, for example, table and column in a tabular database or collection and document in a document database.

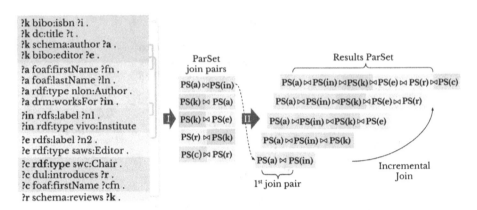

Fig. 5. From query to ParSets to joins between ParSets.

Data Wrapper. In the classical OBDA, a SPARQL query has to be translated to the query language of the relevant data sources. This is, in practice, hard to achieve in the highly heterogeneous Data Lake settings. Therefore, numerous recent publications advocated for the use of an intermediate query language. In our case, the intermediate query language is DEE's query language, dictated by its internal data structure. The Data Wrapper generates data in POA's data structure at query-time, which allows for the parallel execution of expensive operations, *e.g.*, join. There must exist wrappers to convert data entities from the source to DEE's data structure, either fully or partially if parts of the data can be pushed down to the original source. Each identified star from step (1) will generate exactly one ParSet. If more than an entity is relevant, the ParSet is formed as a union. An auxiliary user input Config is used to guide the conversion process, *e.g.*, authentication, or deployment specifications.

Distributed Query Processor. Finally, ParSets are joined together forming the final results. ParSets in the DEE can undergo any query operation, *e.g.*, selection, aggregation, ordering, etc. However, since our focus is on querying multiple data sources, the emphasis is on the join operation. Joins between stars translate into joins between ParSets (Fig. 5 phase I). Next, ParSet pairs are all iteratively joined to form the Results ParSet (Fig. 5 phase II). In short, extracted join pairs are initially stored in an array. After the first pair is joined, it iterates through each remaining pair to attempt further joins or, else, add to a queue. Next, the queue is similarly iterated; when a pair is joined, it is unqueued. The algorithm completes when the queue is empty. As the Results ParSet is a ParSet, it can also undergo query operations. The join capability of ParSets in the DEE replaces the lack of the join common in many NoSQL databases, *e.g.*, Cassandra, MongoDB. Sometimes ParSets cannot be readily joined due to a syntactic mismatch between attribute values; nevertheless, SANSA provides a method to correct these mismatches, thereby enabling the joins.

3.3 Inference

Both RDFS and OWL contain schema information in addition to links between different resources. This additional information and rules allows users to perform reasoning on the knowledge bases in order to infer new knowledge and expand existing knowledge. The core of the inference process is to continuously apply schema-related rules on the input data to infer new facts. This process is helpful for deriving new knowledge and for detecting inconsistencies. SANSA provides an adaptive rule engine that can use a given set of arbitrary rules and derive an efficient execution plan from those. Later, that execution plan is evaluated and run against underlying engines, i.e. Spark SQL, for an efficient and scalable inference process.

3.4 Machine Learning

SANSA-ML is the Machine Learning (ML) library in SANSA. Algorithms in this repository perform various machine learning tasks directly on RDF/OWL input data. While most machine learning algorithms are based on processing simple features, the machine learning algorithms in SANSA-ML exploit the graph structure and semantics of the background knowledge specified using the RDF and OWL standards. In many cases, this allows users to obtain either more accurate or more human-understandable results. In contrast to most other algorithms supporting background knowledge, the algorithms in SANSA scale horizontally using Apache Spark. The ML layer currently supports numerous algorithms for Clustering, Similarity Assessment of entities, Entity Linking, Anomaly Detection and Classification using Graph Kernels. We will cover these algorithms in the context of knowledge graphs in the following section.

3.5 Semantic Similarity Measures

SANSA covers the semantic similarities used to estimate the similarity of concepts defined in ontologies and, hence, to assess the semantic proximity of the resources indexed by them. Most of the approaches covered in the SANSA similarity assessment module are feature-based. The feature model requires the semantic objects to be represented as sets of features. Tversky was the first to formulate the concept of semantic similarity using the feature model, from which a family of semantic measures has been derived. The similarity measure in this context is defined as a function (set-based or distance-based measure) on the common features of the objects under assessment.

Jaccard Similarity. For any two nodes u and v of a data set, the Jaccard similarity is defined as:

$$\text{Sim}_{Jaccard}(u, v) = \frac{|f(u) \cap f(v)|}{|f(u) \cup f(v)|} \tag{1}$$

Here, $f(u)$ is the subset of all neighbours of the node u and $|f(u)|$ the cardinality of $f(u)$ that counts the number of elements in $f(u)$.

Rodríguez and Egenhofer Similarity. Another example of feature-based measure implemented in SANSA is by Rodríguez and Egenhofer [181].

$$\text{Sim}_{RE}(u,v) = \frac{|f(u) \cap f(v)|}{\gamma \cdot |f(u) \setminus f(v)| + (1 - \gamma) \cdot |f(v) \setminus f(u)| + |f(u) \cap f(v)|} \tag{2}$$

where $\gamma \in [0,1]$ allows to adjust measure symmetry.

Ratio Model. Tversky defined a parameterized semantic similarity measure which is called the ratio model (SimRM) [181]. It can be used to compare two semantic objects $(u; v)$ through its respective sets of features U and V:

$$\text{Sim}_{RM}(u,v) = \frac{|f(u) \cap f(v))|}{\alpha |f(u) \setminus f(v)|) + \beta |f(v) \setminus f(u)| + \gamma |f(u) \cap f(v))|} \tag{3}$$

with α, β and $\gamma \geq 0$.

Here, $|f(u)|$ is the cardinality of the set $f(u)$ composed of all neighbours of u. Setting Sim_{RM} with $\alpha = \beta = 1$ leads to the Jaccard index, and setting $\alpha = \beta = 0.5$ leads to the Dice coefficient. In other words, set-based measures can be used to easily express abstract formulations of similarity measures. Here, we set $\alpha = \beta = 0.5$.

Batet Similarity. Batet et al. represent the taxonomic distance as the ratio between distinct and shared features [31]. Batet similarity can be defined as follows:

$$\text{Sim}_{Batet}(u,v) = \log_2 \left(1 + \frac{|f(u) \setminus f(v)| + |f(v) \setminus f(u)|}{|f(u) \setminus f(v)| + |f(v) \setminus f(u)| + |f(u) \cap f(v)|} \right) \tag{4}$$

For any node u, the notation $f(u)$ stands for the set of all neighbours of u.

3.6 Clustering

Clustering is the class of unsupervised learning algorithms that can learn without the need for the training data. Clustering is aimed to search for common patterns and similar trends in the knowledge graphs. The similarity of patterns is mostly measured by a given similarity measure, e.g the measures covered in the previous section. Below, we cover the clustering algorithms implemented in SANSA for knowledge graphs.

PowerIteration Clustering. PowerIteration (PIC) [284] is a fast spectral clustering technique. It is a simple (it only requires a matrix-vector multiplication process) and scalable algorithm in terms of time complexity, O(n). PIC requires pairwise vertices and their similarities as input and outputs the clusters of vertices by using a pseudo-eigenvector of the normalized affinity matrix of the graph. Although the PowerIteration method approximates only one eigenvalue of a matrix, it remains useful for certain computational problems. For instance, Google uses it to calculate the PageRank of documents in its search engine, and Twitter uses it to show follow recommendations. Spark.mllib includes an implementation of PIC using GraphX. It takes an RDD of tuples, which are vertices of an edge, and the similarity among the two vertices and outputs a model with clustering assignments.

BorderFlow Clustering. BorderFlow [325] is a local graph clustering which takes each node as the starting seed and iteratively builds clusters by merging the nodes using BorderFlow-ratio. The clusters must have a maximal intra-cluster density and inter-cluster sparseness. When considering a graph as the description of a flow system, this definition of a cluster implies that a cluster X is a set of nodes such that the flow within X is maximal while the flow from X to the outside is minimal. At each step, a pair of nodes is merged if the border flow ratio is maximised and this process is repeated until the termination criterion is met. BorderFlow is a parameter-free algorithm and it has been used successfully in diverse applications including clustering protein-protein interaction (PPI) data [324] and query clustering for benchmarking [313].

Linked-Based Clustering. Link information plays an important role in discovering knowledge from data. The link-based graph clustering [156] algorithm results in overlapping clusters. Initially, each link represents its own group; the algorithm recursively merges the links using similarity criteria to optimize the partition density until all links are merged into one, or until the termination condition is met. To optimize performance, instead of selecting arbitrary links, the algorithm only considers the pair of links that share a node for merging.

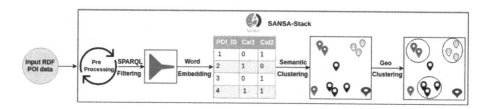

Fig. 6. A semantic-geo clustering flow.

Building Clustering Processes [95]. SANSA proposes a flexible architecture to design clustering pipelines. For example, having points of interest (POI) datasets, SANSA can aggregate them according to several dimensions in one pipeline: their labels on the first hand and their localisation on the other hand. Such an architecture is presented in Fig. 6.

The approach contains up to five main components (which could be enabled/disabled if necessary), namely: data pre-processing, SPARQL filtering, word embedding, semantic clustering and geo-clustering. In semantic-based clustering algorithms (which do not consider POI locations but rather aim at grouping POIs according to shared labels), there is a need to transform the POIs categorical values to numerical vectors to find the distance between them. So far, any word-embedding technique can be selected among the three available ones, namely one-hot encoding, Word2Vec and Multi-Dimensional Scaling. All the abovementioned methods convert categorical variables into a form that could be provided to semantic clustering algorithms to form groups of non-location-based similarities. For example, all restaurants are in one cluster whereas all the ATMs are in another one. On the other hand, the geo-clustering methods help to group the spatially closed coordinates within each semantic cluster.

More generically, SANSA's architecture and implementation allow users to design any kind of clustering combinations they would like. Actually, the solution is flexible enough to pipe together more than two clustering "blocks" and even to add additional RDF datasets into the process after several clustering rounds.

3.7   Anomaly Detection

With the recent advances in data integration and the concept of data lakes, massive pools of heterogeneous data are being curated as Knowledge Graphs (KGs). In addition to data collection, it is of the utmost importance to gain meaningful insights from this composite data. However, given the graph-like representation, the multimodal nature, and large size of data, most of the traditional analytic approaches are no longer directly applicable. The traditional approaches collect all values of a particular attribute, e.g. height, and perform anomaly detection for this attribute. However, it is conceptually inaccurate to compare one attribute representing different entities, e.g. the height of buildings against the height of animals. Therefore, there is a strong need to develop fundamentally new approaches for outlier detection in KGs. SANSA presents a scalable approach that can deal with multimodal data and performs adaptive outlier detection against the cohorts of classes they represent, where a cohort is a set of classes that are similar based on a set of selected properties. An overview of the scalable anomaly detection [216] in SANSA can be seen in Fig. 7.

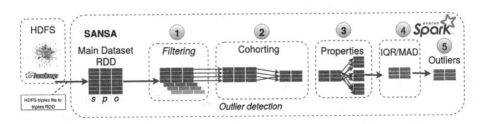

Fig. 7. Anomaly detection execution pipeline.

3.8   Entity Linking

Entity resolution is the crucial task of recognizing and linking entities that point to the same real-world object in various information spaces. Entity linking finds its application in numerous tasks like de-duplicating entities in federal datasets related to medicine, finance, transportation, business and law enforcement, etc. With the growth of the web in terms of volume and velocity, the task of linking records in heterogeneous data collections has become more complicated. It is difficult to find semantic relations between entities across different datasets containing noisy data and missing values with loose schema bindings. At the same time, pairwise comparison of entities over large datasets implies and exhibits quadratic complexity. Some recent approaches reduce this complexity by aggregating similar entities into blocks. In SANSA, we implement a more generic method for entity resolution that does not use blocking and significantly reduces the quadratic comparisons. In SANSA, we use scalable techniques like vectorization using hashingTF, count-vectorization and Locality Sensitive Hashing [190] to achieve almost linear performance for large-scale entity resolution. An overview of the approach used in SANSA can be seen in Fig. 8.

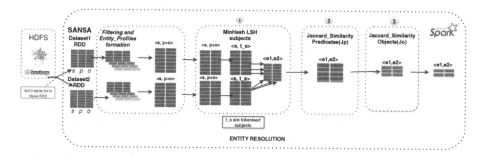

Fig. 8. Overview of scalable Entity Linking.

3.9   Graph Kernels for RDF

Many machine learning algorithms strongly depend on the specific structure of the data, which forces users to fit their observations in a particular predefined setting or re-implement the algorithms to fit their requirements. For dynamic data models like Knowledge Graphs that can operate on schema-free structures, techniques like propositionalization or graph kernels are used. Inspired by [287], we developed graph kernels in SANSA. The walk kernel corresponds to a weighted sum of the cardinality of walks up to a given length. The number of paths can be calculated either by breadth-first search or by multiplication of the adjacency matrix. A path kernel is similar to walk kernel, but it counts the number of paths instead. Unlike walks, paths must consist of distinct vertices. SubtreekKernels attempt to limit the calculations of kernels by selecting subgraphs identified with a central entity, and sharing a common structure. This enables a replacement of the intersection graph with other suitable structures. The full subtree kernels are based on the number of full subtrees contained in the intersection graph. The kernels, in general, return the set of feature vectors for the entities that can be further used in algorithms, like neural networks support vector machines or similar algorithms working on numerical data.

Apart from the analytics mentioned in this section, SANSA provides additional algorithms for rule mining, cluster evaluation, graph kernels as well. All of these algorithms are being continuously extended and improved. In addition, more algorithms are being added with time.

4   Grand Challenges and Conclusions

In this chapter, we provide an overview of SANSA's functionalities: an engine that attempts to fill the gap pointed in Chap. 3. SANSA is the only comprehensive system that addresses several challenges and provides libraries for the development of a knowledge graph value chain ranging from acquisition, distribution, and querying to complex analytics (see for instance [170,415] where complex analyses were successfully computed on the Ethereum blockchain using SANSA).

The SANSA stack is a step in the direction of offering a seamless solution to help users dealing with big knowledge graphs. As a consequence, there are still **grand challenges** to face:

- Availability of data in RDF. This challenge is to be linked to the research directions on federated queries (Chap. 5) and to the design of mappings (Chap. 4) to pave the road for datalake-oriented solutions such as the one presented by Mami *et al.* [295]. While the representation of data as knowledge graphs has gained lots of traction and large-scale knowledge graphs are being created, a majority of data being created and stored is not-RDF and therefore challenges such as the necessary efforts for data cleaning, and/or data maintenance should be taken into account.
- RDF and Query layer. The distributed context requires smart partitioning methods (see [53] and [235] for detailed taxonomies) aligned with the querying strategies. One possibility would be to have dynamic partitioning paradigms which could be automatically selected based on data shape and/or query patterns, as envisioned in [14].
- In a distributed context, processes often share resources with concurrent processes, and therefore the definition itself of what is a "good" query answer time may vary, as reviewed in the context of distributed RDF solutions by Graux *et al.* in [169]. One could think of basing this performance evaluation on use-cases.
- Machine Learning and Partial access to data. Most machine learning algorithms generally require access to all the training data and work by iterating over the training data to fit the desired loss function. This is challenging in the distributed setting where one might need to use multiple local learners or

query processors (each working on a subset of the data) and optimize globally over (or collect) partial local results. For very large-scale distributed data, this working model may not be suitable [343]. Hence, there is a strong need to develop fundamentally new algorithms that can work with partial access to the data.

– Challenge on the Semantic Web itself. At the moment, using W3C standards, it is hard to be as expressive as with Property Graphs. This has led to the creation of RDF* [184,185] in order to allow Semantic Web users to express statements of statements within an RDF extension. These new possibilities imply that the current landscape incorporates this extension while guaranteeing the same performances as before.

Chapter 8
Context-Based Entity Matching
for Big Data

Mayesha Tasnim[1], Diego Collarana[1]🆔, Damien Graux[2]🆔,
and Maria-Esther Vidal[3(✉)]🆔

[1] Fraunhofer IAIS, Sankt Augustin, Germany
[2] ADAPT SFI Research Centre, Trinity College, Dublin, Ireland
[3] TIB Leibniz Information Centre For Science and Technology, Hannover, Germany
maria.vidal@tib.eu

Abstract. In the Big Data era, where variety is the most dominant
dimension, the RDF data model enables the creation and integration
of actionable knowledge from heterogeneous data sources. However, the
RDF data model allows for describing entities under various contexts,
e.g., people can be described from its demographic context, but as well
from their professional contexts. Context-aware description poses challenges during entity matching of RDF datasets—the match might not
be valid in every context. To perform a contextually relevant entity
matching, the specific context under which a data-driven task, e.g., data
integration is performed, must be taken into account. However, existing
approaches only consider inter-schema and properties mapping of different data sources and prevent users from selecting contexts and conditions
during a data integration process. We devise COMET, an entity matching technique that relies on both the knowledge stated in RDF vocabularies and a context-based similarity metric to map contextually equivalent
RDF graphs. COMET follows a two-fold approach to solve the problem
of entity matching in RDF graphs in a context-aware manner. In the first
step, COMET computes the similarity measures across RDF entities and
resorts to the Formal Concept Analysis algorithm to map contextually
equivalent RDF entities. Finally, COMET combines the results of the
first step and executes a 1-1 perfect matching algorithm for matching
RDF entities based on the combined scores. We empirically evaluate the
performance of COMET on testbed from DBpedia. The experimental
results suggest that COMET accurately matches equivalent RDF graphs
in a context-dependent manner.

1 Introduction

In the Big Data era, variety is one of the most dominant dimensions bringing
new challenges for data-driven tasks. Variety alludes to the types and sources
of data that are becoming increasingly heterogeneous with new forms of data

V. Janev et al. (Eds.): Knowledge Graphs and Big Data Processing, LNCS 12072, pp. 122–146, 2020.
https://doi.org/10.1007/978-3-030-53199-7_8

collection being introduced with time. At one point in time, the only source of digital data was spreadsheets and databases. Today data is collected from emails, photographs, digital documents, or audio. The variety of unstructured and semi-structured data creates issues during data analysis. Therefore, these varying forms of data must be integrated for consistency in storage, mining, and analysis. The process of integrating these complex and semi-structured data poses its own set of challenges. For example, the same real-world object may be represented in different data sources as different entities; it therefore challenging to identify entities that refer to the same real-world object.

The Resource Description Framework (RDF) data model enables the description of data integrated from heterogeneous data sources. RDF is designed to have a simple data model with formal semantics to provide inference capabilities. The syntax of RDF describes a simple graph-based data model, along with formal semantics, which allows for well-defined entailment regimes that provide the basis for logical deductions. RDF has the following principal use cases as a method for describing web metadata: (i) to allow applications to use an information model which is open rather than constrained; (ii) to allow web data to be machine-processable; and (iii) to combine and integrate data from several sources incrementally. RDF is designed to represent information in a minimally constraining and flexible way; it can be used in isolated applications, where individually designed formats might be easily understood, and the RDF generality offers higher value from sharing. Thus, the value of RDF data increases as it becomes accessible to more applications across the entire internet.

RDF is a semi-structured data model that allows for the encoding of multiple contexts of an entity within the same graph. A context describes a situation that limits the validity of particular information. The so-called "Context as a Box" approach [63] considers context as the conditions and constraints which define whether or not a piece of information is accurate. Contextual information (or meta information) represents the conditions and constraints which describe the situation of a context. For example, the fact "Donald Trump is the President of the United States of America" is valid only in the context of "the presidential period between the years 2017 and 2021". The RDF data model allows for representing entities of the same type with different properties. This in turn allows for the encoding of multiple contexts of an entity within the same graph. For example, the entity *Donald Trump* in an RDF graph can have properties relating to the context of his career as a politician, and also the ones that describe his role as a reality TV celebrity. This feature of RDF is useful for addressing the data complexity challenge of variety– a dominant dimension of data in the Big Data era [218]. Nevertheless, enabling diverse representations of the same entity poses new challenges during the analysis of RDF graphs. This is particularly prevalent in cases where specific contexts need to be considered for the effective identification of similar entities [35]. Two entities may be similar in one context but dissimilar in another. In this chapter[1], we present a novel approach to tackle

---

[1] This chapter is based on the master thesis of Mayesha Tasnim.

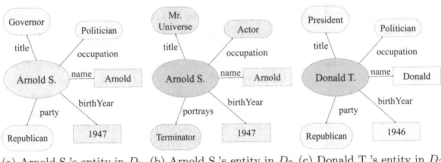

(a) Arnold S.'s entity in D_1 (b) Arnold S.'s entity in D_2 (c) Donald T.'s entity in D_2

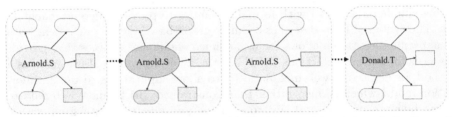

(d) Entity matching using similarity   (e) Entity matching using similarity and context

Fig. 1. Motivation Example. The top row shows three entities across two datasets. The bottom row shows two matching scenarios, the left one not considering context during entity matching, and the right one taking context into consideration.

the problem of entity matching considering context as a new dimension of the matching algorithm.

1.1 Motivating Example

Following the principle of the web of linked data, RDF allows for the representation of different contexts of an entity within the same graph. This means that applications attempting to match entities from different graphs have to deal with entities that are valid in different contexts. In order to match entities in such a way that they comply with the context specified by the user of the application, the system context must be taken into account. A system's context represents any kind of information that describes the system and its requirements. If this system context is not considered, the entity matching operation will match entities that are not relevant or valid under the definition of system context.

This can be demonstrated using the example of a context-based entity matching scenario using RDF entities representing persons. *Arnold Schwarzenegger* is a person with an extensive career in both politics and acting. Consequently, there is data available regarding both his career in politics and his achievements in the movie industry. Consider a system that contains data about American politicians and is searching other data sources to match relevant data. The system's dataset D_1 contains information about Arnold Schwarzenegger and his political career. In another dataset D_2 available on the web there exists information about Arnold's acting career, e.g. the movies he has acted in and the roles he has played. The same dataset D_2 also contains information about other celebrities, like Donald Trump, President of the United States. These entities are presented in Figs. 1a, 1b and 1c, respectively.

In a typical entity matching scenario where context is not considered, entities are matched to the ones that are most similar to them. In such a case, Arnold Schwarzenegger's entity from D_1 will be matched with the entity in D_2 containing information about his acting career, as shown in Fig. 1d. However, in the context of politics, Arnold's political career is more similar to Donald Trump's than his own career in acting. They are politicians of almost the same age who both support the Republican party. In a political context, their careers are far more similar than when Arnold's post as the Governor of California is compared with his portrayal of the Terminator in Terminator 2. Therefore, when the context of American politics is considered, the entity of Arnold S. from D_1 should be matched with the Donald T. entity from D_2. This is an example of *context-aware entity matching*.

1.2 Challenges and Problems

To match entities from heterogeneous sources in a unified way, Bellazi et al. [37] explain the importance of analyzing all data sources to identify interoperability conflicts. Vidal et al. [447] characterize the interoperability conflicts into six categories. We summarizes the main characteristics of each interoperability conflict.

1. Structuredness (C1): data sources may be described at different levels of structuredness, i.e. structured, semi-structured, and unstructured. The entities in a structured data source are described in terms of fixed schema and attributes, e.g. the entity-relationship model. In semi-structured data sources, a fixed schema is not required, and entities can be represented using different attributes and properties. Examples of semi-structured data models are the Resource Description Framework (RDF) or XML. Lastly, in unstructured data sources, the no data model is used, so the data does not follow any structured. Typically unstructured data formats are: textual, numerical, images, or videos.

2. Schematic (C2): the following conflicts arise when data sources are modeled with different schema. i) the same entity is represented by different attributes; ii) different structures model the same entity, e.g., classes versus properties; iii) the same property is represented with different data types, e.g., string versus integer; iv) different levels of specialization/generalization describe the same entity; v) the same entity is named differently; and vi) different ontologies are used, e.g., to describe a gene function the following ontologies may be used UMLS, SNOMED-CT, NCIT, or GO.

3. Domain (C3): various interpretations of the same domain exist on different data sources. These interpretations include: homonyms, synonyms,

acronyms, and semantic constraints—different integrity constraints are used to model a concept.

4. Representation (C4): different representations are used to model the same entity. These representation conflicts include: different scales and units, values of precision, incorrect spellings, different identifiers, and various encodings.

5. Language (C5): the data and schema may be specified using different languages, e.g. English and Spanish.

6. Granularity (C6): the data may be collected under different levels of granularity, e.g. samples of the same measurement observed at different time-frequency, various criteria of aggregation, and data model at different levels of detail.

2   Applications of Entity Matching

Entity Matching (EM) is an important operation in the field of data science and data management, and as such there are many practical applications where entity matching is necessary. In this section, we explore two applications of entity matching, namely *Data Integration* and *Knowledge Summarization*.

2.1   Semantic Data Integration

Semantic data integration is a research field that deals with integrating and reconciling *semantic heterogeneity* in different data sources. Towards this goal, the inclusion of semantics as a tool to aid data integration makes the entire process more powerful [101]. Using semantics in data integration means building data integration systems where the semantics of data are explicitly defined, and these semantics are used in turn during all the phases of data integration. It is unrealistic to entertain the idea that various data sources across the web will publish data using the same set of rules and conventions. Indeed, in reality data available across the World Wide Web have very different representations of the same information and concepts (entities). The stack of semantic technologies allows the opportunity for describing data semantically, and for interlinking disparate data sources. Thus, semantic integration is a useful approach for integrating semantically heterogeneous data. The bulk of the work done surrounding semantic data integration revolves around three aspects [332]. The first aspect is *mapping discovery*, or the process of automatically finding similarities between two ontologies and mapping properties that present the same real-world concept. The second is *mapping representation*, which is concerned with the specific method of representing mappings between two ontologies. The third and final aspect is *enabling reasoning*, which concerns itself with the process of performing reasoning over ontologies once the mapping has been established.

An example of an approach to achieve semantic data integration is the MINTE framework proposed by Collarana et al. [84]. MINTE is a *semantic integration technique* that is able to match and merge semantically equivalent

RDF entities in a single step through the utilization of semantics present in the vocabularies. MINTE uses both semantic similarity measures and the implicit knowledge present in the RDF vocabularies in order to match and merge RDF graphs that refer to the same real-world entity. MINTE's performance is powered by *semantic similarity measures, ontologies*, and *fusion policies* that consider not only textual data content but also logical axioms encoded into the graphs.

MINTE implements a two-step approach for determining the similarity between two RDF entities and then merging them. In the first step, MINTE implements a 1-1 weighted perfect matching algorithm to identify semantically equivalent RDF entities in input data sources. Then MINTE relies on *fusion policies* to merge triples from these semantically equivalent RDF entities. Fusion policies are rules operating on RDF triples, which are triggered by certain configurations of predicates and objects. Fusion policies can also resort to an ontology O to resolve possible conflicts. Collarana et al. define multiple fusion policies, e.g. *union policy, subproperty policy* and *authoritative graph policy*, which are each designed for flexible management and targeted control of an integrated knowledge graph. Figure *MINTE architecture* depicts the main components of the MINTE architecture. The accuracy of the process of determining when two RDF molecules are semantically equivalent in MINTE is impacted by the characteristics of the similarity measure Sim_f. Collarana et al. report the best performance when the GADES [371] similarity metric is used.

2.2   Summarization of Knowledge Graph

Another application of entity matching lies in the summarization of knowledge graphs. A knowledge graph is an ontology combined with a collection of instances that represents a collection of interlinked descriptions of entities. Knowledge graphs often capture domain-specific knowledge in the form of a graph. It has a data layer that contains the actual information and a semantic layer that represents the schema or the ontology. Typically knowledge graphs contain millions of entities and billions of properties describing these entities. This can lead to information overload, and therefore it is important to compress and summarize knowledge graphs for efficient representation of data [175].

The task of entity summarization is an essential part of knowledge graph summarization. Entity summaries allow the concise representation of the most important information about a certain real-world object. In the process of entity summarization, *entity matching* plays an important role. In order to summarize entities that either refer to the same real-world entity or are similar according to some summarization paradigm, it is first necessary to *identify* entities that belong in the same summary unit. For example, several knowledge graphs contain information about Marie Curie, each containing hundreds of facts about her life. For typical use cases, a summary containing a few basic items of information, namely her name, birth year, occupation and notable contributions, is enough to distinguish the most relevant aspects about her. To achieve this goal, it is first required to isolate entities from each knowledge graph that refer to Marie Curie. This is done using an entity matching technique. Knowledge graph summarization can either be *concise* – containing only a subset of original facts, or *comprehensive* – containing an overview for all the original facts. The need for either a concise or a comprehensive summary depends on the particular case.

Knowledge graphs can also be summarized along different axes. For example, information can be summarized based on the semantic layer, i.e. ontology. It can also be summarized along different contextual layers, e.g., along time, geographic location, etc. In Chapter *Use Cases*, a temporal summarization technique for knowledge graph entities using COMET is described.

3   Novel Entity Matching Approaches

The problem of entity matching between disparate data sources is essential to the field of data integration. This is because one of the primary tasks in data integration is to reconcile varying schemas, thereby creating mapping entities between different data sources. Multiple approaches for inter-schema mapping exist both in the relational and graph database community. Multiple approaches also exist for the Entity Summarization – another application of entity matching.

A substantial amount of research has also been done over the idea of context and its role in data-driven tasks, particularly in the semantic web where the concept of data is intricately related to its semantics. The bulk of this research is limited to the formalization of context, although not much work has been done in practically implementing this concept. The following are some of the related carried out in formalizing context as well as a few practical approaches towards data integration and entity summarization.

3.1   Context in the Semantic Web

Principles for Formalizing Context: Bozzato et al. [63] present an argument that context needs to be represented in a more advanced manner in the Semantic Web and Linked Open Data (LOD). They further define a set of properties that a representation of context *should* abide by. These properties allow context to be an integral part of RDF data and its reasoning. The properties are as follows:

1. *Encapsulation*: data that share the same context must be encapsulated for ease in access and identification.
2. *Explicit meta knowledge*: contextual information must be represented in a logical language.
3. *Separation*: there must be a way to clearly distinguish meta knowledge from object knowledge.
4. *Relationship*: relationships between contexts must be explicitly represented.
5. *Encapsulation*: data that share the same context must be encapsulated for ease in access and identification.
6. *Contextual reasoning*: the representation should allow for reasoning to be done using the contextual knowledge.
7. *Locality*: each unit of context representation should allow the definition of axioms which are valid only within the local scope.

8. *Knowledge Lifting*: it should be possible to reuse knowledge from one context and apply it in another.
9. *Overlap*: the representation should allow for overlaps of knowledge between different contexts.
10. *Complexity invariance*: the addition of this contextual layer should not increase the complexity of reasoning.

The definition of context in COMET is guided by the principles defined above. Our definition particularly focuses on implementing the properties of *Explicit meta knowledge* and *Contextual reasoning*.

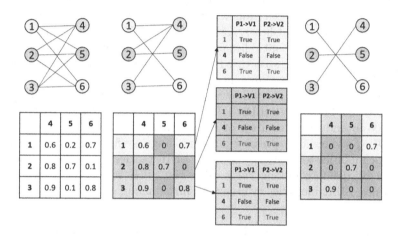

Fig. 2. Context Ontology for Data Integration (CODI) [409]. An overview of contextual elements (CE) defined in the context ontology

Context Ontology for Data Integration (CODI). The Context Ontology for Data Integration [409] was developed by Souza et al. to formally represent context in data integration processes. They first define the concept of Contextual Elements (CE) to represent the context of any domain-specific scenario. This is shown in Fig. 2. They then build a context ontology suited to the domain-specific scenario after having meetings with domain experts. This context ontology is then used during the reconciliation of schema during data integration. Although this approach works with the formal definition of context in data integration scenarios, it is still quite expensive since it cannot work without extensive input from domain experts in the modeling of the Context Ontology. It also does not make use of the semantics already existing in the data instances to guide its modeling of context.

3.2   Entity Matching Approaches

Applications in Data Integration. Data Integration (DI) is one of the most common applications that require entity matching. This matching is done at either at a schema-level or at an instance-level. There are a number of approaches that aim at the integration of disparate RDF data sources. We divide these works based on whether they match ontologies, or the instances themselves.

Ontology Matching Approaches. Many of the data integration approaches based on RDF data apply the concept of mapping heterogeneous data sources to a common ontology. One approach using ontologies is KARMA, proposed by Knoblock et al. [247]. This is a framework for integrating a variety of data sources including databases, spreadsheets, XML, JSON, and Web APIs. KARMA implements a hybrid approach that relies on supervised machine algorithms for identifying mapping rules from structured sources to ontologies; these mapping rules can be refined by users via a user interface.

Another approach is suggested by Schultz et al. [388], who describe the Linked Data Integration Framework (LDIF). LDIF is oriented to integrate RDF datasets from the Web and provides a set of independent tools to support interlinking tasks. LDIF provides an expressive mapping language for translating data from various vocabularies to a unified ontology. LDIF tackles the problem of identity resolution by defining linking rules using the SILK tool [213]. Based on the defined rules, SILK identifies `owl:sameAs` links among entities of two datasets.

Instance Matching Approaches. In the task of identifying whether given entities refer to the same real-world entity, growing attention in the relational databases field is given to crowdsourcing mechanisms [242,445]. Reporting impressive results, such approaches, however, might struggle in sophisticated domains with multiple contexts due to a lack of human experts who could reliably provide necessary example data.

ODCleanStore [307] and UnifiedViews [246] are ETL frameworks for integrating RDF data. ODCleanStore relies on SILK to perform instance matching and provides custom data fusion modules to merge the data of the discovered matches.

The MINTE framework proposed by Collarana et al. [84] also tackles the task of matching entities in different datasets that correspond to the same real-world entity by making use of the semantics encoded in the data itself. They first apply a *semantic similarity metric* in order to identify *semantically equivalent* entities from two different RDF graphs. Next they make use of a set of novel *fusion policies* to merge these semantically equivalent entities. Although MINTE makes use of the semantics encoded into the RDF graph itself, it does not consider the context during the step of entity matching. The work done in COMET is in essence a context-based extension of MINTE (Fig. 3).

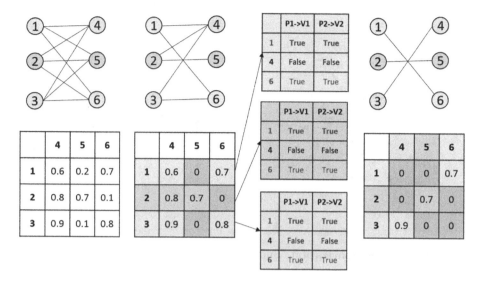

Fig. 3. Entity Summarization. Summarizing a single entity as envisioned by LinkSum [424]

Applications in Entity Summarization. Entity summarization is the process of creating a concise representation of an entity in order to describe the whole entity. A number of approaches have been formulated in order to generate summaries of entities [175]. One such approach is RELIN [79] by Cheng et al. where they defined the problem of entity summarization using RDF graphs and demonstrated its utility in entity identification. RELIN makes use of the PageRank algorithm to select relevant features in the creation of the summary entity. In 2014, Thalhammer and Rettinger proposed SUMMARUM [425], a dbpedia-based entity summarization framework that also uses PageRank in order to rank the features of an entity. It also uses the global popularity of DBPedia resources corresponding to their Wikipedia pages. They later proposed LinkSum [424], which in addition to PageRank also makes use of an adaptation of the Back-Link method combined with new methods for predicate selection. These entity summarization frameworks focus on the rank of features (attributes) in order to create the summary, but do not take into consideration any contextual dimension of the data. The above-mentioned integration frameworks aim at mapping different data sources with possibly varying schema, i.e., they perform inter-schema mapping. ontext-based integration could only be supported in these frameworks on a superficial level via filtering query results without applying many inherent semantics. Similarly, the entity summarization frameworks aim at summarizing via some order of properties instead of considering contextual information present in the data. Therefore, we identify a need for context-based entity matching mechanisms and present our approach, which can be adapted for both integration and summarization of RDF data (Fig. 4).

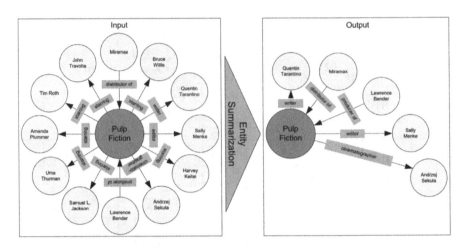

Fig. 4. Entity Summarization. Summarizing a single entity as envisioned by LinkSum [424]

4   COMET: A Context-Aware Matching Technique

To provide a solution to the *problem of contextually matching* RDF entities, COMET – a context-aware RDF molecule matching technique – is proposed. This technique is grounded on the semantic data integration techniques proposed by Collarana et al. [84], whose work deals with matching and merging RDF molecules that are semantically similar using semantic similarity metric and fusion policies. This work makes use of the concepts of RDF molecules but contributes a new approach as to taking into consideration the *context* of the system while matching entities. COMET is an entity matching framework designed to create, identify, and match contextually equivalent RDF entities. Grounded on the entity matching component from the data integration technique proposed by Collarana et al. [84], we propose COMET, an entity matching approach to merge equivalent RDF entities based on context. Thus, a solution to the *problem of contextually matching entities* is provided (Fig. 5).

4.1   Problem Definition

RDF Molecule [84] – If $\Phi(G)$ is a given RDF Graph, we define RDF Molecule M as a subgraph of $\Phi(G)$ such that,

$$M = \{t_1, \ldots, t_n\}$$

$$\forall \quad i, j \in \{1, \ldots, n\}\big(subject(t_i) = subject(t_j)\big)$$

Where $t_1, t_2, \ldots, t_n$ denote the triples in M. In other words, an RDF Molecule M consists of triples which have the same subject. That is, it can be represented by a tuple $M = (R, T)$, where R denotes the URI of the molecule's

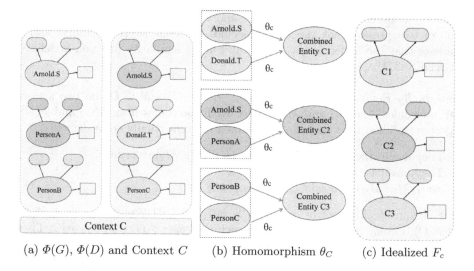

(a) $\Phi(G)$, $\Phi(D)$ and Context C (b) Homomorphism θ_C (c) Idealized F_c

Fig. 5. Problem Definition. The left side shows two RDF Graphs the system Context. The right side shows the application of homomorphism θ_C on the RDF graphs, resulting in the formation of Contextualized RDF Graph F_c.

subject, and T denotes a set of property and value pairs $p = $ *(prop, val)* such that the triple *(R, prop, val)* belongs to M. For example, the RDF molecule for *Arnold Schwarzenegger* is (dbr:Arnold-Schwarzenegger, { (dbo:occupation, *Politician*), (dbp:title, *Governor*)}). An RDF Graph $\Phi(G)$ described in terms of RDF molecules is defined as follows:

$$\Phi(G) = \{M = (R, T) | t = (R, prop, val) \in G \land (prop, val) \in T\}$$

Context – We define a context C as any Boolean expression which represents the criteria of a system. Two entities, such as an RDF molecule M_1 and M_2, can be either similar or not similar with respect to a given context. That is, C is a Boolean function that takes as input two molecules M_1 and M_2 and returns true if they are similar according to system context, and false otherwise. Below is an example of context C, modeled after the example presented in Fig. 1, where two molecules are similar if they have the same occupation. If $P = (p, v)$ is the predicate representing the occupation property of a molecule, then context.

$$C(M_1, M_2) = \begin{cases} \text{true}, & \text{if } P \in M_1 \land P \in M_2. \\ \text{false}, & \text{otherwise.} \end{cases}$$

Depending on the requirements of the integration scenario, this context can be any Boolean expression.

Semantic Similarity Function – Let M_1 and M_2 be any two RDF molecules. Then *semantic similarity function* Sim_f is a function that measures the *semantic similarity* between these two molecules and returns a value between $[0, 1]$. A value of 0 expresses that the two molecules are completely dissimilar and 1 expresses that the molecules are identical. Such a similarity function is defined in GADES [371].

Contextually Equivalent RDF Molecule – Let $\Phi(G)$ and $\Phi(D)$ be two sets of RDF molecules. Let M_G and M_D be two RDF molecules from $\Phi(G)$ and $\Phi(D)$, respectively. Then, M_G and M_D are defined as contextually equivalent iff

1. They are in the same context. That is, $C(M_1, M_2) = \texttt{true}$
2. They have the highest similarity value, i.e.,
   $Sim_f(M_G, M_D) = max(\forall_{m \in \Phi(D)} Sim_f(M_G, m))$

Let F_c be an idealized set of *contextually integrated* RDF molecules from $\Phi(G)$ and $\Phi(D)$. Let θ_C be a homomorphism such that $\theta_C : \Phi(G) \cup \Phi(D) \to F_c$. Then there is an RDF Molecule M_F from F_c such that $\theta(M_D) = \theta(M_G) = M_F$. From the motivation example, this means that the molecule of *Arnold Schwarzenegger*, the politician, is *contextually equivalent* to the molecule of *Donald Trump* as they are similar *and* they satisfy the context condition of having the same occupation.

In this work, we tackle the problem of explicitly modeling the context and then matching RDF molecules from RDF graphs that are both highly similar and equivalent in terms of this context. This problem is defined as follows: given RDF graphs $\Phi(G)$ and $\Phi(D)$, let M_G and M_D be two RDF molecules such that $M_G \in \Phi(G)$ and $M_D \in \Phi(D)$. The system is supplied with a context parameter C, which is a Boolean function evaluating if two molecules are in the same context. It is also supplied with a similarity function Sim_f, which evaluates the semantic similarity between M_G and M_D.

The problem of creating a contextualized graph Φ_C consists of building a homomorphism $\theta_C : \Phi(G) \cup \Phi(D) \to F_c$, such that for every pair of RDF molecules belonging to Φ_C there are none that are *contextually equivalent* according to system context C. If M_G and M_D are contextually equivalent molecules belonging to F_c, then $\theta_C(M_G) = \theta_C(M_D)$, otherwise $\theta_C(M_G) \neq \theta_C(M_D)$.

An example of this problem is illustrated in Figure X, which depicts a use case with two RDF graphs and a single context condition C. With respect to C, the RDF molecule *Arnold.S* from $\Phi(G)$ is in the same context as *Donald.T* from $\Phi(D)$, but not in the same context as the molecule *Arnold.S* from $\Phi(G)$. So the problem is to identify a homomorphism θ_C which evaluates the RDF molecules based on system context and maps these RDF molecules in a way that they can be integrated into a contextualized graph.

4.2   The COMET Architecture

We propose COMET, an approach to match contextually equivalent RDF graphs according to a given context, thus providing a solution to the problem of *contextually matching* RDF graphs. Figure 6 depicts the main components of the COMET architecture. COMET follows a two-fold approach to solve the problem of entity matching in RDF graphs in a context-aware manner: First, COMET computes the similarity measures across RDF entities and resorts to the Formal Concept Analysis algorithm to map contextually equivalent RDF entities. Finally, COMET combines the results of the first step and executes a 1-1 perfect matching algorithm for matching RDF entities based on the combined scores to finally synthesize the matching into a contextualized RDF graph.

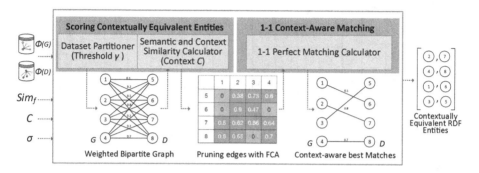

Fig. 6. The COMET Architecture. COMET receives two RDF datasets, e.g., G and D; a similarity function Sim_f; and a context C. The output is a set of contextually matching RDF entities.

4.3   Identifying Contextually Equivalent Entities

Building a Bipartite Graph. The COMET pipeline receives two RDF graphs $\Phi(G), \Phi(D)$ as input, along with context parameter C, and a similarity function Sim_f. COMET first constructs a bipartite graph between the sets $\phi(G)$ and $\phi(D)$. The *Dataset Partitioner* employs a similarity function Sim_f and ontology O to compute the similarity between RDF molecules in $\phi(G)$ and $\phi(D)$ assigning the similarity score as vertices weight in the bipartite graph. COMET allows for arbitrary, user-supplied similarity functions that leverage different algorithms to estimate similarity between RDF molecules. Thus, COMET supports a variety of similarity functions including simple string similarity. However, as shown in [84], semantic similarity measures are advocated (in the implementation of this work we particularly use GADES [371]) as they achieve better results by considering semantics encoded in RDF graphs.

After RDF molecules similarity comparison, the result of the similarity function is tested against a threshold γ to determine entity similarity (the similarity threshold's minimum acceptable score). Thus, edges are discarded from the bipartite graph whose weights are lower than γ. A threshold equal to 0.0 does not impose any restriction on the values of similarity; thus the bipartite graph includes all the edges. High thresholds, e.g. 0.8, restrict the values of similarity, resulting in a bipartite graph comprising just a few edges.

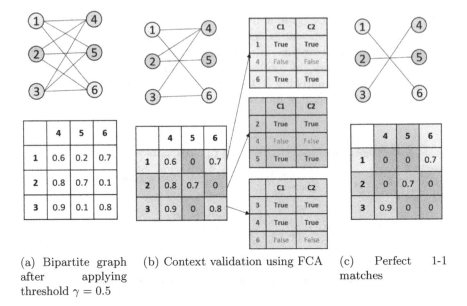

(a) Bipartite graph after applying threshold $\gamma = 0.5$ (b) Context validation using FCA   (c) Perfect 1-1 matches

Fig. 7. Context Validation. The left side shows a bipartite graph after the application of threshold. The remaining edges go through a special 1-1 matching algorithm which takes into account the system context using FCA. The result is a perfect match between contextually equivalent molecules.

Pruning RDF Entities According to ContexB. The main step on the COMET pipeline is to validate and prune pairs of RDF molecules that do not comply with the input context C, making COMET a context-aware approach. For identifying contextually equivalent RDF entities, the *Context Validator* component employs the Formal Concept Analysis (FCA) algorithm. FCA is the study of binary data tables that describe the relationship between objects and their attributes. Applying this context validation step over the RDF molecules ensures that only contextually relevant tuples are kept. In COMET, context is modeled as any Boolean function. Two molecules are matched if they satisfy this condition, otherwise they are not matched. The algorithm by V. Vychodil [451] is applied in COMET; it performs formal concept analysis to compute formal concepts within a set of objects and their attributes. This algorithm is extended in our approach for validating complex *Boolean conditions*. A typical formal concept analysis table is shown in Table 1.

Table 1. Object-Attribute table for performing FCA.

	Attribute 1	Attribute 2	Attribute 3
Object 1		X	X
Object 2		X	
Object 3	X		X

Instead of using attributes in the column of the FCA matrix, in our approach, we replace the attributes with a *boolean condition* C. This is the same as the context condition C used in our approach. For example, the context C from the motivating example can be broken down into $C = C_1 \wedge C_2$ where $C_1 = $ "contains property dbo:occupation", and $C_2 = $ "has the same value for property dbo:occupation". The execution of the FCA algorithm remains unchanged by this adaptation since the format of the input to FCA is still a binary matrix.

When applied to RDF molecules, formal concept analysis returns a set of formal concepts $< M, C >$ where M is a set of all the molecules that contain all conditions contained in C. That is, by applying FCA, the set of molecules that satisfy a certain context condition can be obtained. Thus, the molecules that do not meet the context condition are pruned. In Fig. 7, an example of context validation is demonstrated. Edges in a bipartite graph are filtered according to a threshold value γ as detailed in the previous section. Next, the remaining edges are validated by constructing an FCA matrix according to context condition C. The FCA algorithm returns the edge satisfying the context conditions. The edges that do not satisfy the context condition are discarded.

4.4 The 1-1 Perfect Matching Calculator

COMET solves the problem of *context-aware entity matching* by computing a 1-1 weighted perfect matching between the sets of RDF molecules. The input of the 1-1 weighted perfect matching component is the weighted bipartite graph created on the previous step. Since each weight of an edge between two RDF molecules corresponds to a combined score of semantic similarity and context equivalence value, we call this a 1-1 context-aware matching calculator. The effect of this 1-1 context aware matching calculator is demonstrated in Fig. 9 Finally, a combinatorial optimization algorithm like the Hungarian algorithm [267] is utilized to compute the matching.

4.5 Integration Use Case: Applying Fusion Policies

In order to apply this context-aware entity matching pipeline into a data integration scenario, we envision the usage of *fusion policies* defined by Collarana et al. [84]. To consolidate entities identified as contextually equivalent, COMET can make use of synthesis policies, i.e. a user-supplied function that defines how the RDF molecules should be combined to form a connected whole. COMET can adopt the following synthesis policies:

1. The *Union Policy*, which includes all predicates-object pairs, removing the one that is syntactically the same;
2. The *Linking Policy*, which produces `owl:sameAs` links between contextually equivalent RDF molecules;
3. The *Authoritative Policy*, which allows for defining one RDF graph as a prevalent source selecting its properties in case of property conflicts, i.e., properties annotated as `owl:FunctionalProperty`, equivalent properties `owl:equivalentProperty`, and equivalent classes annotated with `owl:sameAs` or `owl:equivalentClass`.

Algorithm 1: closure(B,y)
1   for $j \leftarrow 0$ to n do
2     $D[j] \leftarrow 1$;
3   foreach i in $rows[y]$ do
4     $match \leftarrow$ True;
5   for $j \leftarrow 0$ to n do
6   if $\begin{cases} B[j]=1 \\ context[i,j]=0 \end{cases}$ then
7        $match \leftarrow$ False;
8   break for loop;
9   if $match =$ *True* then
10   for $j \leftarrow 0$ to n do
11   if $context[i,j]=0$ then
12        $D[j] \leftarrow 0$;
13   return D

Algorithm 2: generate(B,y)
1   process B ;   // Printing B
2   if $B = Y \mid y > n$ then
3   return
4   for $j \leftarrow y$ to n do
5   if $B[j] = 0$ then
6       $B[j] \leftarrow 1$;
7       $D \leftarrow$ closure(B,j);
8       $skip \leftarrow$ False;
9   for $k \leftarrow 0$ to $j-1$ do
10   if $D[k] \neq B[k]$ then
11         $skip \leftarrow$ True;
12   break for loop;
13   if $skip =$ *False* then
14   generate(D,j + 1);
15       $B[j] \leftarrow 0$;
16   return

Fig. 8. Implemented algorithms (extended from [451]).

By applying these policies, the end output is a synthesized graph with linked entities that are *contextually equivalent*. In the next chapter, we take a look at another use case of context-aware entity matching: the temporal summarization of knowledge graph entities.

5 Empirical Evaluation

This section presents an overview of the technical details, execution and the results obtained in the empirical evaluation.

5.1 Research Questions

We conducted an empirical evaluation to study the effectiveness and performance of COMET in solving the entity matching problem among RDF graphs. We address the following research questions:

- **(RQ1)** Is COMET able to perform entity matching with regard to context more accurately than the MINTE [84] entity matching component?
- **(RQ2)** Does the content of the dataset with respect to the context condition affect the accuracy of COMET?
- **(RQ3)** How much overhead does the context-evaluation step in COMET add to the overall pipeline?

(RQ1) and **(RQ2)** are combined to conduct **Experiment 1** in order to evaluate the effectiveness or accuracy of COMET. **(RQ3)** is addressed by **Experiment 2** where the overhead of the context-evaluation step is measured.

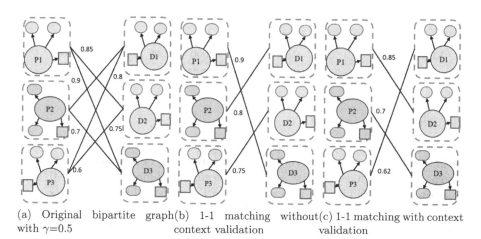

(a) Original bipartite graph with γ=0.5   (b) 1-1 matching without context validation   (c) 1-1 matching with context validation

Fig. 9. The **1-1 Perfect Matching.** COMET applies a special 1-1 perfect matching algorithm which evaluates context as well as similarity between two molecules. A traditional 1-1 perfect matching algorithm only considers similarity (weight of edges). Without evaluating context, the 1-1 matching algorithm matches molecules that are not in the same context. When context is evaluated alongside similarity, molecules in the same context are matched.

5.2   Implementation

Practically, COMET is implemented in Python and hosted in GitHub[2] along with the datasets and logs used in this evaluation. The experiments were executed on a Windows 10 (64 bits) machine with CPU: Intel Core i7-8650U 1.9 GHz (4 physical cores) and 16 GB RAM. For the COMET pipeline we use the semantic similarity measure *GADES* [371], which Collarana et al. have previously demonstrated to have the best performance in terms of accuracy when added to their MINTE pipeline [84]. *GADES* relies on semantic description encoded in ontologies to determine relatedness. *GADES* examines both string similarity and hierarchy similarity by making use of graph neighbourhoods.

---

[2] https://github.com/RDF-Molecules/COMET.

Table 2. Benchmark Description. Datasets used in the evaluation including: number of RDF molecules (M), number of triples (T), evaluated contexts (C).

Configuration	Experiment 1: Effectiveness					
	A		**B**		**C**	
Datasets	*A1*	*A2*	*B1*	*B2*	*C1*	*C2*
Molecules	1000	1000	1000	1000	1000	1000
Triples	70,660	70,660	70,776	70,776	71,124	71,124
Context	$C(M_{D1}, M_{D2}) = \texttt{true}$, if $\texttt{dbo:occupation}$ match					

	Experiment 2: Runtime							
Datasets	*XS1*	*XS2*	*S1*	*S2*	*M1*	*M2*	L1	L2
Molecules	100	100	500	500	1,000	1,000	2,000	2,000
Triples	7,084	7,084	33,916	33,916	71,124	71,124	138,856	138,856

5.3 Baseline

As a baseline, we compare the effectiveness of COMET against the MINTE pipeline proposed by Collarana et al. [84]. Towards **(RQ1)** and **(RQ2)** we design an experiment to measure the *precision, recall* and *f-measure* of COMET in comparison to MINTE. We also run COMET and MINTE on datasets with different compositions of molecules with respect to context in order to observe the effect of contextual content of datasets on the effectiveness of COMET. Towards **(RQ3)**, we observe the impact of COMET context-evaluation step on temporal and memory performance.

5.4 Effectiveness Evaluation

Metrics. Although each experiment has different datasets and gold standards, we use the same metrics for all the experiments: *Precision, Recall,* and *F-meaure. Precision* measures what proportion of the performed entity matches are actually correct. That is, *precision* is the fraction of RDF molecules that has been identified as contextually equivalent by COMET (C), which intersects with the Gold Standard (GS). On the other hand, *recall* measures the overall proportion of integrated RDF molecules that were identified correctly. That is, *recall* is measured by the fraction of correctly identified similar molecules with respect to the Gold Standard, i.e., $Precision = \frac{|C \cap GS|}{|C|}$ and $Recall = \frac{|C \cap GS|}{|GS|}$. *F-measure* is the harmonic mean of *Precision* and *Recall*.

Datasets. For this experiment, we use datasets containing 1,000 people entities from DBpedia. In order to test the effect of contextual data content on the accuracy of COMET, three pairs of datasets *(A1, A2), (B1, B2),* and *(C1, C2)* are generated using configurations *A, B,* and *C,* respectively. These configurations are as follows:

1. **Configuration A:** Every molecule *a1* in dataset A1 has **2** *highly similar* molecules *a2* and *a3* in dataset A2, such that *a2* satisfies context condition, but *a3* does not. That is, $C(a1, a2) = \texttt{true}$ and $C(a1, a3) = \texttt{false}$.
2. **Configuration B:** Every molecule *b1* in dataset B1 has **3** *highly similar* molecules *b2*, *b3* and *b4* in dataset B2, such that *b2* and *b3* satisfy the context but *b4* does not.
3. **Configuration C:** Every molecule *c1* in dataset C1 has **4** *highly similar* molecules in dataset C2, two of which satisfy the context condition, and two that do not.

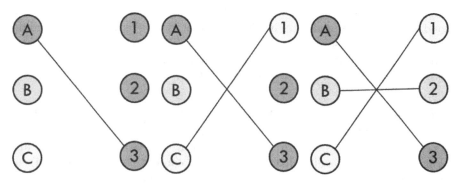

(a) Molecule A has only one perfect match

(b) Molecule A has two perfect matches

(c) Molecule A has three perfect matches.

Fig. 10. Effect of dataset content on matching accuracy. The goal of COMET is to choose the most similar molecule which is also in the same context. With a higher number of similar molecules within the same context, the probability of COMET choosing the correct match every time decreases.

The motivation of curating datasets using these three configurations is as follows: As seen in Sect. 4, COMET applies a special 1-1 perfect matching algorithm to find the best match according to both similarity and context condition. For this reason, the varying number of highly similar molecules that are also in the same context will affect the way COMET performs on the dataset. A higher number of similar molecules in the same context means a lesser chance of COMET identifying the correct match.

This is demonstrated in Fig. 10. Here, circles displaying the same color denote that they are molecules in the same context. In Fig. 10a, molecule A has only one perfect match available in the matching dataset and COMET makes this match accordingly. But in Fig. 10b and 10c, the number of perfect matches within the same context increases to two and three, respectively. This means that the probability of COMET identifying the true match for Molecule A decreases. Therefore we aim to evaluate exactly how the varying numbers of similar molecules in a dataset affect the accuracy of COMET.

Table 3. Effectiveness evaluation of COMET.

Configuration	COMET			MINTE		
	Precision	*Recall*	*F-Measure*	*Precision*	*Recall*	*F-Measure*
A	1.0	1.0	1.0	0.54	0.54	0.54
B	0.708	0.708	0.708	0.449	0.449	0.449
C	0.558	0.558	0.558	0.408	0.408	0.408

Every pair of datasets is synthesized as follows: First, molecules from the original set of 1,000 DBpedia person entities are duplicated according to the configuration condition to create n number of highly similar molecules in the second dataset. Then predicates inside the similar molecules are randomly edited and deleted to create some variation of similarity. The predicates are then edited to ensure that the correct number of similar molecules in the second dataset satisfy the context according to the original dataset.

Context and Gold Standard. Similar to the motivation example shown in Fig. 1, the context C used in this experiment checks if two molecules have the same value for the predicate dbo:occupation. The Gold Standard contains matches between molecules that (i) satisfy the context condition; and (ii) are highest in similarity among all other molecules. For every pair of datasets belonging to the three configurations (i.e. configuration A, B and C), there is a corresponding Gold Standard G_A, G_B and G_C. The datasets, gold standard and the experiment code are all available on GitHub.

Experiment 1: Contextually Matching DBpedia RDF Molecules. Table 2 describes the dataset used during our evaluations. This experiment was conducted on MINTE and COMET once for each pair of datasets *(A1, A2)*, *(B1, B2)* and *(C1, C2)*, with the context condition requiring that every pair of matched molecules must have the same value for dbo:occupation property. The threshold value γ for this experiment is applied at the 97th percentile in every case. Then comparing against the Gold Standard G_A, G_B and G_C for configurations A, B and C respectively, the metrics Precision and Recall were calculated each time. The results are presented in Table 3.

Experiment 2: Impact of Context Evaluation on Performance. In addition to the previous reported experiments focusing on effectiveness, we also pay particular attention to the evaluation of performance. Indeed, we specifically design an experiment to analyze how much overhead is added to COMET for evaluating context in its entity matching pipeline with respect to MINTE, which does not evaluate context.

Metrics. During our tests, we monitored each task by measuring not only execution time but a broader set of metrics:

- *Time* (seconds): measures the time used to process the various tasks and sub-tasks relevant in our study;
- *Memory (& SWAP)* (Bytes): allows for keeping track of the memory allocations during the experiments; the idea is to search for possible bottlenecks caused due to adding context evaluation to our approach.
- *CPU usage* (Percentage): simply records the processing activity.

Datasets. Table 2 reports on the datasets used during this set of experiments. As shown, we fed COMET with four datasets, each one involving more triples than the previous ones; they contain from 7 000 up to 100,000 triples. The molecules range from sets of 100 to 2,000.

Since COMET performs analysis of molecules both in its creation of bipartite graphs and context evaluation step, we wanted to observe how the performance is affected by increases in molecule number.

Temporal Performance. In Fig. 11, we present the obtained results with the datasets XS, S, M, and L. This representation is twofold. Firstly, the bar chart represents for each dataset the time distribution according to the various phases which COMET involved: i.e. computing similarity in a bipartite graph, evaluating context using FCA computation, and performing 1-1 perfect matching in blue, purple, and yellow, respectively. Secondly, the red curve presents for each dataset the total time required to run the experiment; notice that we use a logarithmic scale. As a consequence, we successfully find experimentally that the context evaluation step does not take any more time than the other phases. As shown in the bars of Fig. 11, the purple section representing the context evaluation step does occupy a greater percentage of the total runtime as the size of the dataset increases, but it still consumes less than half of the runtime in comparison to the other phases.

Memory Consumption. To analyze how the memory is used by COMET during its experimental runs, we pay attention to the RAM & SWAP consumption for each dataset tested; in addition we also recorded the CPU usage. It appears that COMET did not use much of the resources to run the experiments with the datasets. Moreover, we even observed that the pressure on the CPU and the amount of memory used by the system at every second is almost the same for all the considered datasets. This, therefore, means that the current implementation of COMET rather spreads its computations along the time (see again the red curve of Fig. 11) instead of allocating more resources when the dataset size increases.

5.5   Discussion of Observed Results

Based on the values of Precision, Recall, and F-measure reported in Experiment 1 (Table 3), we can positively answer **(RQ1)**, and **(RQ2)** i.e., COMET is able to effectively match entities across RDF graphs according to context, and indeed the content of the datasets does affect the accuracy. In every case, COMET performs better than MINTE, and the reason is clear – MINTE does not take context into consideration during its 1-1 perfect matching whereas COMET does.

Moreover, the decrease in precision in recall of COMET with the increase of the number of highly similar molecules within the dataset also makes sense. With a higher number of similar molecules to choose from, COMET has less of a chance of correctly identifying the perfect match. On the other hand, in the case of *configuration A*, the precision and recall is perfect. This is because the dataset in *configuration A* supplies only 1 perfect option (a highly similar molecule that also meets the context). The perfect precision and recall demonstrate that in an ideal condition with only 1 perfect option, COMET will always match correctly.

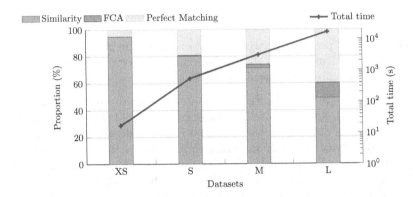

Fig. 11. Temporal performance for datasets XS, S, M and L. The bars along the y-axis represent the time distribution required for each of the phases of COMET. The red curve presents the total time required to run the experiment in logarithmic scale (Color figure online).

By observing the temporal performance (Fig. 11) and memory consumption of COMET when supplied with datasets of increasing volumes, we can also answer (**RQ3**), i.e., by measuring the amount of overhead the context-evaluation step of COMET adds to the overall pipeline. We show that the context evaluation step adds a fraction of the temporal overhead with respect to a traditional 1-1 matching algorithm, and does not have any observable overhead in terms of memory consumption.

6   Grand Challenges and Conclusions

In the age of data variety, adding and considering data context is more important than ever. Context lends information to its scope of validity and affects most data-driven tasks, such as data integration. In this chapter, we presented COMET – an approach to match contextually equivalent RDF entities from different sources into a set of 1-1 perfect matches between entities. COMET follows a two-fold approach where first contextually equivalent RDF molecules are identified according to a combined score of semantic and context similarity. Then, a 1-1 perfect matching is executed to produce a set of matches considering context. COMET utilizes the Formal Concept Analysis algorithm to decide whenever two RDF molecules are contextually equivalent. The behavior of COMET was empirically studied on two real-world RDF graphs under different context configurations. The observed results suggest that COMET is able to effectively identify and merge contextually equivalent entities in comparison to a baseline framework which does not consider context. We also envision an approach for creating entity summaries automatically out of different temporal versions of a knowledge graph. To do so, the proposed approach utilizes the concepts of RDF molecules, Formal Concept Analysis, and Fusion Policies. The entity evolution summaries created by the approach may serve to create documentation, to display a visualization of the entity evolution, or to make an analysis of changes.

This work is a first step in the direction of the formalization of context and its effect on data-driven tasks. Therefore, there are still **grand challenges** to face towards consolidating context-based similarity approaches. Thus, we present the four grand challenges that should be tackled as next steps, i.e.: 1) *measuring context* with probabilistic functions; 2) the *performance* of the context-aware matching algorithms; 3) full *usage of the semantic representation* of entities as knowledge graphs; and furthermore, 4) the *application* of context-aware entity matching on a variety of data-driven tasks.

We now describe them in detail:

1. **Measuring context with probabilistic functions:** In this chapter, we employ a straightforward definition of context conditions, i.e. modeling context as a Boolean function of entities. According to this model, an entity is either valid within a context or invalid. The real-world meaning and scope of context are much more general, and therefore context should be modeled in a more generalized way. For example, the measure of the validity of an entity concerning different contexts can be a probabilistic function. Meaning the range of the context function could be any value between the interval [0,1] instead of being only 0 or 1. We suggest the use of Probabilistic Soft Logic (PSL) to implement this concept.

2. **Performance:** Although in this chapter, we focus on the variety dimension of big data, context-based approaches should apply to the volume dimension as well. In COMET, for example, the complexity of the 1-1 matching algorithm is quadratic as COMET employs the original Formal Concept Analysis algorithm. As such, it is possible to evaluate a distributed version of the Formal Concept Analysis algorithm that may improve the run-time overhead in this work. Big data frameworks such as Hadoop and Spark can be used in the implementation of this distributed version of COMET.

3. **Exploitation of the semantic representation of entities:** The proposed approach, presented in this chapter, utilizes the knowledge encoded in RDF graphs themselves to create context parameters. Nevertheless, not all the potential of semantics has been studied to improve the accuracy of context-based matching approaches. A natural next step, for example, would be to take advantage of the implicit knowledge encoded in RDF Knowledge Graphs. Employing a reasoner additional contextual data can be inferred, empowering the modeling and evaluating of context.

4. **Application of context-aware matching on various data-driven tasks:** We mentioned during the chapter the application of the COMET approach in the entity summarization use-case. Tasnim et al. [422] show the architecture and pipeline modifications to COMET in order to produce a summary along one contextual axis, i.e. temporal axis. The approach can be adapted to other contextual axes, e.g., geographic location, hierarchical position, and more. Depending on the contextual axis, many more use cases of context-aware entity matching can be explored. Also, the elements used in the creation of the entity evolution summary, e.g., the ontology, can be investigated and further developed to empower the approach.

Applications

Appendix

Chapter 9
Survey on Big Data Applications

Valentina Janev[1](✉) (ID), Dea Pujić[1] (ID), Marko Jelić[1] (ID),
and Maria-Esther Vidal[2] (ID)

[1] Institute Mihajlo Pupin, University of Belgrade, Belgrade, Serbia
valentina.janev@institutepupin.com
[2] TIB Leibniz Information Centre For Science and Technology, Hannover, Germany

Abstract. The goal of this chapter is to shed light on different types of big data applications needed in various industries including healthcare, transportation, energy, banking and insurance, digital media and e-commerce, environment, safety and security, telecommunications, and manufacturing. In response to the problems of analyzing large-scale data, different tools, techniques, and technologies have bee developed and are available for experimentation. In our analysis, we focused on literature (review articles) accessible via the Elsevier ScienceDirect service and the Springer Link service from more recent years, mainly from the last two decades. For the selected industries, this chapter also discusses challenges that can be addressed and overcome using the semantic processing approaches and knowledge reasoning approaches discussed in this book.

1 Introduction

In the last decade, the **Big Data** paradigm has gain momentum and is generally employed by businesses on a large scale to create value that surpasses the investment and maintenance costs of data. Novel applications have been created for different industries allowing (1) storing as much data as possible in a cost-effective manner (volume-based value); (2) rapid analysis capabilities (velocity-based value); (3) structured and unstructured data to be harvested, stored, and used simultaneously (variety-based value); (4) accuracy of data processing (Veracity-based value); etc. In the next decade, the amount of data will continue to grow and is expected to reach 175 zetabytes in 2025 [85]. This will fundamentally affect worldwide enterprises. This chapter is interested in identifying:

- **RQ1:** What are the main application areas of big data analytics and the specific data processing aspects that drive value for a selected industry domain?
- **RQ2:** Which are the main tools, techniques, and technologies available for experimentation in the field of big data analytics?

In December 2018, within the LAMBDA project framework, a literature review was initiated that included an extensive and comprehensive analysis of journal

V. Janev et al. (Eds.): Knowledge Graphs and Big Data Processing, LNCS 12072, pp. 149–164, 2020.
https://doi.org/10.1007/978-3-030-53199-7_9

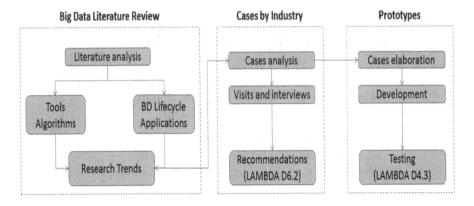

Fig. 1. Research methodology

articles from available sources such as (1) the Elsevier ScienceDirect service[1] and (2) the Springer Link service[2]. Elsevier ScienceDirect is a website which provides subscription-based access to a large database of scientific and medical research. It hosts over 12 million pieces of content from 3,500 academic journals and 34,000 e-books. SpringerLink is the world's most comprehensive online collection of scientific, technological and medical journals, books and reference works printed from Springer-Verlag. In parallel, the market of available commercial and open-source tools was surveyed and monitored[3]. As **Big Data** is a very active area of research nowadays, we are also involved in analysis of different industry cases studies, as is presented in the research methodology depicted in Fig. 1. This chapter outlines the methodology and the process of selecting articles relevant for our research (see Sect. 2) and discusses the main research trends in big data applications in different industries (Sect. 3). In order to answer the second research question, the authors established the catalog of big data tools that is available at the LAMBDA project web page[4].

2   Literature Review

This section presents the literature review approach that was adopted in order to identify the relevant application areas of big data technologies. In April 2020, a simple keyword based query on term *Big Data Analytics* returns:

- 180,736 results in ScienceDirect (or 3% more than in December 2019, 174,470 results), 10,042 of them review articles, where the oldest 2 papers are from 1989 and discuss the challenges to computational science and use of supercomputers for conducting experiments in key scientific and engineering areas such as

---

[1] https://www.sciencedirect.com/.
[2] https://link.springer.com/.
[3] https://project-lambda.org/D2.1.
[4] https://project-lambda.org/tools-for-experimentation.

atmospheric science, astronomy, materials science, molecular biology, aerody-
namics, and elementary particle physics [467];
- 40,317 results in SpringerLink (or 7% more than in December 2019, 33,249
results), where the oldest publications dating from 1950s are related to mathematics.

Big Data Analytics is a broad topic that, depending on the objectives of
the research, can be linked on the one hand to data science and machine learning, and on the other to data and software engineering. Being interested in the
role that analytics plays in business strategy, we limited our search to articles in
the domain of business intelligence. Business intelligence entails the analysis of
past and present data to create actionable insights for informed decision-making.
Thus, the search for *review articles* linked to **Big Data Analytics** and **Business
Intelligence** leads to 615 articles. The number is even smaller if we are looking
for **Business Intelligence** (BI) and **NoSQL** solutions– see Table 1. That means
that the concept of **Business Intelligence** still prevails in the scientific literature but is based on relational database-driven applications. Further on, looking
for the year of publication, the authors have found that there are articles from the
1930s also linked to the topic **Big Data** albeit mainly related to medical studies.
In our analysis, we focused on review articles from more recent years, mainly from
the last two decades.

Table 1. Number of review articles in ScienceDirect database

Keywords	1995–1999	2000–2005	2006–2009	2010–2015	2016–2020	*Total*
BDA	388	718	1349	2190	4,605	10,042
BDA and BI	12	15	45	80	437	615
BDA and BI and NoSQL				3	31	35
BDA and Apps and NoSQL				8	46	54

Hence, in order to identify the main application area, we first identified journals (using ScienceDirect service) that most frequently publish research articles about **Big Data Analytics, Business Intelligence**, and **Applications** in
Industry. ThetTable below points to a number of articles published in international journals between 2015 and 2019, as well as the journals relevant for the
search criteria. What can be noticed is that there are three times more articles
related to **Big Data and Applications**, then to **Big Data Analytics and
Applications**. The number of retrieved results is drastically smaller if we introduce the topic '**Business Intelligence**'.

Some of the journals listed in Table 2 refer to scientific fields that are not
in direct relation to the research conducted in the LAMBDA project, such as
Nuclear Physics and Astrophysics, Materials Science, Construction and Architecture, Chemistry and Chromatography. Big data research is conducted in these

Table 2. Journals that match the search criteria

'Big Data' and 'Application' (128,033)	Neurocomputing, Journal of Cleaner Production, Procedia Computer Science, IFAC Proceedings Volumes, Expert Systems with Applications, Physica A: Statistical Mechanics and its Applications, Sensors and Actuators B: Chemical, Journal of Chromatography A, Nuclear Physics B, European Journal of Operational Research
'Big Data' and 'Industry' (59,734)	Journal of Cleaner Production, Future Generation Computer Systems, Energy Policy, Journal of Membrane Science, Expert Systems with Applications, Procedia Computer Science, Journal of Banking and Finance, Research Policy, European Journal of Operational Research
'Big Data Analytics' and 'Applications' (41,031)	Journal of Cleaner Production, Future Generation Computer Systems, Neurocomputing, Journal of Chromatography A, IFAC Proceedings Volumes, Physica A: Statistical Mechanics and its Applications, Sensors and Actuators B: Chemical, Analytica Chimica Acta, Journal of Membrane Science, Nuclear Physics B
'Big Data Analytics' and 'Business Intelligence' (3,539)	Future Generation Computer Systems, Procedia Computer Science, Technological Forecasting and Social Change, Expert Systems with Applications, Decision Support Systems, IFAC Proceedings Volumes, Accounting, Organizations and Society

disciplines and there is a need for enhanced statistical algorithms, modeling and simulation approaches; however, these scientific areas are currently beyond the scope of our research and will not be discussed in the following sections.

Trends: Detailed analysis of the retrieved surveys on **BDA and Apps and NoSQL** (54 papers) showed that there is a shift of focus from operational data management systems, data-warehouses and business intelligent solutions (present for instance in Finance and Insurance domain in 1990s) [336] to parallel and distributed computing [478], as well as scalable architectures [187] for storing and processing data in the cloud ("Analytics in Cloud" [368]). Emerging paradigms such as the Internet of Things [120,369] and blockchain additionally influence cloud computing systems [157]. Interconnected technologies like RFID (Radio Frequency IDentification) and WSAN (Wireless Sensor and Actor Networks) enabled development of smart environments [122] that will be explored further in subsequent sections. Wide availability of cheap processing power and vast amounts of data in recent years have enabled impressive breakthroughs in machine learning [123,178,269], semantic computing [222,316], artificial neural networks and multimodal affective analytics [400].

3   Big Data Analytics in Industrial Sectors

The analysis presented in this section examines the BDA-driven applications in sectors spanning healthcare, transport, telecommunications, energy production and smart grids, energy consumption and home automation, finance, media, e-Government [220] and other public utilities. The research was motivated by the needs of the Mihajlo Pupin Institute to innovate the existing product portfolio that is currently mainly focused on building advanced analytical services for control, monitoring and management of large facilities, for instance from the transport and the energy sector.

Healthcare and Pharma

Healthcare and Data Engineering. Advances in Internet of Things (IoT) and sensor devices have enabled integrated data processing from diverse healthcare data sources in a real-time manner [339]. In addition to existing sources (Electronic Health Record and Clinical reports), healthcare providers can use new data sources such as social media platforms, telematics, and wearable devices in order to personalize treatment plans. However, healthcare organizations face unique challenges when it comes to developing and implementing the smart health concept [11] based on using a remote cloud server with powerful computing capabilities. Besides taking into account the 3Vs (volume, velocity and variety) that raise issues related to scalability, efficiency, speed, transparency, availability, reliability, security, and others, the veracity dimension is very important because the value of health information is directly dependent on the ability to determine the quality of the data in question (accuracy, correctness, reliability). Hence, fog-enabled smart health solutions are proposed where fog nodes create a heterogeneous fog network layer and complement a portion of computation and storage of the centralized cloud server [421].

Personalized medicine is an approach to the practice of medicine that uses information about a patient's unique genetic makeup and environment to customize their medical care to fit their individual requirements. Recently, epigenetics has grown in popularity as a new type of science that refers to the collection of chemical modifications to the DNA and chromatin in the nucleus of a cell, which profoundly influence the functional output of the genome. The identification of novel individual epigenetic-sensitive trajectories at the single cell level might provide additional opportunities to establish predictive, diagnostic and prognostic biomarkers as well as drug targets [386]. Based on emerging trends, patient care can be improved in many ways including using:

- modern healthcare applications that almost every smartphone possesses like Apple Health[5], Google Health[6] or Samsung Health[7] are used for spotting trends and patterns;

---

[5] https://www.apple.com/ios/health/.
[6] https://health.google/.
[7] https://www.samsung.com/global/galaxy/apps/samsung-health/.

- the data obtained by wireless body area networks, implemented with adequate permissions by the user (WBANs) can be integrated (with clinical trials, patient records, various test results and other similar data) and analysed in order to improve the effectiveness of medical institutions and to aid doctors in their decision making;
- advanced data management and processing (patient similarity, risk stratification, and treatment comparison [345]) for better prescription recommendations and optimizations of the drug supply chain, which results in cutting losses and increasing efficiency.

Over the years, the role of Artificial Intelligence in medicine has become increasingly important, for instance for image processing and diagnosis purposes. Also deep-learning neural networks have proved very useful for extracting associations between a patient's condition and possible causes. To summarize opportunities and challenges of using innovative big data tools in healthcare, we point in Table 2 to the COVID-19 outbreak that occurred this year (Table 3).

Table 3. Case study: coronavirus disease 2019 (COVID-19)

Description	The outbreak of the 2019 novel coronavirus disease (COVID-19) has caused more than 5 million people to be infected and hundred of thousands of deaths. In the fight against the disease, almost all countries in the world have taken radical measures utilizing big data technologies. [485]
Key challenges	- Integration of heterogeneous data, which requires governments, businesses, and academic institutions to jointly promote the formulation of relevant policies
	- Rapid collection and aggregation of multi-source big data
	- GIS technologies for rapid visualization of epidemic information
	- Spatial tracking of confirmed cases and estimation of population flow
	- Prediction of regional transmission, spatial segmentation of the epidemic risk and prevention level
	- Balancing and management of the supply and demand of material resources

https://coronavirus-monitor.com/ (checked 22/05/2020).

Pharma. New trends in pharmaceutical research (such as genomic computing [370]) make the process of discovering disease patterns, early epidemic and pandemic detection and forecasting much easier. Das, Rautaray and Pandey [96] outline the general potential uses of big data in medicine like heart attack prediction, brain disease prediction, diagnosis of chronic kidney disease, analysing specific disease data, tuberculosis prediction, early hearth stage detection, HIV/AIDS prediction and some general aspects like disease outbreak and disease outcome prediction. Lee and Yoon [275] discuss some technical aspects of big data applications in medicine like missing values, the effects of high dimensionality, and bias control. Ristevski and Chen [374] mention privacy and security on the topic of big data in healthcare, while Tafti [420] offers an open source toolkit for biomedical sentence classification. Modern concepts relating to mobile health are discussed in [214] with Bayne [32] exploring big data in neonatal health care.

Transportation and Smart Cities

As suggested in Chap. 1, Smart Transportation is one of the key big data vertical applications besides Healthcare, Government, Energy and Utilities, Manufacturing and Natural Resources, Banking and Insurance, the Financial industry, Communications and Media, Environment and Education. The collection of related articles to this topic is possibly the largest of all applications. Zhang [483] offers a methodology for fare reduction in modern traffic congested cities, Liu [285] discusses the Internet of Vehicles, Grant-Muller [165] talks about the impacts that the data extracted from the transport domain has on other spheres, Torre-Bastida [429] talks about recent advances and challenges of modern big data applications in the transportation domain, while Imawan [211] analyses the important concept of visualization in road traffic applications. Also related, Ghofrani [154] surveys big data applications for railways, Gohar [158] discusses data-driven modelling in intelligent transportation systems, and Wang [454] attempts fuzzy control applications in this domain. Herein, we will discuss route planning applications and future challenges related to self-driving cars and user behaviour analysis.

Route Planning Applications. Using Global Positioning System (GPS) data, for instance, a large number of smartphone users benefit from the routing system by receiving information about the shortest or fastest route between two desired points. Some applications like Waze rely on direct user inputs in order to locate closed-off streets, speed traps etc. but at its most rudimentary level, this approach can work with just raw GPS data, calculating average travel times per street segments, and thus forming a live congestion map. Of course, such a system would be of no benefit to end users if it were not precise, but since the aggregated results that are finally presented are obtained based on many different sources, classifying this as a big data processing task, the data uncertainty is averaged out, an accurate results tend to be presented. In order to provide a quick response, geo-distributed edge devices also known as *edge servers* are used that can form an edge cloud for providing computation, storage and networking resources to facilitate big data analytics around the point of capture [91].

Self-driving cars rely on vast amounts of data that are constantly being provided by its users and used for training the algorithms governing the vehicle in auto-pilot mode. Holding on to the automation aspect, big data processing in the transportation domain could even be used to govern traffic light scheduling, which would have a significant impact on this sector, at least until all vehicles become autonomous and traffic lights are no longer required.

User Behaviour Analysis. Furthermore, the transportation domain can be optimized using adequate planning obtained from models with data originating from user behaviour analysis. Ticketing systems in countries with high population density or frequent travellers where reservations have to be made, sometimes, a few months in advance, rely on machine learning algorithms for predictions governing prices and availability. Patterns discovered from toll collecting stations and border crossings can be of huge importance when planning the duration of one's trip and optimizing the selected route.

Energy Production and Smart Grids

Energy Production. The energy sector has been dealing with big data for decades, as tremendous amounts of data are collected from numerous sensors, which are generally attached to different plant subsystems. Recently, modern big data technologies have also been applied to plant industry such as oil and gas plants, hydro, thermal and nuclear power plants, especially in the context of improving operational performance. Thus, some of the applications of big data in the oil and gas industry [311] are analyzing seismic and micro-seismic data, improving reservoir characterization and simulation, reducing drilling time and increasing drilling safety, optimization of the performance of production pumps, improved petrochemical asset management, improved shipping and transportation, and improved occupational safety. Promising applications of big data technology in future nuclear fusion power plants are (1) data/plasma modeling in general [88], (2) real-time emergency planning [276], (3) early detection of accidents in reactors [290], etc. Related to hydro-power plants, many authors have discussed the use of IoT applications for measuring water supply (see Koo [260], Bharat [396] or Ku [418]). Zohrevand [490] talks about the application of Hidden Markov models for problem detection in systems for water supply.

Smart Grids. The smart grid (SG) is the next-generation power grid, which uses two-way flows of electricity and information to create a widely distributed automated energy delivery network [155]. The goal is to optimize the generation, distribution and consumption of electricity. In general, there are three main areas where data analytics have been applied:

- Ensuring smart grid stability, load forecast and prediction of energy demand for planning and managing energy network resources;
- Improving malfunction diagnosis, either on the production side (in plant facilities) or health state estimation, and identifying locations and forecasting future line outages in order to decrease the outage costs and improve system reliability;
- Profiling user behaviours to adjust individual consumption patterns and to design policies for specific users.

Smart metering equipment and sensors provide key insights into load distribution and profiles required by plant operators to sustain system stability. Predictive maintenance also plays a key role in smart grid upkeep since all segments are both critical and expensive, and any unplanned action cuts users from the electricity supply upon which almost all modern devices rely to function. Analytics methodologies or algorithms used in these cases are: 1) statistical methods; 2) signal processing methodologies; 3) supervised regression forecasting (short and long-term forecasts); 4) clustering algorithms; 4) dimensionality reduction techniques; and 5) feature selection and extraction. Tu [431] and Ghorbanian [155] present a long list of various open issues and challenges in the future for smart grids such as

- lack of comprehensive and general standard, specifically concentrated on big data management in SGs;
- interoperability of smart devices dealing with massive data used in the SGs;
- the constraint to work with approximate analytics and data uncertainty due to the increasing size of datasets and real-time necessity of processing [354];
- security and privacy issues and the balance between easier data processing and data access control for big data analytics, etc.

More insight into potential applications of big data-oriented tools and analytical technologies in the energy domain are given in Chap. 10.

Energy Consumption and Home Automation

An unavoidable topic when discussing big data applications, in general, is home automation. One of the challenges that the world is facing nowadays is reducing our energy consumption and improving energy efficiency. The Internet of Things, as a network of modern sensing equipment, plays a crucial role in home automation solutions that based on this data are capable of processing and providing accurate predictions, and energy saving recommendations. Home automation solutions provide optimal device scheduling to maximize comfort and minimize costs, and can even be extended from the operation aspect to planning and offering possible home adjustments or suggesting investments in renewable sources if the location being considered is deemed fit. Having smart appliances initially presented the concept of human-to-machine communication but, governed by big data processing, this concept has been further popularized with machine-to-machine communication where the human input is removed, resulting in less interference. Predictive maintenance and automatic fault detection can also be obtained from sensor data for both basic household appliances and larger mechanical systems like cars, motors, generators, etc. IoT applications require proper cloud frameworks [456]. Ge [151] presents a comprehensive survey of big data applications in the IoT sphere, Martis [300] introduce machine learning to the mix. Kumari [270] gives a survey but with the main focus on multimedia, and Kobusińska [248] talks about current trends and issues.

Banking and Insurance

Business intelligence tools have been used to drive profitability, reduce risk, and create competitive advantage since the 1990s. In the late 1990s, many banks and insurance companies started using machine learning techniques for categorizing and prioritizing clients, assessing the credit risk of individual clients or companies, and survival analysis, etc. As this industry generally adopts new technologies early on, thanks to advances in cognitive computing and artificial intelligence, companies can now use sophisticated algorithms to gain insights into consumer behavior. Performing inference on integrated data from internal and external sources is nowadays the key for detecting fraud and security vulnerabilities. Furthermore, novel approaches state that the applied machine learning can be supplemented with semantic knowledge, thus improving the requested predictions and classifications and enriching them with reasoning explanations that pure machine learning based deduction lacks [40]. Regarding other financial institutions, stock markets, for instance, are also a considerable use case for big data as the sheer volume and frequency of transactions slowly renders traditional processing solutions and computation methods obsolete. Finding patterns and surveilling this fast-paced process is key for proper optimization and scam prevention. Hasan [186] and Huang [204] offer concrete approaches like predicting market conditions by deep learning and applying market profile theory with Tian [427] discussing latency critical applications, Begenau [36] looking at the link between Big Data and corporate growth, and (Óskarsdóttir [492] placing an emphasis on data collected from social networks and mobile phones.

Social Networks and e-Commerce

Social Networks. When considering big data applications, one cannot overlook the massive impact that the development of social networks like YouTube, Facebook and Twitter has had on digital media and e-commerce. Social networks provide a source of personalized big data suitable for data mining with several hundreds of thousands of new posts being published every minute. They are also excellent platforms for implementing big data solutions whether it be for advertising, search suggestions, post querying or connection recommendations. The social network structure has also motivated researchers to pursue alike architectures in the big data domain. From the related literature, Saleh [381] addresses challenges in social networks that can be solved with big data, Persico [352] gives a performance evaluation of Lambda and Kappa architectures, and Ghani [152] classifies analytics solutions in the big data social media domain.

e-Commerce. With all services available to web users, the wide variety of online shopping websites also presents a continuous source of huge volumes of data that can be stored, processed, analysed and inferred to create recommendation engines with predictive analytics. As a means to increase user engagement, multi-channel and cross-channel marketing and analysis are performed to optimize product presence in the media fed to the user. It is no accident that a certain advertisement starts to show right after a user has searched for that specific product category. Examining user behaviour patterns and tendencies allows for offer categorization in the best possible way so that the right offer is presented precisely when it needs to be, thus maximizing sale conversions. Data received from big data analysis can also be used to govern product campaigns and loyalty programs. However, content recommendations (inferred from big data sources) in this domain are not only related to marketing and sales but are also used for proper display of information relating to the user. Some search engines companies have even publicly stated that their infrastructure relies on big data architecture, which is not surprising considering the amount of data that needs to be processed.

Environment Monitoring

Environmental monitoring involves the collection of one or more measurements that are used to assess the status of an environment. Advances in remote sensing using satellite and radar technologies have created new possibilities in oceanography, meteorology, forestry, agriculture and construction (urban planning). Environmental remote sensing can be subdivided into three major categories based on the distance between the sensor and the area being monitored [139]. The first category, satellite-based measurement systems, is primarily employed to study the Earth and its changing environment. The most valuable source of data from this category is the Landsat, a joint satellite program of the USGS and NASA, that has been observing the Earth continuously from 1972 through to the present day. More than 8 million images [207] are available via the NASA website[8] and Google Earth Engine Data Catalog [9]. Additionally, the Earth observation mission from the EU Copernicus Programme produces 12 terabytes of daily observations (optical imagery at high spatial resolution over land and coastal waters) each day that can be freely accessed and analysed with DIAS, or Data and Information Access Services[10].

The second major category of remote sensing encompasses aircraft-borne instruments, for instance, the light detection and ranging (LIDAR) systems that permit better monitoring of important atmospheric species such as ozone, carbon monoxide, water vapor, hydrocarbons, and nitrous oxide as well as meteorological parameters such as atmospheric density, pressure, and temperature [139].

Ground-based instruments (e.g. aerosols measurement instruments) and Wireless Sensor Networks (WSN) [397] are the third major category for outdoor monitoring technologies that create new opportunities to monitor farms and rain forests, cattle, agricultural (soil moisture), water quality, volcanic eruptions and earth-quakes, etc.

The table below points to some social-economic and natural environment applications enabled by big data, IoT and remote sensing (Table 4).

Natural Disasters, Safety and Security

The application of big data analytics techniques is specially important for the Safety and Security industry as it can extract hidden value (e.g. early warning, triggers, predictions) from security-related data, derive actionable intelligence, and propose new forms of surveillance and prevention. Additionally, the number of connected devices is expected to rapidly increase in the coming years with the use of AI-defined 5G networks [477]. **Natural Disasters.** Due to changing climatic

---

[8] https://landsat.gsfc.nasa.gov.
[9] https://developers.google.com/earth-engine/datasets/catalog.
[10] https://www.copernicus.eu/en/access-data/dias.

Table 4. Environment monitoring applications (examples)

Smart farming	Big data research in Smart Farming is still in an early development stage. Challenges foreseen are related both to technical and organizational issues. Technical challenges include the automation of the data acquisition process, the availability and quality of the data, and the semantic integration of these data from a diversity of sources (information on planting, spraying, materials, yields, in-season imagery, soil types, weather, and other practices). Although, from a business perspective, farmers are seeking ways to improve profitability and efficiency, there are challenges related to the governance (incl. data ownership, privacy, security) and business models for integration of the farms in the entire food supply chain [469]
Rainforest monitoring	The contribution of the world's rainforests to the reduction of the impact of climate change is well-known to environment scientists, therefore projects have been started to integrate various low-cost sensors for measuring parameters such as humidity, temperature, total solar radiation (TSR), and photosynthetically active radiation (PAR) [68]
Biodiversity planning	- Machine learning and statistical algorithms have proved to be useful for the prediction of several numeric target attributes simultaneously, for instance, to help natural resource managers to assess vegetation condition and plan biodiversity conservation [249]

conditions, natural disasters such as floods, landslides, droughts, earthquakes are nowadays becoming common events. These events create a substantial volume of data that needs to be processed in real time and thus avoid, for instance, suffering and/or death of the people affected. Advancements in the field of IoT, machine learning, big data, remote sensing, mobile applications can improve the effectiveness of disaster management strategies and facilitate implementation of evacuation processes. The requirements faced by ICT developers are similar to those in the other domains already discussed

- the need to integrate multimodal data (images, audio, text from social sites such as Twitter and Facebook);
- the need to syncronize the activities of many stakeholders involved in four aspects of emergency (preparedness, response, mitigation and recovery);
- the need to install measuring devices for collecting and real-time analysis in order to understand changes (e.g. in water level, ocean waves, ground motions, etc);
- the need to visualize information;
- the need to communicate with people (first responders and/or affected people and track their responses and behaviour) or to alert officials to initiate rescue measures.

The global market offers a wide range of emergency solutions (in the form of web and/or mobile solutions) with intuitive mapping, live field monitoring and multimedia data sharing, such as CommandWear[11], TRACmate[12], and Track24[13]. However, the Linked Data principles and data management techniques discussed in the previous chapters can, to a considerable extend, facilitate integration and monitoring; see for instance the *Intelligent fire risk monitor based on Linked Open Data* [442].

Safety and Security of Critical Infrastructures. Big data processing is especially important for protecting critical infrastructures like airports, railway/metro systems, and power grids. Large infrastructures are difficult to monitor due to their complex layout and the variety of entities that they may contain such as rooms and halls of different sizes, restricted areas, shops, etc. In emergency situations, various control and monitoring systems, e.g. fire protection systems, heating, ventilation and air conditioning systems, evacuation and access control systems and flight information display systems among others, can send altogether thousands of events to the control room each second [309]. By streaming these low-level events and combining them in a meaningful way, increased situation awareness can be achieved. Using big data tools, stream processing solutions, complex event processing/event-condition-action (CEP/ECA) paradigm and combining events, state and emergency management procedures, a wide range of emergency scenarios and emergency procedures can be pre-defined. Besides processing the large amount of heterogeneous data extracted from multiple sources while considering the challenges of volume, velocity and variety, what is also challenging today is

- real-time visualization and subsequent interaction with computational modules in order to improve understanding and speed-up decision making;
- development of advanced semantic analytics and Machine Learning techniques for new pattern recognition that will build upon pre-defined emergency scenarios (e.g. based on rules) and generate new early warning procedures or reliable action plans.

Telecommunications

Following the already mentioned impact of using smart mobile phones as data sources, the telecommunications industry must also be considered when discussing big data. The 5th generation of cellular network (5G) that is now live in 24 markets (GSMA predicts that it will account for 20% of global connections by 2025) will provide real-time data collection and analysis and open possibilities for business intelligence and artificial intelligence-based systems.

Mobile, television and internet service providers have customer retention as their core interest in order to maintain a sustainable business. Therefore, in order to prevent customer churn, behaviour patterns are analysed in order to provide predictions on customers looking to switch their provider and allow the company to act in time and offer various incentives or contract benefits in due course.

---

[11] http://www.commandwear.com/features/.

[12] https://play.google.com/store/apps/details?id=com.gridstone.teamactivator.

[13] https://www.track24.com/smart24/.

Also, besides this business aspect, telecommunication companies using big data analytic solutions on data collected from mobile users can use the information generated in this way to assess problems with their network and perform optimizations, thus improving the quality of their service. Since almost all modern mobile phones rely on wireless 4G (and 5G in the years to come) networks to communicate when their users are not at home or work, all communication is passed through the data provider's services, and in processing this data still lie many useful bits of information as only time will tell what useful applications are yet to be discovered. Papers covering this aspect include Yazti [479] and He [191] outlining mobile big data analytics, while Amin [15] talks about preventing and predicting the mentioned phenomena of customer churn, and Liu [286] talks about collecting data from mobile (phone and wearable) devices.

Manufacturing
Industry 4.0 is about automating processes, improving the efficiency of processes, and introducing edge computing in a distributed and intelligent manner. As discussed previously, more complex requirements are imposed in process operations while the process frequently forfeits robustness, complicating process optimization. In the Industry 4.0 era, smart manufacturing services have to operate over multiple data streams, which are usually generated by distributed sensors in almost real-time. Similarly to other industrial sectors, transforming plants into full digital production sites requires an efficient and flexible infrastructure for data integration and management connected to powerful computational systems and cognitive reasoning engines. Edge computing (distributing computing, storage, communication and control as close as possible to the mediators and objects at the edge) plays an important role in smart manufacturing. Data has to be transferred, stored, processed and transferred again back (bidirectional communications from machine to machine, machine to cloud and machine to gateway) to both users and providers in order to transmit the inferred knowledge from sensor data. In the layered infrastructure (see Fig. 2), cognitive services have a central role and their design (selection of algorithms/models) depends on the problem in place, for instance

- Kumar [268] proposes using the MapReduce framework for automatic pattern recognition based on fault diagnosis in cloud-based manufacturing. Fault diagnosis significantly contributes to reduce product testing cost and enhances manufacturing quality;
- Vater [443] discusses how new technologies, such as IoT, big data, data analytics and cloud computing, are changing production into the next generation of industry.

In the smart manufacturing ecosystem, cognitive applications make use of process data (processed on the edge) and provide high level supervisory control and support the process operators and engineers. Data analytics and AI techniques are combined with digital twins and real-life feedback from the shop floor or production facility to improve the quality of products and processes. Example areas where semantic processing and artificial intelligence can advance this sector are

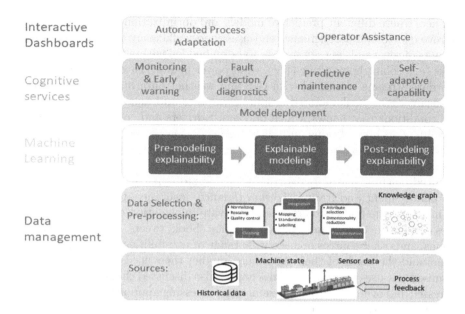

Fig. 2. Multi-layered software architecture

- **Human-Computer Interaction.** In complex situations, operators and machines need to quickly analyze situations, communicate and cooperate with each other, coordinate emergency response efforts, and find reasonable solutions for emerging problems. In such situations, collaborative intelligence services are needed that require fewer human-driven decisions as well as easy-to-use interfaces that accelerate information-seeking and human response. Interpretability and explainability are crucial for achieving fair, accountable and transparent (FAT) machine learning, complying with the needs and standards of the business sector.
- **Dynamic process adaptation.** Many industrial processes are hard to adapt to changes (e.g. related to status and availability of all relevant production resources, or in case of anomaly detection). This affects product quality and can cause damage to equipment and production lines. Hence, a semantic framework for storing contextual information and an explainable AI approach can be used for fine-tuning of process parameters to optimize environmental resources, fast reconfiguration of machines to adapt to production change, or advance fault diagnosis and recovery.

4   Conclusions

This chapter presented applications of big data approaches in different sectors. Research into real-time data analytics by addressing the volume and velocity dimension of big data is a significant area in emerging smart grid technology, for instance, where different predictive models and optimization algorithms serve to improve end-to-end performance, end-user energy efficiency and allow increasing amounts of renewable energy sources to be embedded within the distribution networks (e.g. solar photovoltaic (PV), wind power plants). Next, analytics on real-time data streams combined with GIS and weather data improves detection of significant events, enhances situational awareness and helps identify hazardous road conditions (e.g. snow), which may assist drivers and emergency responders in avoiding such conditions and allow for faster emergency vehicle routing and improved response time. Solutions that address the variety dimension, integration of heterogeneous data sources (including open and social media data) and advanced machine learning algorithms have found application in customer relation management and fraud detection (finance, insurance, telecommunication). For instance, the ability to cross-relate private information on consumer preferences and products with information from Facebook, tweets, blogs, product evaluations, and other sources opens a wide range of possibilities for organisations to understand the needs of their customers, predict their needs and demands, and optimise their use of resources. This chapter also discussed challenges that can be addressed and overcome using the semantic processing approaches and knowledge reasoning approaches discussed in this book.

Chapter 10
Case Study from the Energy Domain

Dea Pujić$^{(\boxtimes)}$, Marko Jelić, Nikola Tomašević, and Marko Batić

Institute Mihajlo Pupin, University of Belgrade, Belgrade, Serbia
dea.pujic@pupin.rs

Abstract. Information systems are most often the main focus when considering applications of Big Data technology. However, the energy domain is more than suitable also given the worldwide coverage of electrification. Additionally, the energy sector has been recognized to be in dire need of modernization, which would include tackling (i.e. processing, storing and interpreting) a vast amount of data. The motivation for including a case study on the applications of big data technologies in the energy domain is clear, and is thus the purpose of this chapter. An application of linked data and post-processing energy data has been covered, whilst a special focus has been put on the analytical services involved, concrete methodologies and their exploitation.

1 Introduction

Big Data technologies are often used in domains where data is generated, stored and processed at rates that cannot be efficiently processed by one computer. One of those domains is definitely that of energy. Here, the processes of energy generation, transmission, distribution and use have to be concurrently monitored and analyzed in order to assure system stability without brownouts or blackouts. The transmission systems (grids) that transport electric energy are in general very large and robust infrastructures that are accompanied by a great deal of monitoring equipment. Novel Internet of Things (IoT) concepts of smart and interconnected homes are also pushing both sensors and actuators into peoples homes. The power supply of any country is considered to be one the most critical systems and as such its stability is of utmost importance. To that effect, a wide variety of systems are deployed for monitoring and control. Some of these tools are presented in this chapter with a few from the perspective of end users (Non-Intrusive Load Monitoring, Energy Conservation Measures and User Benchmarking) and a few from the perspective of the grid (production, demand and price forecasting).

2 Challenges Withing the Big Data Energy Domain

In order to be able to provide advanced smart grid, user-oriented services, which will be discussed further in this chapter, integration with high volume, heterogeneous smart metering data (coming both from the grid side, e.g. placed in power

© The Author(s) 2020
V. Janev et al. (Eds.): Knowledge Graphs and Big Data Processing, LNCS 12072, pp. 165–180, 2020.
https://doi.org/10.1007/978-3-030-53199-7_10

substations, and from the user side, e.g. installed in homes and buildings) is a prerequisite. To specify, suggest and deliver adequate services to end users (i.e. energy consumers) with respect to their requirements and power grid status, various forms of energy data analytics should be applied by distribution system operators (DSO) and grid operators such as precise short- and long-term energy production and consumption forecasting. In order to deliver such energy analytics, historical energy production data from renewable energy sources (RES) and historical consumption data, based on smart metering at consumer premises and LV/MV power substations, must be taken into account.

The main challenge to providing advanced smart grid services is related to the integration and interoperability of high volume heterogeneous data sources as well as adequate processing of the acquired data. Furthermore, making this data interoperable, based on Linked Data API, and interlinked with other data sources, such as weather data for renewable energy sources (RET) production analysis, number of inhabitants per home units, etc., is essential for providing additional efficient user tailored analytical services such as energy conservation action suggestions, comparison with other consumers of the same type, etc.

Another challenge is related to analysis of grid operations, fault diagnostics and detection. To provide such advanced analytics, real-time integration and big data analysis performed upon the high volume data streams coming from metering devices and power grid elements (e.g. switches, transformers, etc.) is necessary, and could be solved using Linked Data principles. Finally, to support next generation technologies enabling smart grids with an increased share of renewables, it is necessary to provide highly modular and adaptable power grids. In addition, adequate tools for off-line analysis of power system optimal design should be deployed. These analytical tools should also incorporate allocation of optimal reconfiguration of power grid elements to provide reliable and flexible operation as an answer to the changing operational conditions. Tools for planning and reconfiguring power distribution networks consider power station infrastructure and its design, number and capacity of power lines, etc. To provide such advanced grid capabilities, integration with historical power grid data, archives of detected alarms and other relevant operational data (such as data from smart metering, consumption data, etc.) is necessary. Therefore, the main challenge is to provide digested input to the batch-processing, big data analytics for power grid infrastructure planning.

Having all of this in mind, the significance of big data processing techniques is obvious. On the other hand, further in this chapter examples of analytical services will be presented and discussed.

3   Energy Conservation Big Data Analytical Services

Improving quality of life through advanced analytics is common nowadays in various domains. Consequently, within the energy domain, collecting data from numerous smart meters, processing it and drawing conclusions are common concepts in the field of developing energy conversation services. The amount of aforementioned data highly depends on the service's principal use. If the focus is put on just one household, data can be undoubtedly processed using only one computer. Nonetheless, if the scale of a problem is a neighbourhood, municipality or city level, data processing and analytical computations can be taken as a big data problem. Therefore, within this chapter, methodologies for smart energy services are going to be discussed.

3.1 Non-Intrusive Load Monitoring

The first of these is so-called Non-Intrusive Load Monitoring (NILM). NILM was motivated by conclusions, such as those from [70], which claimed that up to 12% of residential energy consumption can be decreased by giving users feedback on how the energy has been used. In other words, by providing the user with information about which of their appliances is using electrical energy and how much, significant savings can be reached. Nonetheless, providing this kind of information would require installation of numerous meters all around households, which is usually unacceptable for the end-user. Therefore, instead of the Intrusive Load Monitoring solution which influences users' convenience, Non-Intrusive Load Monitoring was proposed by Hart in [183] with the main goal of providing users with the same information in a harmless way by aggregating entire household consumption at the appliance level, which can be seen in Fig. 1.

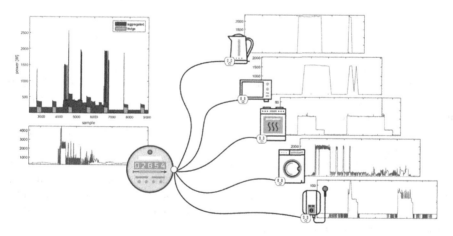

Fig. 1. Non-Intrusive Load Monitoring concept

Having in mind the previous information, two main problems are present within the NILM literature - **classification**, which provides information about the activation on the appliance level, and **regression** for the estimation of the appliance's individual consumption, as shown in the example Fig. 2. As these are some of the most common problems in advanced analytics, typical methodologies employed to address these are leading machine learning approaches, which are going to be presented and discussed further in this section to give an example of the use of applied big data technologies in the energy domain.

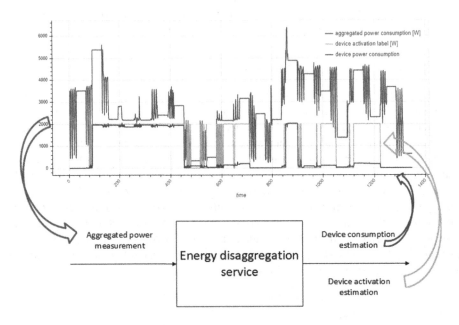

Fig. 2. NILM classification and regression example

As a first step, in this section, the currently present publicly available datasets will be introduced as the basis of data-driven models, which will be discussed further. Depending on the sampling rate, within the NILM literature, data and further corresponding methodologies are usually separated in two groups - **high** and **low** frequency ones. For high frequency, measurements with a sampling time of less than 1 ms are considered. These kind of data are usually unavailable in everyday practice due to the fact that usual residential metering equipment has a sampling period around 1 s and is put as the low frequency group. This difference in sampling rate further influences the choice of the disaggregation methodology and preprocessing approach for the real-time coming data used as the corresponding inputs.

When discussing publicly available data sets, methodologies are not strictly separated in accordance with the chosen sampling rate but rather by the geographical location. In other words, measurements usually correspond to some localized neighbourhood from which both high and low frequency data might be found in the same data set. The first published dataset we refer to is REDD (Reference Energy Disaggregation Data Set, 2011) [256]. It includes both low and high sampling frequency measurements from six homes in the USA. For the first group, both individual and aggregated power measurements were covered for 16 different appliances, allowing the development of various models, which require labeled data. By contrast, high frequency measurements contain only aggregated data from the household, so the developers have to use unsupervised techniques. Another widely spread and used data set published with [238] is UK-DALE (UK Domestic Appliance-Level Electricity) collected in the United Kingdom from five houses. It, again, covers the whole range of sampling rates, and, similarly to REDD, contains labeled data only for those with a sampling period bigger than 1 s. Additional data sets that should be addressed are REFIT [318], ECO (Electricity Consumption and Occupancy) [33], IHEPCDS (Individual household electric power consumption Data Set) [319] for low sampling rate and BLUED [137] and PLAID [145] for the high one[1].

After presenting the available data, potential and common problems with data processing as part of the theme of big data will be discussed. The first one, present in most of the data sets, is the presence of the **missing data**. Depending on the data set and the specific household appliance, the scale of this problem varies. For example, in the case of refrigerators, this is a minor problem which can be neglected because it works circularly, so each approximately 20 min it turns on or off, leading to numerous examples of both active and inactive working periods. By contrast, when, for example, a washing machine is considered, dropping down the sequence of its activation is unacceptable as it is turned on twice a week in a household on average, so it is difficult to collect enough data for training purposes. Therefore, different techniques were adapted in different papers for additional data synthesization from simply adding existing individual measurements of the appliance's consumption on the aggregated power measurements in some intervals when the considered appliance has not been working to more sophisticated approaches such as generative modeling, which was used to enrich data from commercial sector measurements [193].

It is worth mentioning here that characteristics of the data from these different sets significantly deviate in some aspects as a result of differences in location, habits, choice of domestic appliance, number of occupants, the average age of the occupant etc. The NILM literature has attempted to address this **generalization problem**. Even though the problem of achieving as high performance as possible on the testing rather than training domain is a hot topic in many fields of research within Machine Learning (ML) and Big Data, the generalization problem is even more crucial for NILM. As different houses might include different types of the same appliances, the performance on the data coming from the house whose measurements have not been used in the training process might be significantly lower than the estimated one. Additionally, it is obvious that the only application of the NILM models would be in houses which have not been used in the training phase, as they do not have labeled data (otherwise, there would be no need for NILM). Bearing all of this in mind, validating the results from the data coming from the house whose measurements have already been used in the training process is considered inadequate. Thus, it is accepted that for validation and testing purposes one, so called, unseen house is set aside and

---

[1] http://wiki.nilm.eu/datasets.html.

all further validation and testing is done for that specific house. Nonetheless, the houses covered by some publicly available dataset are by the rule in the same neighbourhood, which leads to the fact that data-driven models learn patterns which are characteristics of the domain rather than the problem. Therefore, separation of the house from the same dataset might be adequate. Finally, the last option would be validating and testing the measurements from the house using a different data set.

State-of-the-art NILM methodologies will be presented later in this section alongside corresponding estimated performance evaluations. Historically, the first ones were Hidden Markov Models and their advancements. They were designed to model the processes with unobservable states, which is indeed the case with the NILM problem. In other words, the goal is to estimate individual consumption in accordance with the observable output (aggregated consumption). This approach and its improvements have been exploited in numerous papers such as [227, 245, 255, 293, 294], and [56]. However, in all of the previously listed papers which cover the application of numerous HMM advancements to the NILM problem, the problem of error propagation is present. Namely, as HMM presumes that a current state depends on a previous one, mistakes in estimating previous states have a significant influence on predicting current ones.

Apart from HMMs, there are numerous unsupervised techniques applied for NILM. The main cause of this is the fact that labeled data for the houses in which services are going to be installed are not available, as already discussed. Therefore, many authors choose to use unsupervised learning techniques instead of improving generalization on the supervised ones. Examples of these attempts are shown in [194] where clusterization and histogram analysis has been employed before using the conditional random fields approach, in [344] where adaptation over unlabeled data has been carried out in order to improve performance on the gaining houses, and in [136] where disaggregation was described as a single-channel source separation problem and Non Negative Matrix Factorization and Separation Via Tensor and Matrix Factorization were used. Most of these approaches were compared with the HMM-based one and showed significant improvements. Another approach to gain the best generalization capabilities possible that can be found in the literature is semi-supervised concept in which a combination of supervised and unsupervised learning is present. In [30], self-training has been carried out using internal and external information in order to decrease the necessity of labeled data. Further, [208] proposes the application of transfer learning and blind learning, which exploits data from training and testing houses.

Finally, supervised techniques were widely spread in the literature as well. Currently, various ML algorithms hold a prime position with regards to supervised approaches, as they have proven themselves to be an adequate solution for the discussed problem, as reviewed in [419]. The biggest group currently popular in the literature is neural networks (NNs). Their ability to extract complex features from an input sequence was confirmed to increase their final prediction performance. Namely, two groups stood out to be most frequently used - Recurrent Neural Networks (RNNs) with the accent on Long Short Term Memory (LSTM) [302], and

Convolutional Neural Networks (CNNs) with a specific subcategory of Denoising Autoencoders [239].

After presenting various analytical approaches for solving the NILM problem, it is crucial to finish this subsection with the conclusion that results obtained by this service could be further post-processed and exploited. Namely, disaggregated consumption at the appliance level could be utilized for developing failure detection services in cooperation with other heterogeneous data.

3.2   Energy Conservation Measures (ECM)

When discussing the appeal and benefits of energy savings and energy conservation amongst end users, especially residential ones, it is no surprise that users react most positively and vocally when potential cost savings are mentioned. Of course, when this is the main focus, retrofitting old technologies, improving insulation materials, replacing windows and installing newer and more energy-efficient technologies is usually included in the course of action first recommended. This is mainly because the aspects that are tackled by these modifications are the largest source of potential heat losses and energy conversion inefficiencies. However, there is a significant and still untapped potential for achieving significant energy savings by correcting some aspects of user behaviour.

Besides inefficient materials, bad habits are one of the main causes of high energy loss, especially in heating and cooling applications with the thermal demand being a distinct issue due to the high volume of energy being spent in the residential sector on it. Finding the crucial behavioral patterns that users exhibit when unnecessarily wasting energy is key for efficient mitigation and, therefore, a smart home concept is proposed in order to analyze user behavior and facilitate the necessary changes. In order to obtain data to be able to suggest energy conservation measures, a set of smart sensors should be deployed to monitor various parameters. Some of these sensors could include but are not limited to:

- Smart external meter interfaces (measurement of total energy consumption in real-time);
- Smart electricity plugs and cables (measurement of energy consumption per appliance in real time and possibility of on/off control);
- Smart thermostats (measurement and continuous control of reference temperature and possibly consumed energy);
- Occupancy sensors (measurement of occupancy and motion and ambient temperature also);
- Window sensors (measurements of open/close status of windows and doors and ambient temperature also);
- Volatile organic compound (VOC) sensors (measurement of air quality and ambient temperature)

In some cases where installing smart plugs and cables is not deemed to be economical, a NILM algorithm described in Subsect. 3.1 can be employed in order to infer individual appliance activity statuses using only the data from the external meter. When widespread deployment of such sensors is being done, the amount of data that should be collected, stored and processed quickly grows due to the fact that multiple sensors are to be deployed in each room and that each of the sensors usually reports multiple measurements (e.g. the window sensor reports the temperature besides the open/close status, but also has a set of utility measurements such is the network status strength, battery status, etc. which should also be monitored as they provide crucial data regarding the health of the device itself). Therefore, efficient solutions, possibly from the realm of big data, should be employed in order to facilitate efficient storage and processing of data as the problematic user behavior is time-limited and should be pointed out to the user in due course while a problematic event is ongoing.

A small-scale use case of such a system was tested on around two dozen apartments in the suburbs of Leers, France with the proposed architecture of the system illustrated in Fig. 3. Using such an architecture, the back-end of the

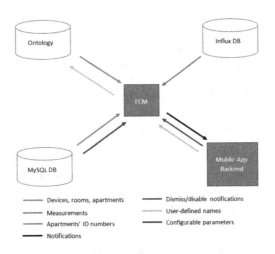

Fig. 3. Proposed architecture of a small-scalle ECM system

system that employs a MySQL database for static data storage regarding the apartment IDs and custom notification settings in conjunction with an ontology for storing room layouts and detailed sensor deployment data provides support for the main ECM engine that analyses data from the real-time IoT-optimized NoSQL Influx database and sends push notifications to the end users notifying them of energy-inefficient behaviour by cross-correlating different measurements from different sensors. For example, when a heating or cooling device is observed to be turned on in an unoccupied space, the user is warned. If the user acts upon such information and resolves the issue, the notification is dismissed automatically, or if the user does not react and the problematic event goes unresolved, he or she is re-notified after a predefined period of time. These events are analyzed with different scopes for individual rooms but also for entire apartments. Also, since smart sensors are already deployed, the energy conservation analysis can also be extended to regard security (no occupancy whilst a door or window is open) and health (poor air quality and windows closed) aspects also. Of course, each event is analyzed separately and appropriate notifications with corrective actions are issued to the end user.

3.3   User Benchmark

Besides the most obvious motivating factor of energy savings – monetary savings – another factor that can greatly impact users' behavior is social pressure. Namely, in a hypothetical scenario where different users were placed in a competition-like environment where the main goal is to be as energy-efficient as possible or, in other words, where each user's score is determined by how efficiently they consume energy, those users would be more likely to strive to perform better and hence consume energy in a more environmentally friendly way. In order to facilitate such an environment, a benchmarking engine has to be developed in order to provide an algorithm that would rank the users.

[81,113] and [329] in the literature point out that the benchmarking procedures in the residential sector have long been neglected in favor of industrial applications. Different algorithms and technologies proposed as core include:

- Simple normalization
- Ordinary least squares (OLS)
- Stochastic frontier analysis (SFA)
- Data envelopment analysis (DEA)
- Simulation (model-based) rankings
- Artificial neural networsk (ANNs)
- Fuzzy reasoning

with related literature [171] offering several dozens of additional related algorithms for multi-criteria decision making (MCDM). The applications of the aforementioned algorithms found in the literature are generally focused on schools, other public buildings and offices, with very few papers, such as [259,291] and [461], analyzing the residential sector.

One of the most prominent standards in energy efficiency ranking is the acclaimed Energy Star program [182], which rates buildings on a scale from 1 to 100 based on models and normalization methods of statistical analysis performed over a database from the US Energy Information Administration (EIA). However, the Energy Star rating does not take into account dynamic data obtained by observing the ongoing behavior of residents. This is where the concept of an IoT-powered smart home can provide a new dimension to energy efficiency benchmarking through real-time analysis of incoming data on how people use the space and appliances at their disposal.

The basis of every ranking algorithm is a set of static parameters that roughly determines the thermal demand of the considered property. These parameters generally include: total heated area, total heated volume, outward wall area, wall thickness, wall conductivity or material, number of reported tenants. This data generally is not massive in volume and is sufficient for some elementary ranking methods. However, an energy efficiency rating that only takes into consideration this data would only have to be calculated once the building is constructed or if some major renovations or retrofits are being made. As such, it would not be able to facilitate a dynamic competition-based environment in which users would compete on a daily or weekly basis on who is consuming their energy in the most economical way.

Given the reasoning above, the static construction and occupancy parameters are extended with a set of dynamic parameters that are inferred based on sensor data collected by the smart home. This data could, for example, include: total consumed energy, occupancy for the entire household, cooling and heating degree days, responsiveness to user-tailored behavior-correcting messages, alignment of load with production from renewable sources, etc. As these parameters are changing on a day-to-day basis, their dynamic nature would provide a fast-paced source that would power the fluctuations in energy efficiency scores of individual users and ultimately help users to see that their change in behaviour has made an impact on their ranking. Also, it is worth mentioning that when users within a same micro-climate are to be ranked, using heating and cooling degree days may prove to be redundant as all users would have the same parameters in this regard. Therefore, this data can be augmented using indoor ambient temperature measurements in order to monitor overheating in winter and overcooling in summer.

The most important procedure that should be conducted within user benchmarking solutions in order to provide a fair comparison between different users with different habits and daily routines is to provide a so-called normalization of consumed energy. This means that, for example, larger consumers should not be discriminated just based on higher consumption; rather, other factors such as the amount of space that requires air conditioning or the number of people using the considered space should be taken into account. In this regard, simply dividing the total consumed energy by the, for example, heated area provides a good first estimate of how energy-efficient different users are per unit of surface, but also implies that a linear relation between area and energy is assumed, which might not be their inherent relationship. In order to mitigate against this issue, vast amounts of data should be collected from individual households using IoT sensors and analyzed in order to either deduce appropriate relations required for normalization or to provide a basis for the aforementioned algorithms (DEA, SFA, etc.), which assign different weights to each of the parameters taken into account.

4   Forecasters

Following the widespread deployment of renewable sources such as wind turbines, photovolotaic panels, geothermal sources, biomass plants, solar thermal collectors and others, mainly as a result of various government-enforced schemes, programs and applicable feed-in tariffs, the stability of the grid has been significantly compromised. The integration of these novel sources has proven to be a relatively cumbersome task due to their stochastic nature and variable production profile, which will be covered in greater depth in Subsect. 4.2. Since the production of most of these sources is highly correlated with meteorological data (wind turbine production with wind speed and photovoltaic production with irradiance and cloud coverage), legacy electrical generation capacities (coal, nuclear and hydro power plants) which have a significantly shorter transient between different states of power output have to balance the fast-paced variations in generation that are a byproduct of the introduction of renewable sources. Since total generation is planned in order to be able to fulfill the total demand that will be requested, being able to know beforehand how much energy will be required in the future and how much energy will be available can provide a basis for potential energy and cost savings through optimal resource planning.

4.1 Demand Forecaster

Given the importance of demand forecasting, it is expected that this topic will be covered by more than a few authors in their published research. However, even though there is a noticeable number of publications in this regard, the topic of energy demand forecasting and the methods used for its estimation still appear to be under-explored without a unified proposed approach and most of the studies being case-specific. In that regard, a probabilistic approach for peak demand production is analyzed in [322], an autoregressive model for intra-hour and hourly demand in [450] and ANN-powered short-term forecasting in [401]. Short-term forecasting is also analyzed whilst making use of MARS, SVR and ARIMA models in [9] and [463] presenting a predictive ML approach. Deep learning frameworks are discussed by [34] and [466]. DSM in connection with time-of-use tariffs is analyzed by [200] and simultaneous predictions of electricity price and demand in smart grids in [314].

Some authors like [105, 149, 195] and [12] also discuss demand forecasting but place the focus of their research on the predictors that can be used to predict and correlate with the demand values. In this regard, [486] analyzes the correlation of indoor thermal performance and energy consumption. However, again, very few studies focus on residential users, i.e. households and apartments, especially with regard to dynamic data that depicts the ongoing use of that household.

In line with what other authors have noted in their work, the crucial factors that affect demand and that are to be taken into account when building predictive models are the meteorological conditions of the analyzed site. In essence, this correlation is not direct, but rather the temperature, wind speed and direction and irradiance have a significant impact on the use of heating and cooling devices, which are usually the largest consumers of energy in residential households without district heating and cooling. Besides, the current season of the year in moderate climates greatly determines what climatic conditions can be expected, and, therefore, the geographic properties of the analyzed site have to be taken into account since it is the location that determines how severe the seasonal variations in climatic conditions will be. As for the static data, the total floor space or heated volume are also said to be closely correlated with total consumption, but cannot be used to dynamically estimate demand with high time resolution. Here is where large volumes of IoT sensor data collected directly from homes can be of great help in increasing the precision of predictive models. Namely, indoor ambient temperature coupled with outdoor meteorological conditions with live occupancy data in real time can provide a precise short-term estimation of the consumption profile. Furthermore, if past behaviour is taken into account (in the form of previous demand curves both as an average over a larger time period in the past and the more current ones from the previous couple of days) with current day indicators (i.e. whether it is a working day or weekend/holiday), relatively precise hourly and possibly even inter-hourly profiles can be generated.

The presence of smart measuring devices in the form of smart plugs and cables which report real-time consumption per appliance in a home, or their substitution with an NILM algorithm as described in Subsect. 3.1 where bad performance due to insufficient generalization is not an issue, provides the possibility of predicting demand on a per-appliance level. This approach is scarcely depicted in contemporary research articles with only a few papers like [28,312] and [226] exploring this subject. Alternatively, the problem of demand forecasting is most often approached from an aggregated perspective, through the prediction of neighbourhood, city or state-level consumption, with data availability generally being the driving factor that ultimately decides what type of demand will be estimated. Time series from Figs. 4, 5 and 6 illustrate the different dynamics of the demand signals from a single appliance, all appliances of one home and several aggregated homes. Since each of these applications usually requires different levels of prediction precision, the raw data used for these illustrations was averaged with different sample intervals (15 s, 60 s and 15 min) in accordance with the appropriate use case.

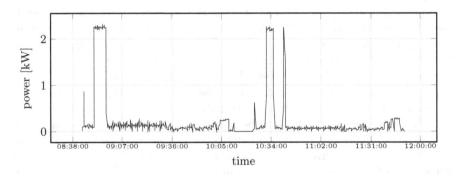

Fig. 4. Typical washing machine demand profile with 15 s averages (showing what appear to be two activations in the span of 4 h)

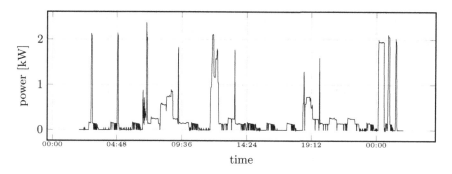

Fig. 5. Total household demand profile with 60 s averages (showing several appliance activations during a full 24-h period)

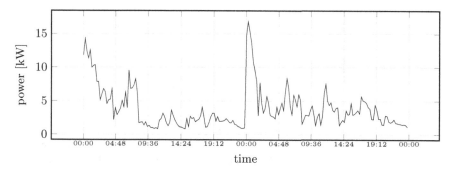

Fig. 6. Aggregate household demand profile with 15 min averages (showing consumption for 2 days with time-of-use tariff)

4.2 Production Forecaster

It has already been mentioned that energy planning is crucial for grid stability, and that it highly depends on the forecast renewable energy sources (RES) production. Therefore, in this subsection different methodologies used for production forecasting are going to be covered as well as their relation to the field of big data.

The production of RES technologies is highly influenced by weather conditions. For example, there is very high dependency between PV production and solar radiation, similar to the relationship between wind turbines and wind speed and direction. In Table 1, the selection of weather services is given followed by their main characteristics. Namely, depending on the practical application, production forecasters can have different time resolutions and horizons, which dictates the necessary weather forecast parameters. Therefore, from the above-mentioned table, it can be seen that Darksky can provide estimations in terms of minutes, whilst its horizon, as some kind of compromise, is only 7 days. Additionally, depending on the approach, historical weather data might be necessary for the purpose of the training process, as, currently, the most popular approaches in the field of RES production are data-driven algorithms. Finally, the choice of weather service highly influences its price. All of those characteristics can be found in the table.

Table 1. Overview of forecasting data providers

Name	Min. forecast resolution	Max. horizon [days]	Historical data	Free up to	Coverage
OpenWeatherMap	hourly	30	Yes	60 calls/minute	Global
Weatherbit	hourly	16	Yes	500 calls/day	Global
AccuWeather	hourly	15	prev. 24 h	50 calls/day	Global
Darksky	minute	7	Yes	1000 calls/day	Global
weathersteak	hourly	14	Yes	1000 calls/month	
Yahoo! Weather	hourly	10	No	2000 calls/day	Global
The Weather Channel	15 min	30	Yes		Global
World Weather Online	hourly	15	Yes	Not free	Global

Depending on the practical application apart from input weather parameters developed methodology varies, as well. For the use cases in which few measurements are available, physical models are usually chosen. These models are based on mathematical models and are usually deployed when there are not enough real world measurements. These models are characterized with the lowest performances in comparison with the following ones, but exist in cases of missing data. This methodology is present in the literature for various RES such as photo-voltaic panels (PVs) [115,334], wind turbines (WTs) [273] and solar-thermal collectors (STCs) [80,394]. However, even though they do not require huge amounts of measurements, physical characteristics such as number of solar panels, position of panels and wind turbines, capacity etc. are needed and sometimes, again, inaccessible. Taking into account suppliers' tendency to equip the grid with numerous IoT sensors nowadays, the necessity of physical models is decreasing, leaving room for data-driven models, which are a more important part of this chapter and within the field of big data.

Currently the most popular and explored topic in the field of RES production forecasters is statistical and machine learning (ML) based techniques, which were proven to achieve higher performances but require substantial amounts of data. Nonetheless, bearing in mind that a huge amount of big data is currently available in the energy domain, these approaches are not common only amongst researchers but also in real practice. The first group that stands out are the statistical autoregressive methodologies SARIMA, NARIMA, ARMA, etc. [437]. They are followed by probabilistic approaches, such as in [452]. Finally, neural networks and machine learning-based approaches are proven as one of the most suitable choices [205,236,453], similar to numerous other fields.

Apart from the similar inputs regarding weather parameters and applied models for RES production forecasters, all of the methodologies are dependent on the estimation time horizon. Depending on the practical application, the orders of magnitude can range from minutes to years. Further post-processing of the obtained forecast results is another important factor. Apart from the grid control and stability, from the perspective of big data the analytical tool developed on top of the results provided by the forecaster could be exploited for failure and irregularity detection in the system together with its high level metadata. By contrast, outputs with the big time horizon could be seen as adequate for extracting conclusions on a yearly basis using big data tools already presented in this book.

4.3 Pricing Prediction

Another important application of prediction algorithms in the energy domain are price predictions. As energy sectors worldwide are becoming increasingly deregulated, variable pricing in energy trading is becoming increasingly prominent with some envisioning a not-so-distant future where the cost of energy in the wholesale and maybe even retail markets will be changing every 15 min while the standard nowadays is usually hourly changes at most. Having accurate predictions of wholesale market prices presents key information for large-scale energy traders because it provides an insight into future trends in the same way as stock price predictions do and allows for sound investment planning.

Wholesale price variations greatly impact retail prices, which, in turn, have a key influence on the shape of the expected demand curve from end users. Moving from fixed pricing to first time-of-use tariffs and later hourly variable pricing has allowed for energy retailers to have granular control of load levels through what is essentially implicit demand response (DR) where load increase or decrease events are defined by the current prices. Energy prices are also influenced by the availability of renewable sources. For example, systems with high PV penetration tend to have lower prices during mid-day production peaks to try and motivate users to consume more energy when there is a surplus in the system. In that way, demand predictions, production predictions and pricing productions are mutually interconnected in such a way that should result in a balanced system of equal supply and demand.

5 Conclusion

The brief overview laid out in this chapter provides an insight into some potential applications of big data-oriented tools and analytical technologies in the energy domain. With the importance of climate change mitigation growing by the day, the number of solutions working towards increasing energy efficiency and responsible energy use is only expected to rise. As such, this domain provides an interesting and challenging realm for novel research approaches.

References

1. OZON Open Source Projects: A distributed, reliable key-value store for the most critical data of a distributed system (2014)
2. CGI Inc.: Internet of things (2015). https://www.cgi-group.co.uk/sites/default/files/files_uk/brochures/uk_iot_overview_brochure_nov_15.pdf
3. Abadi, M.J.S., Zamanifar, K.: Producing complete modules in ontology partitioning. In: 2011 International Conference on Semantic Technology and Information Retrieval, pp. 137–143. IEEE (2011)
4. Abdelaziz, I., Mansour, E., Ouzzani, M., Aboulnaga, A., Kalnis, P.: Lusail: a system for querying linked data at scale. Proc. VLDB Endowment **11**(4), 485–498 (2017)
5. Acosta, M., Hartig, O., Sequeda, J.F.: Federated RDF query processing. In: Sakr, S., Zomaya, A.Y. (eds.) Encyclopedia of Big Data Technologies. Springer, Cham (2019). https://doi.org/10.1007/978-3-319-77525-8
6. Acosta, M., Vidal, M., Lampo, T., Castillo, J., Ruckhaus E.: ANAPSID: an adaptive query processing engine for SPARQL endpoints. In: The Semantic Web - ISWC 2011–10th International Semantic Web Conference, Bonn, Germany, 23–27 October 2011, Proceedings Part I, pp. 18–34 (2011)
7. Agarwal, B.L.: Basic Statistics, 6th edn. New Age International, New Delhi (2015)
8. Al Hasan, M., Zaki, M.J.: A survey of link prediction in social networks. In: Aggarwal, C. (ed.) Social Network Data Analytics, pp. 243–275. Springer, Boston (2011). https://doi.org/10.1007/978-1-4419-8462-3_9
9. Al-Musaylh, M.S., Deo, R.C., Adamowski, J.F., Li, Y.: Short-term electricity demand forecasting with MARS, SVR and ARIMA models using aggregated demand data in queensland, australia. Adv. Eng. Inform. **35**, 1–16 (2016)
10. Alexander, K., Cyganiak, R., Hausenblas, M., Zhao, J.: Describing linked datasets. In: Proceedings of the WWW2009 Workshop on Linked Data on the Web, LDOW 2009, Madrid, Spain, 20 April 2009 (2009)
11. Alharthi, H.: Healthcare predictive analytics: an overview with a focus on Saudi Arabia. J. Infection Public Health **11**(6), 749–756 (2018)
12. Ali, M., Iqbal, M.J., Sharif, M.: Relationship between extreme temperature and electricity demand in Pakistan. Int. J. Energy Environ. Eng. **4**(1), 36 (2013)
13. Allen, J.F., Frisch, A.M.: What's in a semantic network? In: Proceedings of the 20th Annual Meeting on Association for Computational Linguistics, pp. 19–27. Association for Computational Linguistics (1982)
14. Aluç, G., Ozsu, M.T., Daudjee, K., Hartig, O.: Chameleon-DB: a workload-aware robust RDF data management system. University of Waterloo, Technical report CS-2013-10 (2013)
15. Amin, A., Al-Obeidat, F., Shah, B., Adnan, A., Loo, J., Anwar, S.: Customer churn prediction in telecommunication industry using data certainty. J. Bus. Res. **94**, 290–301 (2019)
16. Ancin, D., Almirall, G.: 5G to account for 15 percentage of global mobile industry by 2025 as 5G network launches accelerate (2019)
17. Angeli, G., Manning, C.: Philosophers are mortal: inferring the truth of unseen facts. In: Proceedings of the Seventeenth Conference on Computational Natural Language Learning, pp. 133–142 (2013)

18. Arenas, M., Barceló, P., Libkin, L., Murlak, F.: Foundations of Data Exchange. Cambridge University Press, Cambridge (2014)
19. Arenas, M., Bertossi, L.E., Chomicki, J.: Consistent query answers in inconsistent databases. In: PODS, pp. 68–79. ACM Press (1999)
20. Arenas, M., Pérez, J., Reutter, J.L., Riveros, C.: Foundations of schema mapping management. In: PODS, pp. 227–238. ACM (2010)
21. Arenas, M., Pérez, J., Sallinger, E.: Towards general representability in knowledge exchange. In: AMW, CEUR Workshop Proceedings, vol. 1087. CEUR-WS.org (2013)
22. Arming, S., Pichler, R., Sallinger, E.: Combined complexity of repair checking and consistent query answering. In: AMW, CEUR Workshop Proceedings, vol. 1189. CEUR-WS.org (2014)
23. Assunçãoa, M.D.: Big data computing and clouds: trends and future directions. J. Parallel Distrib. Comput. **79–80**, 3–15 (2015)
24. Atzeni, P., Bellomarini, L., Iezzi, M., Sallinger, E., Vlad, A.: Weaving enterprise knowledge graphs: the case of company ownership graphs. In: EDBT, pp. 555–566. OpenProceedings.org (2020)
25. Auer, S., Bizer, C., Kobilarov, G., Lehmann, J., Cyganiak, R., Ives, Z.: DBpedia: a nucleus for a web of open data. In: Aberer, K., et al. (eds.) ASWC/ISWC -2007. LNCS, vol. 4825, pp. 722–735. Springer, Heidelberg (2007). https://doi.org/10.1007/978-3-540-76298-0_52
26. Auer, S., et al.: Managing the life-cycle of linked data with the LOD2 stack. In: Cudré-Mauroux, P., et al. (eds.) ISWC 2012. LNCS, vol. 7650, pp. 1–16. Springer, Heidelberg (2012). https://doi.org/10.1007/978-3-642-35173-0_1
27. Auer, S., et al.: The bigdataeurope platform - supporting the variety dimension of big data. In: Web Engineering - 17th International Conference, ICWE 2017, Rome, Italy, 5–8 June 2017, Proceedings, pp. 41–59 (2017)
28. Barbato, A., Capone, A., Rodolfi, M., Tagliaferri, D.: Forecasting the usage of household appliances through power meter sensors for demand management in the smart grid. In: 2011 IEEE International Conference on Smart Grid Communications, SmartGridComm 2011 (2011)
29. Bardi, A., Manghi, P.: Enhanced publications: data models and information systems. Liber Q. **23**(4), 240–273 (2014)
30. Barsim, K.S., Yang, B.: Toward a semi-supervised non-intrusive load monitoring system for event-based energy disaggregation. In: 2015 IEEE Global Conference on Signal and Information Processing (GlobalSIP), pp. 58–62 (2015). ISBN 978-1-4799-7591-4
31. Batet, M., Sánchez, D., Valls, A.: An ontology-based measure to compute semantic similarity in biomedicine. J. Biomed. Inform. **44**(1), 118–125 (2011)
32. Bayne, L.E.: Big data in neonatal health care: big reach, big reward? critical nursing clinics of North America. Crit. Care Nurs. Clin. North Am. **30**(4), 481–497 (2018)
33. Beckel, C., Kleiminger, W., Cicchetti, R., Staake, T., Santini, S.: The eco data set and the performance of non-intrusive load monitoring algorithms. In: Proceedings of the 1st ACM Conference on Embedded Systems for Energy-Efficient Buildings, pp. 80–89 (2014)
34. Bedi, J., Toshniwal, D.: Deep learning framework to forecast electricity demand. Appl. Energy **238**, 1312–1326 (2019)
35. Beek, W., Schlobach, S., van Harmelen, F.: A contextualised semantics for owl: sameAs. In: The Semantic Web. Latest Advances and New Domains - 13th International Conference, ESWC, pp. 405–419 (2016)

36. Begenau, J., Farboodi, M., Veldkamp, L.: Big data in finance and the growth of large firms. J. Monetary Econ. **97**, 71–87 (2018)
37. Bellazzi, R.: Big data and biomedical informatics: a challenging opportunity. Yearb Med. Inform. **9**(1), 8–13 (2014)
38. Bellomarini, L., Sallinger, E., Gottlob, G.: The vadalog system: datalog-based reasoning for knowledge graphs. In: Proceedings of the VLDB Endowment, vol. 11 (2018)
39. Bellomarini, L., et al.: COVID-19 and company knowledge graphs: assessing golden powers and economic impact of selective lockdown via AI reasoning. CoRR, abs/2004.10119 (2020)
40. Bellomarini, L., Fakhoury, D., Gottlob, G., Sallinger, E.: Knowledge graphs and enterprise AI: the promise of an enabling technology. In: 2019 IEEE 35th International Conference on Data Engineering (ICDE), pp. 26–37. IEEE (2019)
41. Bellomarini, L., et al.: Data science with vadalog: bridging machine learning and reasoning. In: Abdelwahed, E.H., Bellatreche, L., Golfarelli, M., Méry, D., Ordonez, C. (eds.) MEDI 2018. LNCS, vol. 11163, pp. 3–21. Springer, Cham (2018). https://doi.org/10.1007/978-3-030-00856-7_1
42. Bellomarini, L., Gottlob, G., Pieris, A., Sallinger, E.: Swift logic for big data and knowledge graphs. In: IJCAI, pp. 2–10. ijcai.org (2017)
43. Bellomarini, L., Gottlob, G., Pieris, A., Sallinger, E.: Swift logic for big data and knowledge graphs. In: Tjoa, A.M., Bellatreche, L., Biffl, S., van Leeuwen, J., Wiedermann, J. (eds.) SOFSEM 2018. LNCS, vol. 10706, pp. 3–16. Springer, Cham (2018). https://doi.org/10.1007/978-3-319-73117-9_1
44. Bellomarini, L., Gottlob, G., Pieris, A., Sallinger, E.: The vadalog system: swift logic for big data and enterprise knowledge graphs. In: AMW, CEUR Workshop Proceedings, vol. 2100. CEUR-WS.org (2018)
45. Bellomarini, L., Gottlob, G., Sallinger, E.: Datalog-based reasoning for knowledge graphs. In: AMW, CEUR Workshop Proceedings, vol. 2369. CEUR-WS.org (2019)
46. Ben-Kiki, O., Evans, C., Ingerson, B.: YAML Ain't Markup Language (YAML). Ghent University, Working Draft (2004)
47. Berbakov, L., Tomasevic, N., Batic, M.: Architecture and implementation of IoT system for energy efficient living. In: 26th Telecommunications Forum, TELFOR 2018, Belgrade, Serbia (2018)
48. Berbers, Y., Zwaenepoel, W. (eds.): Google Dataset Search: Building a Search Engine for Datasets in an Open Web Ecosystem. ACM (2019)
49. Berger, G., Gottlob, G., Pieris, A., Sallinger, E.: The space-efficient core of vadalog. In: PODS, pp. 270–284. ACM (2019)
50. Bermudez, I., Traverso, S., Mellia, M., Munafo, M.: Exploring the cloud from passive measurements: the Amazon AWS case. In: 2013 Proceedings IEEE INFOCOM, pp. 230–234. IEEE (2013)
51. Berners-Lee, T.: Linked data (2006). https://www.w3.org/DesignIssues/LinkedData.html
52. Bernstein, P.A., Melnik, S.: Model management 2.0: manipulating richer mappings. In: SIGMOD Conference, pp. 1–12. ACM (2007)
53. Blin, G., Curé, O., Faye, D.C.: A survey of RDF storage approaches. Revue Africaine de la Recherche en Informatique et Mathématiques Appliquées, 15 (2012)
54. Blumauer, A.: From taxonomies over ontologies to knowledge graphs (2014)
55. Bonatti, P.A., Decker, S., Polleres, A., Presutti, V.: Knowledge graphs: new directions for knowledge representation on the semantic web (Dagstuhl Seminar 18371). Dagstuhl Rep. **8**(9), 29–111 (2019)

56. Bonfigli, R., Principi, E., Fagiani, M., Severini, M., Squartini, S., Piazza, F.: Non-intrusive load monitoring by using active and reactive power in additive factorial hidden markov models. Appl. Energy **208**, 1590–1607 (2017)
57. Bordes, A., Usunier, N., Garcia-Duran, A., Weston, J., Yakhnenko, O.: Translating embeddings for modeling multi-relational data. In: Advances in Neural Information Processing Systems, pp. 2787–2795 (2013)
58. Borgwardt, S., Ceylan, I.I., Lukasiewicz, T.: Ontology-mediated queries for probabilistic databases. In: Thirty-First AAAI Conference on Artificial Intelligence (2017)
59. Borgwardt, S., Ceylan, I.I., Lukasiewicz, T.: Recent advances in querying probabilistic knowledge bases. In: Proceedings of the Twenty-Seventh International Joint Conference on Artificial Intelligence, IJCAI 2018, 13–19 July 2018, Stockholm, Sweden. International Joint Conferences on Artificial Intelligence (2018)
60. Borne, K.: Top 10 big data challenges - a serious look at 10 big data v's (2014)
61. Bornmann, L., Mutz, R.: Growth rates of modern science: a bibliometric analysis based on the number of publications and cited references. J. Assoc. Inf. Sci. Technol. **66**(11), 2215–2222 (2015)
62. Borthakur, D., et al.: HDFs architecture guide. Hadoop Apache Project **53**(1–13), 2 (2008)
63. Bozzato, L., Homola, M., Serafini, L.: Context on the semantic web: why and how. ARCOE-12, p. 11 (2012)
64. Burgstaller, F., Neumayr, B., Sallinger, E., Schrefl, M.: Rule module inheritance with modification restrictions. In: Panetto, H., Debruyne, C., Proper, H.A., Ardagna, C.A., Roman, D., Meersman, R. (eds.) OTM 2018. LNCS, vol. 11230, pp. 404–422. Springer, Cham (2018). https://doi.org/10.1007/978-3-030-02671-4_25
65. Bush, V., Bush, V.: As we may think. Resonance **5**(11), 101–108 (1945)
66. Cadene, R., Ben-Younes, H., Cord, M., Thome. N.: MUREL: multimodal relational reasoning for visual question answering. In: Proceedings of the IEEE Conference on Computer Vision and Pattern Recognition, pp. 1989–1998 (2019)
67. Calvanese, D., et al.: The mastro system for ontology-based data access. Semant. Web **2**(1), 43–53 (2011). ISSN 1570-0844. IOS Press
68. Cama, A., Montoya, F.G., Gómez, J., Cruz, J.L.D.L., Manzano-Agugliaro, F.: Integration of communication technologies in sensor networks to monitor the Amazon environment. J. Cleaner Prod. **59**, 32–42 (2013)
69. Carbone, P., Katsifodimos, A., Ewen, S., Markl, V., Haridi, S., Tzoumas, K.: Apache flink: stream and batch processing in a single engine. In: Bulletin of the IEEE Computer Society Technical Committee on Data Engineering, vol. 36, no. 4 (2015)
70. Carrie Armel, K., Gupta, A., Shrimali, G., Albert, A.: Is disaggregation the holy grail of energy efficiency? the case of electricity. Energy Policy **52**, 213–234 (2013)
71. Catherine, R., et al.: Short Paper: Weather Station Data Publication at IRSTEA: An Implementation Report, TC-SSN2014, pp. 89–104 (2014). http://ceur-ws.org/Vol-1401/#paper-07
72. Ceravolo, P., Azzini, A., Angelini, M., et al.: Big data semantics. J. Data Semant. **7**, 65–85 (2018)
73. Ceri, S., Gottlob, G., Tanca, L.: What you always wanted to know about datalog (and never dared to ask). IEEE Trans. Knowl. Data Eng. **1**(1), 146–166 (1989)
74. Ceylan, I.I.: Query answering in probabilistic data and knowledge bases. Gesellschaft für Informatik eV (2018)

75. Charalambidis, A., Troumpoukis, A., Konstantopoulos, S.: Semagrow: optimizing federated SPARQL queries. In: Polleres, A., Pellegrini, T., Hellmann, S., Parreira, J.X. (eds.) Proceedings of the 11th International Conference on Semantic Systems, SEMANTICS 2015, Vienna, Austria, 15–17 September 2015, pp. 121–128. ACM (2015)

76. Chen, C., Chiang, R., Storey, V.: Business intelligence and analytics: from big data to big impact. MIS Q. **36**(4), 1165–1188 (2012)

77. Chen, M., Mao, S., Liu, Y.: Big data: a survey. MONET **19**(2), 171–209 (2014)

78. Chen, X., Chen, H., Zhang, N., Zhang, S.: SparkRDF: elastic discreted RDF graph processing engine with distributed memory. In: 2015 IEEE/WIC/ACM International Conference on Web Intelligence and Intelligent Agent Technology (WIIAT), vol. 1, pp. 292–300. IEEE (2015)

79. Cheng, G., Tran, T., Qu, Y.: RELIN: relatedness and informativeness-based centrality for entity summarization. In: Aroyo, L., et al. (eds.) ISWC 2011. LNCS, vol. 7031, pp. 114–129. Springer, Heidelberg (2011). https://doi.org/10.1007/978-3-642-25073-6_8

80. Chow, T.: Performance analysis of photovoltaic-thermal collector by explicit dynamic model. Sol. Energy **75**(2), 143–152 (2003)

81. Chung, W.: Review of building energy-use performance benchmarking methodologies. Appl. Energy **88**(5), 1470–1479 (2011)

82. Clearman, J., et al.: Feature engineering and explainability with vadalog: a recommender systems application. In: Datalog, volume 2368 of CEUR Workshop Proceedings, pp. 39–43. CEUR-WS.org (2019)

83. Clement, J.: Worldwide digital population as of April 2020 (2020)

84. Collarana, D., Galkin, M., Ribón, I.T., Vidal, M., Lange, C., Auer, S.: MINTE: semantically integrating RDF graphs. In: Proceedings of the 7th International Conference on Web Intelligence, Mining and Semantics, WIMS, pp. 22:1–22:11 (2017)

85. European Commission. Communication from the commission to the European parliament, the council, the European economic and social committee and the committee of the regions: European data strategy, com (2020) 66 final. https://ec.europa.eu/digital-single-market/en/policies/75981/3489

86. European Commission: The rolling plan on ICT standardisation (2020). https://ec.europa.eu/digital-single-market/en/news/rolling-plan-ict-standardisation

87. Cox, M., Ellsworth, D.: Application-controlled demand paging for out-of-core visualization. In: Proceedings of the Visualization 1997 (Cat. No. 97CB36155), pp. 235–244. IEEE (1997)

88. Rea, C., Granetz, R.S.: Exploratory machine learning studies for disruption prediction using large databases on DIII-D. Fusion Sci. Technol. **74**(1–2), 89–100 (2017)

89. Csar, T., Lackner, M., Pichler, R., Sallinger, E.: Computational social choice in the clouds. In: BTW (Workshops), LNI, vol. P-266, pp. 163–167. GI (2017)

90. Csar, T., Lackner, M., Pichler, R., Sallinger, E.: Winner determination in huge elections with mapreduce. In: AAAI, pp. 451–458. AAAI Press (2017)

91. Cui, Q., et al.: Stochastic online learning for mobile edge computing: learning from changes. IEEE Commun. Mag. **57**(3), 63–69 (2019)

92. Cuzzocrea, A., Sellis, T.: Semantics-aware approaches to big data engineering. J. Data Semant. **6**, 55–56 (2017)

93. Cyganiak, R., Bizer, C., Garbers, J., Maresch, O., Becker, C.: The D2RQ Mapping Language. Technical report, FU Berlin, DERI, UCB, JP Morgan Chase, AGFA, HP Labs, Johannes Kepler Universität Linz (2012)

94. Cyganiak, R., Wood, D., Lanthaler, M.: RDF 1.1 Concepts and Abstract Syntax. Recommendation, World Wide Web Consortium (W3C) (2014)
95. Dadwal, R., Graux, D., Sejdiu, G., Jabeen, H., Lehmann, J.: Clustering pipelines of large RDF POI data. In: Hitzler, P., et al. (eds.) ESWC 2019. LNCS, vol. 11762, pp. 24–27. Springer, Cham (2019). https://doi.org/10.1007/978-3-030-32327-1_5
96. Das, N., Rautaray, S., Pandey, M.: Big data analytics for medical applications. Int. J. Modern Educ. Comput. Sci. **10**, 2 (2018)
97. Das, S., Sundara, S., Cyganiak, R.: R2RML: RDB to RDF mapping language. In: Working group recommendation, World Wide Web Consortium (W3C) (2012)
98. Big Data: A new world of opportunities. NESSI White Paper, pp. 1–25 (2012)
99. Big Data: Principles and best practices of scalable realtime data systems. N. Marz J. Warren, Henning (2014)
100. Davenport, T.H.: Analytics 3.0 (2013). https://hbr.org/2013/12/analytics-30
101. De Giacomo, G., Lembo, D., Lenzerini, M., Poggi, A., Rosati, R.: Using ontologies for semantic data integration. In: Flesca, S., Greco, S., Masciari, E., Saccà, D. (eds.) A Comprehensive Guide Through the Italian Database Research Over the Last 25 Years. SBD, vol. 31, pp. 187–202. Springer, Cham (2018). https://doi.org/10.1007/978-3-319-61893-7_11
102. De Meester, B., Dimou, A.: The Function Ontology. Ghent University - imec - IDLab, Unofficial Draft (2016)
103. De Meester, B., Heyvaert, P., Dimou, A.: YARRRML. Unofficial draft, imec - Ghent University - IDLab, August 2019
104. De Meester, B., Maroy, W., Dimou, A., Verborgh, R., Mannens, E.: Declarative data transformations for linked data generation: the case of DBpedia. In: Blomqvist, E., Maynard, D., Gangemi, A., Hoekstra, R., Hitzler, P., Hartig, O. (eds.) ESWC 2017. LNCS, vol. 10250, pp. 33–48. Springer, Cham (2017). https://doi.org/10.1007/978-3-319-58451-5_3
105. Dedinec, A., Dedinec, A.: Correlation of variables with electricity consumption data. In: Konjović, Z., Zdravković, M., Trajanović, M. (Eds.) ICIST 2016 Proceedings, vol. 1, pp. 118–123. Eventonic (2016)
106. der Scheer, W. V.: 4 vs (2015)
107. Dettmers, T., Minervini, P., Stenetorp, P., Riedel, S.: Convolutional 2D knowledge graph embeddings. In: Thirty-Second AAAI Conference on Artificial Intelligence (2018)
108. Dhingra, B., Jin, Q., Yang, Z., Cohen, W.W., Salakhutdinov, R.: Neural models for reasoning over multiple mentions using coreference. arXiv preprint arXiv:1804.05922 (2018)
109. Dimou, A., Vahdati, S., Di Iorio, A., Lange, C., Verborgh, R., Mannens, E.: Challenges as enablers for high quality linked data: insights from the semantic publishing challenge. PeerJ Comput. Sci. **3**, e105 (2017)
110. Dimou, A., Vander Sande, M.: RDF Mapping Language (RML). Unofficial draft, Ghent University - iMinds - Multimedia Lab, September 2014
111. Dimou, A., Vander Sande, M., Colpaert, P., Verborgh, R., Mannens, E., Van de Walle, R.: RML: a generic language for integrated RDF mappings of heterogeneous data. In: Proceedings of the 7th Workshop on Linked Data on the Web, CEUR Workshop Proceedings, CEUR, vol. 1184 (2014)
112. Dimou, A., Verborgh, R., Sande, M.V., Mannens, E., Van de Walle, R.: Machine-interpretable dataset and service descriptions for heterogeneous data access and retrieval. In: Proceedings of the 11th International Conference on Semantic Systems, New York, NY, USA. ACM (2015)

113. Do, H., Cetin, K.S.: Residential building energy consumption: a review of energy data availability, characteristics, and energy performance prediction methods. Current Sust. Renew. Energy Rep. **5**(1), 76–85 (2018)

114. Doan, A., Halevy, A.Y., Ives, Z.G.: Principles of Data Integration. Morgan Kaufmann, San Francisco (2012)

115. Dolara, A., Leva, S., Manzolini, G.: Comparison of different physical models for PV power output prediction. Sol. Energy **119**, 83–99 (2015)

116. Dong, X.L., Gabrilovich, E., Heitz, G., Horn, W., Murphy, K., Sun, S., Zhang, W.: From data fusion to knowledge fusion. Proc. VLDB Endowment **7**(10), 881–892 (2014)

117. Dou, J., Qin, J., Jin, Z., Li, Z.: Knowledge graph based on domain ontology and natural language processing technology for chinese intangible cultural heritage. J Vis. Lang. Comput **48**, 19–28 (2018)

118. Duerst, M., Suignard, M.: Internationalized Resource Identifiers (IRIs). Standard track, IETF (2005)

119. Duggan, J., et al.: The BigDAWG polystore system. SIGMOD Rec. **44**(2), 11–16 (2015)

120. Díaz, M., Martín, C., Rubio, B.: State-of-the-art, challenges, and open issues in the integration of internet of things and cloud computing. J. Network Comput. Appl. **67**, 99–117 (2016)

121. Ehrlinger, L., Wöß, W.: Towards a definition of knowledge graphs. SEMANTiCS (Posters, Demos, SuCCESS), p. 48 (2016)

122. Elazhary, H.: Internet of things (IoT), mobile cloud, cloudlet, mobile IoT, IoT cloud, fog, mobile edge, and edge emerging computing paradigms: Disambiguation and research directions. J. Network Comput. Appl. **128**, 105–140 (2019)

123. Elshawi, R., Sakr, S., Talia, D., Trunfio, P.: Big data systems meet machine learning challenges: towards big data science as a service. Big Data Res. **14**, 1–11 (2018)

124. Endris, K.M., Galkin, M., Lytra, I., Mami, M.N., Vidal, M., Auer, S.: MULDER: querying the linked data web by bridging RDF molecule templates. Database Exp. Syst. Appl. **2017**, 3–18 (2017)

125. Endris, K.M., Rohde, P.D., Vidal, M., Auer, S.: Ontario: federated query processing against a semantic data lake. In: Database and Expert Systems Applications - 30th International Conference, DEXA 2019, Linz, Austria, 26–29 August 2019, Proceedings, Part I, pp. 379–395 (2019)

126. Euzenat, J., Shvaiko, P.: Ontology Matching. Springer, Heidelberg (2013). https://doi.org/10.1007/978-3-642-38721-0

127. Fagin, R., Haas, L.M., Hernández, M., Miller, R.J., Popa, L., Velegrakis, Y.: Clio: schema mapping creation and data exchange. In: Borgida, A.T., Chaudhri, V.K., Giorgini, P., Yu, E.S. (eds.) Conceptual Modeling: Foundations and Applications. LNCS, vol. 5600, pp. 198–236. Springer, Heidelberg (2009). https://doi.org/10.1007/978-3-642-02463-4_12

128. Fagin, R., Kolaitis, P.G., Popa, L., Tan, W.C.: Composing schema mappings: second-order dependencies to the rescue. ACM Trans. Database Syst. **30**(4), 994–1055 (2005)

129. Färber, M.: The Microsoft academic knowledge graph: a linked data source with 8 billion triples of scholarly data. In: Ghidini, C., et al. (eds.) ISWC 2019. LNCS, vol. 11779, pp. 113–129. Springer, Cham (2019). https://doi.org/10.1007/978-3-030-30796-7_8

130. Faria, D., Pesquita, C., Santos, E., Palmonari, M., Cruz, I.F., Couto, F.M.: The agreementmakerlight ontology matching system. In: Meersman, R., et al. (eds.) OTM 2013. LNCS, vol. 8185, pp. 527–541. Springer, Heidelberg (2013). https://doi.org/10.1007/978-3-642-41030-7_38

131. Faye, D.C., Cure, O., Blin, G.: A survey of RDF storage approaches. ARIMA J. **15**, 11–35 (2012)

132. Fayzrakhmanov, R.R., Sallinger, E., Spencer, B., Furche, T., Gottlob, G.: Browserless web data extraction: challenges and opportunities. In: WWW, pp. 1095–1104. ACM (2018)

133. Feinerer, I., Pichler, R., Sallinger, E., Savenkov, V.: On the undecidability of the equivalence of second-order tuple generating dependencies. In: AMW,CEUR Workshop Proceedings, vol. 749. CEUR-WS.org (2011)

134. Feinerer, I., Pichler, R., Sallinger, E., Savenkov, V.: On the undecidability of the equivalence of second-order tuple generating dependencies. Inf. Syst. **48**, 113–129 (2015)

135. Figueiras, P., Antunes, H., Guerreiro, G., Costa, R., Jardim-Gonçalves, R.: Visualisation and detection of road traffic events using complex event processing. In: Volume 2: Advanced Manufacturing, ASME International Mechanical Engineering Congress and Exposition, 11 (2018). V002T02A081

136. Figueiredo, M., Ribeiro, B., de Almeida, A.: Electrical signal source separation via nonnegative tensor factorization using on site measurements in a smart home. IEEE Trans. Instrum. Meas. **63**(2), 364–373 (2014)

137. Filip, A.: Blued: a fully labeled public dataset for event-based nonintrusive load monitoring research. In: 2nd Workshop on Data Mining Applications in Sustainability (SustKDD), p. 2012 (2011)

138. Firican, G.: The 10 vs of big data (2017). https://tdwi.org/articles/2017/02/08/10-vs-of-big-data.aspx

139. Friedman, D.: Iv.1 - the changing face of environmental monitoring. In: Twardowska, I. (ed.) Solid Waste: Assessment, Monitoring and Remediation, Waste Management Series, vol. 4, pp. 453–464. Elsevier (2004)

140. Friedman, M., Levy, A.Y., Millstein, T.D.: Navigational plans for data integration. In: Proceedings of the IJCAI-99 Workshop on Intelligent Information Integration, Held on July 31: in conjunction with the Sixteenth International Joint Conference on Artificial Intelligence City Conference Center, p. 1999. Stockholm, Sweden (1999)

141. Furche, T., Gottlob, G., Neumayr, B., Sallinger, E.: Data wrangling for big data: towards a lingua franca for data wrangling. In: AMW, CEUR Workshop Proceedings, vol. 1644 . CEUR-WS.org (2016)

142. Fuxman, A., Hernández, M.A., Ho, C.T.H., Miller, R.J., Papotti, P., Popa, L.: Nested mappings: schema mapping reloaded. In: VLDB, pp. 67–78. ACM (2006)

143. Gadepally, V., Kepner, J.: Big data dimensional analysis. In: IEEE High Performance Extreme Computing Conference (2014)

144. Galárraga, L.A., Teflioudi, C., Hose, K., Suchanek, F.: Amie: association rule mining under incomplete evidence in ontological knowledge bases. In: Proceedings of the 22nd International Conference on World Wide Web, pp. 413–422 (2013)

145. Gao, J., Giri, S., Kara, E.C., Bergés, M.: Plaid: a public dataset of high-resoultion electrical appliance measurements for load identification research: demo abstract. In: Proceedings of the 1st ACM Conference on Embedded Systems for Energy-Efficient Buildings, pp. 198–199 (2014)

146. Gao, Y., Liang, J., Han, B., Yakout, M., Mohamed, A.: Building a large-scale, accurate and fresh knowledge graph. In: SigKDD (2018)

147. Garg, N.: Apache Kafka. Packt Publishing Ltd., Birmingham (2013)
148. Garlaschelli, D., Battiston, S., Castri, M., Servedio, V., Caldarelli, G.: The scale-free topology of market investments. Technical report. http://www.lps.ens.fr/~battiston/SF_TopoShareNets.pdf
149. Gastli, A., Charabi, Y., Alammari, R.A., Al-Ali, A.M.: Correlation between climate data and maximum electricity demand in Gatar. In: 2013 7th IEEE GCC Conference and Exhibition (GCC), pp. 565–570 (2013). ISBN 978-1-4799-0721-2
150. Gates, A., Dai, D.: Programming Pig: Dataflow Scripting with Hadoop. O'Reilly Media Inc., Sebastopol (2016)
151. Ge, M., Bangui, H., Buhnova, B.: Big data for Internet of Things: a survey. Fut. Gener. Comput. Syst. **87**, 601–614 (2018)
152. Ghani, N.A., Hamid, S., Hashem, I.A.T., Ahmed, E.: Social media big data analytics: a survey. Comput. Hum. Behav. **101**, 417–428 (2019)
153. Ghazi, M.R., Gangodkar, D.: Hadoop, mapreduce and HDFs: a developers perspective. Procedia Comput. Sci. **48**(C), 45–50 (2015)
154. Ghofrani, F., He, Q., Goverde, R.M., Liu, X.: Recent applications of big data analytics in railway transportation systems: a survey. Transp. Res. Part C: Emerg. Technol. **90**, 226–246 (2018)
155. Ghorbanian, M.,, Hacopian Dolatabadi, S., Siano, P.: Big data issues in smart grids: a survey. IEEE Syst. J. **PP**, 1–12 (2019)
156. Giannini, S.: RDF data clustering. In: Abramowicz, W. (ed.) BIS 2013. LNBIP, vol. 160, pp. 220–231. Springer, Heidelberg (2013). https://doi.org/10.1007/978-3-642-41687-3_21
157. Gill, S.S., et al.: Transformative effects of iot, blockchain and artificial intelligence on cloud computing: evolution, vision, trends and open challenges. Internet Things **8**, 100118 (2019)
158. Gohar, M., Muzammal, M., Rahman, A.U.: Mart TSS: defining transportation system behavior using big data analytics in smart cities. Sustain. Cities Soc. **41**, 114–119 (2018)
159. Golshan, B., Halevy, A.Y., Mihaila, G.A.,. Tan, W.: Data integration: after the teenage years. In: Proceedings of the 36th ACM SIGMOD-SIGACT-SIGAI Symposium on Principles of Database Systems, PODS 2017, Chicago, IL, USA, 14–19 May 2017, pp. 101–106 (2017)
160. Görlitz, O., Staab, S.: SPLENDID: SPARQL endpoint federation exploiting VOID descriptions. In: Proceedings of the Second International Workshop on Consuming Linked Data (COLD2011), Bonn, Germany, 23 October 2011 (2011)
161. Gottlob, G., Pichler, R., Sallinger, E.: Function symbols in tuple-generating dependencies: expressive power and computability. In: PODS, pp. 65–77. ACM (2015)
162. Gottlob, G., Pichler, R., Sallinger, E.: Function symbols in tuple-generating dependencies: expressive power and computability. In: AMW, CEUR Workshop Proceedings, vol. 1912. CEUR-WS.org (2017)
163. Gottlob, G., Pichler, R., Sallinger, E.: Function symbols in tuple-generating dependencies: expressive power and computability. In: AMW, CEUR Workshop Proceedings, vol. 1912. CEUR-WS.org (2017)
164. Gottlob, G., Pieris, A., Sallinger, E.: Vadalog: recent advances and applications. In: Calimeri, F., Leone, N., Manna, M. (eds.) JELIA 2019. LNCS (LNAI), vol. 11468, pp. 21–37. Springer, Cham (2019). https://doi.org/10.1007/978-3-030-19570-0_2

165. Grant-Muller, S., Hodgson, F., Malleson, N.: Enhancing energy, health and security policy by extracting, enriching and interfacing next generation data in the transport domain (a study on the use of big data in cross-sectoral policy development). In: IEEE International Congress on Big Data (BigData Congress), Honolulu, HI, USA, 2017

166. Grau, B.C., Horrocks, I., Kazakov, Y., Sattler, U.: A logical framework for modularity of ontologies. In: IJCAI 2007, pp. 298–303 (2007)

167. Grau, B.C., Horrocks, I., Kazakov, Y., Sattler, U.: Modular reuse of ontologies: theory and practice. J. Artif. Intell. Res. **31**, 273–318 (2008)

168. Graux, D., Jachiet, L., Genevès, P., Layaïda, N.: SPARQLGX: efficient distributed evaluation of SPARQL with Apache Spark. In: Groth, P., et al. (eds.) ISWC 2016. LNCS, vol. 9982, pp. 80–87. Springer, Cham (2016). https://doi.org/10.1007/978-3-319-46547-0_9

169. Graux, D., Jachiet, L., Geneves, P., Layaïda, N.: A multi-criteria experimental ranking of distributed SPARQL evaluators. In: 2018 IEEE International Conference on Big Data (Big Data), pp. 693–702. IEEE (2018)

170. Graux, D., et al.: Profiting from kitties on Ethereum: leveraging blockchain RDF data with SANSA. In: SEMANTiCS Conference (2018)

171. Figueira, J.É., Greco, S., Ehrogott, M.: Multiple Criteria Decision Analysis: State of the Art Surveys. International Series in Operations Research & Management Science. Springer, New York (2005). https://doi.org/10.1007/b100605

172. Gruber, T.R.: A translation approach to portable ontology specifications. Knowl. Acquisition **5**(2), 199–220 (1993)

173. Guagliardo, P., Pichler, R., Sallinger, E.: Enhancing the updatability of projective views. In: AMW. CEUR Workshop Proceedings, vol. 1087. CEUR-WS.org (2013)

174. Gudivada, V., Irfan, M., Fathi, E., Rao, D.L.: Cognitive analytics: going beyond big data analytics and machine learning, Chap. 5. Elsevier (2016)

175. Gunaratna, K.: Semantics-based summarization of entities in knowledge graphs. Ph.D. thesis, Wright State University (2017)

176. Gupta, S., Arpan Kumar Kar, A., Baabdullah, A., Al-Khowaiter, W.: Big data with cognitive computing: a review for the future. Int. J. Inf. Manage. **42**, 78–89 (2018)

177. Haase, P.: Hybrid enterprise knowledge graphs. Technical report, metaphacts GmbH, October 2019

178. Habeeb, R.A.A., Nasaruddin, F., Gani, A., Hashem, I.A.T., Ahmed, E., Imran, M.: Real-time big data processing for anomaly detection: a survey. Int. J. Inf. Manage. **45**, 289–307 (2019)

179. Hai, R., Geisler, S., Quix, C.: Constance: an intelligent data lake system. In: Proceedings of the 2016 International Conference on Management of Data, SIGMOD Conference 2016, San Francisco, CA, USA, 26 June–01 July 2016, pp. 2097–2100 (2016)

180. Halevy, A.Y.: Answering queries using views: a survey. VLDB J. **10**(4), 270–294 (2001)

181. Harispe, S., Sánchez, D., Ranwez, S., Janaqi, S., Montmain, J.: A framework for unifying ontology-based semantic similarity measures: a study in the biomedical domain. J. Biomed. Inform. **48**, 38–53 (2014)

182. Harris, R.: Energy star - the power to protect the environment through energy efficiency (2003)

183. Hart, G.: Nonintrusive appliance load monitoring. Proc. IEEE **80**(12), 1870–1891 (1992)

184. Hartig, O.: Reconciliation of RDF* and property graphs. arXiv preprint arXiv:1409.3288 (2014)

185. Hartig, O., Thompson, B.: Foundations of an alternative approach to reification in RDF. arXiv preprint arXiv:1406.3399 (2014)

186. Hasan, A., Kalıpsız, O., Akyokuş, S.: Predicting financial market in big data: deep learning. In: 2017 International Conference on Computer Science and Engineering (UBMK), pp. 510–515 (2017)

187. Hashem, I.A.T., Yaqoob, I., Anuar, N.B., Mokhtar, S., Gani, A., Khan, S.U.: The rise of "big data" on cloud computing: review and open research issues. Inf. Syst. **47**, 98–115 (2015)

188. Haslhofer, B., Isaac, A., Simon, R.: Knowledge graphs in the libraries and digital humanities domain. arXiv preprint arXiv:1803.03198 (2018)

189. Haussmann, S., et al.: FoodKG: a semantics-driven knowledge graph for food recommendation. In: Ghidini, C., et al. (eds.) ISWC 2019. LNCS, vol. 11779, pp. 146–162. Springer, Cham (2019). https://doi.org/10.1007/978-3-030-30796-7_10

190. Havrlant, L., Kreinovich, V.: A simple probabilistic explanation of term frequency-inverse document frequency (tf-idf) heuristic (and variations motivated by this explanation). Int. J. Gen Syst **46**(1), 27–36 (2017)

191. He, Y., Yu, F.R., Zhao, N., Yin, H., Yao, H., Qiu, R.C.: Big data analytics in mobile cellular networks. IEEE Access **4**, 1985–1996 (2016)

192. Heidari, S., Simmhan, Y., Calheiros, R.N., Buyya, R.: Scalable graph processing frameworks: a taxonomy and open challenges. ACM Comput. Sur. (CSUR) **51**(3), 1–53 (2018)

193. Henriet, S., Simsekli, U., Richard, G., Fuentes, B.: Synthetic dataset generation for non-intrusive load monitoring in commercial buildings. In: Proceedings of the 4th ACM International Conference on Systems for Energy-Efficient Built Environments, pp. 1–2 (2017)

194. Heracleous, P., Angkititrakul, P., Kitaoka, N., Takeda, K.: Unsupervised energy disaggregation using conditional random fields. In: IEEE PES Innovative Smart Grid Technologies, Europe, pp. 1–5 (2014). ISSN: 2165-4824

195. Hernández, L., et al.: A study of the relationship between weather variables and electric power demand inside a smart grid/smart world framework. Sens. (Basel, Switz.) **12**(9), 11571–11591 (2012)

196. Heyvaert, P., De Meester, B., Dimou, A., Verborgh, R.: Declarative rules for linked data generation at your fingertips! In Proceedings of the 15th ESWC: Posters and Demos (2018)

197. Hoff, T.: The architecture Twitter uses to deal with 150M active users, 300K QPS, a 22 MB/s firehose, and send tweets in under 5 seconds (2013). http://highscalability.com/blog/2013/7/8/the-architecture-twitter-uses-to-deal-with-150m-active-users.html

198. Hoffman, S.: Apache Flume: Distributed Log Collection for Hadoop. Packt Publishing Ltd., Birmingham (2013)

199. Hogan, A., et al.: Knowledge graphs. arXiv preprint arXiv:2003.02320 (2020)

200. Hoiles, W., Krishnamurthy, V.: Nonparametric demand forecasting and detection of energy aware consumers. IEEE Trans. Smart Grid **6**(2), 695–704 (2015)

201. Hu, Z., Huang, P., Deng, Y., Gao, Y., Xing, E.: Entity hierarchy embedding. In: Proceedings of the 53rd Annual Meeting of the Association for Computational Linguistics and the 7th International Joint Conference on Natural Language Processing (Volume 1: Long Papers), vol. 1, pp. 1292–1300 (2015)

202. Hu, Z., Ma, X., Liu, Z., Hovy, E., Xing, E.: Harnessing deep neural networks with logic rules. arXiv preprint arXiv:1603.06318 (2016)

203. Huai, Y., et al.: Major technical advancements in Apache Hive. In: Proceedings of the 2014 ACM SIGMOD international conference on Management of Data, pp. 1235–1246 (2014)
204. Huang, W., Chen, A., Hsu, Y., Chang, H., Tsai, M.: Applying market profile theory to analyze financial big data and discover financial market trading behavior - a case study of Taiwan futures market. In: 2016 7th International Conference on Cloud Computing and Big Data (CCBD), pp. 166–169 (2016)
205. Huang, Y., Lu, J., Liu, C., Xu, X., Wang, W., Zhou, X.: Comparative study of power forecasting methods for PV stations. In: 2010 International Conference on Power System Technology, pp. 1–6. IEEE (2010)
206. Hubauer, T., Lamparter, S., Haase, P., Herzig, D.M.: Use cases of the industrial knowledge graph at Siemens. In: International Semantic Web Conference (P&D/Industry/BlueSky) (2018)
207. Hult, J.: Image of the week - 8 million landsat scenes! (2018). https://www.usgs.gov/media/videos/image-week-8-million-landsat-scenes
208. Humala, B., Nambi, A., Prsad, V.: UniversalNILM: a semi-supervised energy disaggregation framework using general appliance models. In: e-Energy (2018)
209. Hunt, P., Konar, M., Junqueira, F.P., Reed, B.: ZooKeeper: wait-free coordination for internet-scale systems. In: USENIX Annual Technical Conference, vol. 8, no. 9 (2010)
210. Ibaraki, T., Kameda, T.: On the optimal nesting order for computing n-relational joins. ACM Trans. Database Syst. **9**(3), 482–502 (1984)
211. Imawan, A., Kwon, J.: A timeline visualization system for road traffic big data. In: IEEE International Conference on Big Data (Big Data), Santa Clara, CA, USA (2015)
212. Imieliński, T., Lipski Jr., W.: Incomplete information in relational databases. In: Readings in Artificial Intelligence and Databases, pp. 342–360. Elsevier (1989)
213. Isele, R., Bizer, C.: Active learning of expressive linkage rules using genetic programming. J. Web Semant. **23**, 2–15 (2013)
214. Istepanian, R.S., Al-Anzi, T.: m-Health 2.0: new perspectives on mobile health, machine learning and big data analytics. Methods **151**, 34–40 (2018)
215. Dix, D.: Linkedin pumps water down to its server racks, uses an interesting spine and leaf network fabric (2017). https://www.networkworld.com/article/3161184/linkedin-pumps-water-down-to-its-server-racks-uses-an-interesting-spine-and-leaf-network-fabric.html
216. Jabeen, H., Dadwal, R., Sejdiu, G., Lehmann, J.: Divided we stand out! Forging Cohorts fOr Numeric Outlier Detection in large scale knowledge graphs (CONOD). In: Faron Zucker, C., Ghidini, C., Napoli, A., Toussaint, Y. (eds.) EKAW 2018. LNCS (LNAI), vol. 11313, pp. 534–548. Springer, Cham (2018). https://doi.org/10.1007/978-3-030-03667-6_34
217. Jacobs, A.: The pathologies of big data. ACM Queue **7**, 10–19 (2009)
218. Jagadish, H.V., et al.: Big data and its technical challenges. Commun. ACM **57**(7), 86–94 (2014)
219. James, P.: Linguistic instruments in knowledge engineering. In: van de Riet, R.P, Meersman, R.A. (eds.) 1992 Elsevier Science publishers bv all rights reserved. 97. In: Linguistic Instruments in Knowledge Engineering: Proceedings of the 1991 Workshop on Linguistic Instruments in Knowledge Engineering, Tilburg, The Netherlands, 17–18 January 1991, p. 97. North Holland (1992)
220. Janev, V., Mijovic, V., Vranes, S.: Using the linked data approach in European e-government systems: example from Serbia. Int. J. Semant. Web Inf. Syst. **14**(2), 27–46 (2018)

221. Janev, V., Vraneš, S.: The role of knowledge management solutions in enterprise business processes. J. Univ. Comput. Sci. **11**(4), 526–546 (2005)
222. Janev, V., Vraneš, S.: Applicability assessment of semantic web technologies. Inf. Process. Manag. **47**, 507–517 (2011)
223. Janev, V., Vraneš, S.: Semantic web. In: Encyclopedia of Information Systems and Technology, vol. 2. Taylor and Francis (2015)
224. Jeusfeld, M.A., Jarke, M., Mylopouos, J.: Metamodeling for Method Engineering. MIT Press, Cambridge (2010)
225. Ji, G., He, S., Xu, L., Liu, K., Zhao, J. : Knowledge graph embedding via dynamic mapping matrix. In: Proceedings of the 53rd Annual Meeting of the Association for Computational Linguistics and the 7th International Joint Conference on Natural Language Processing (Volume 1: Long Papers), vol. 1, pp. 687–696 (2015)
226. Ji, Y., Buechler, E., Rajagopal, R.: Data-driven load modeling and forecasting of residential appliances. arXiv:1810.03727 [stat] (2018)
227. Jia, R., Gao, Y., Spanos, C.J.: A fully unsupervised non-intrusive load monitoring framework. In: 2015 IEEE International Conference on Smart Grid Communications (SmartGridComm), pp. 872–878 (2015)
228. Jiménez-Ruiz, E., Cuenca Grau, B.: LogMap: logic-based and scalable ontology matching. In: Aroyo, L., et al. (eds.) ISWC 2011. LNCS, vol. 7031, pp. 273–288. Springer, Heidelberg (2011). https://doi.org/10.1007/978-3-642-25073-6_18
229. Jiménez-Ruiz, E., Grau, B.C., Horrocks, I., Berlanga, R.: Logic-based assessment of the compatibility of umls ontology sources. J. Biomed. Semant. **2**(1), S2 (2011)
230. Jiménez-Ruiz, E., Grau, B.C., Zhou, Y., Horrocks, I.: Large-scale interactive ontology matching: algorithms and implementation. In: ECAI, vol. 242, pp. 444–449 (2012)
231. Jin, X., Wah, B., Cheng, X., Wang, Y.: Significance and challenges of big data research. Big Data Res. **2**(2), 59–64 (2015)
232. Junior, A.C., Debruyne, C., Brennan, R., O'Sullivan, D.: FunUL: a method to incorporate functions into uplift mapping languages. In: Proceedings of the 18th International Conference on Information Integration and Web-Based Applications and Services. ACM, New York (2016)
233. Kakadia, D.: Apache Mesos Essentials. Packt Publishing Ltd., Birmingham (2015)
234. Kakas, A.C., Kowalski, R.A., Toni, F.: Abductive logic programming. J. Logic Comput. **2**(6), 719–770 (1992)
235. Kaoudi, Z., Manolescu, I.: Rdf in the clouds: a survey. VLDB J. Int. J. Very Large Data Bases **24**(1), 67–91 (2015)
236. Kardakos, E.G., Alexiadis, M.C., Vagropoulos, S.I., Simoglou, C.K., Biskas, P.N., Bakirtzis, A.G.: Application of time series and artificial neural network models in short-term forecasting of PV power generation. In: 2013 48th International Universities' Power Engineering Conference (UPEC), pp. 1–6. IEEE (2013)
237. Kejriwal, M.: What is a knowledge graph? In: Kejriwal, M. (ed.) Domain-Specific Knowledge Graph Construction, pp. 1–7. Springer, Cham (2019). https://doi.org/10.1007/978-3-030-12375-8_1
238. Kelly, J., Knottenbelt, W.: The uk-dale dataset, domestic appliance-level electricity demand and whole-house demand from five uk homes. Sci. Data **2**(1), 1–14 (2015)
239. Kelly, J., Knottenbelt, W.: Neural NILM: deep neural networks applied to energy disaggregation. In: BuildSys@SenSys (2015)
240. Khabsa, M., Giles, C.L.: The number of scholarly documents on the public web. PLoS ONE **9**(5), e93949 (2014)

241. Khadilkar, V., Kantarcioglu, M., Thuraisingham, B., Castagna, P.: Jena-HBase: a distributed, scalable and efficient RDF triple store. In: Proceedings of the 11th International Semantic Web Conference Posters & Demonstrations Track, ISWC-PD, vol. 12, pp. 85–88. Citeseer (2012)

242. Khan, A.R., Garcia-Molina, H.: Attribute-based crowd entity resolution. In: International Conference on Information and Knowledge Management, pp. 549–558 (2016)

243. Khan, N., Naim, A., Hussain, M.R., Naveed, Q.N., Ahmad, N., Qamar, S.: The 51 V's of big data: survey, technologies, characteristics, opportunities, issues and challenges. In: Proceedings of the International Conference on Omni-Layer Intelligent Systems, pp. 19–24 (2019)

244. Khan, Y., Zimmermann, A., Jha, A., Gadepally, V., D'Aquin, M., Sahay, R.: One size does not fit all: querying web polystores. IEEE Access **7**, 9598–9617 (2019)

245. Kim, H., Marwah, M., Arlitt, M., Lyon, G., Han, J.: Unsupervised disaggregation of low frequency power measurements. In: Proceedings of the 2011 SIAM International Conference on Data Mining, pp. 747–758. Society for Industrial and Applied Mathematics (2011)

246. Knap, T., Kukhar, M., Machac, B., Skoda, P., Tomes, J., Vojt, J.: UnifiedViews: an ETL framework for sustainable RDF data processing. In: The Semantic Web: ESWC 2014 Satellite Events, Revised Selected Papers, Anissaras, Crete, Greece, 25–29 May 2014, pp. 379–383 (2014)

247. Knoblock, C.A., et al.: Semi-automatically mapping structured sources into the semantic web. In: Proceedings of the 9th Extended Semantic Web Conference ESWC, Heraklion, Crete, Greece, 27–31 May 2012, pp. 375–390 (2012)

248. Kobusińska, A., Leung, C., Hsu, C.-H., Raghavendra, S., Chang, V.: Emerging trends, issues and challenges in Internet of Things, Big Data and cloud computing. Future Gener. Comput. Syst. **87**, 416–419 (2018)

249. Kocev, D., Džeroski, S., White, M.D., Newell, G.R., Griffioen, P.: Using single- and multi-target regression trees and ensembles to model a compound index of vegetation condition. Ecol. Model. **220**(8), 1159–1168 (2009)

250. Kok, S., Domingos, P.: Learning the structure of Markov logic networks. In: Proceedings of the 22nd International Conference on Machine Learning, pp. 441–448 (2005)

251. Kolaitis, P.G.: Reflections on schema mappings, data exchange, and metadata management. In: PODS, pp. 107–109. ACM (2018)

252. Kolaitis, P.G., Pichler, R., Sallinger, E., Savenkov, V.: Nested dependencies: structure and reasoning. In: PODS, pp. 176–187. ACM (2014)

253. Kolaitis, P.G., Pichler, R., Sallinger, E., Savenkov, V.: Limits of schema mappings. Theory Comput. Syst. **62**(4), 899–940 (2018)

254. Koller, D., Friedman, N.: Probabilistic Graphical Models: Principles and Techniques. MIT Press, Cambridge (2009)

255. Kolter, J.Z., Jaakkola, T.: Approximate inference in additive factorial HMMs with application to energy disaggregation. In: Artificial Intelligence and Statistics, pp. 1472–1482 (2012)

256. Kolter, J.Z., Johnson, M.J.: REDD: a public data set for energy disaggregation research. In: Workshop on Data Mining Applications in Sustainability (SIGKDD), San Diego, CA, vol. 25, pp. 59–62 (2011)

257. Konstantinou, N., et al.: VADA: an architecture for end user informed data preparation. J. Big Data **6**, 74 (2019)

258. Konstantinou, N., et al.: The VADA architecture for cost-effective data wrangling. In: SIGMOD Conference, pp. 1599–1602. ACM (2017)

259. Koo, C., Hong, T., Lee, M., Seon Park, H.: Development of a new energy efficiency rating system for existing residential buildings. Energy Policy **68**, 218–231 (2014)

260. Koo, D., Piratla, K., Matthews, C.J.: Towards sustainable water supply: schematic development of big data collection using Internet of Things (IoT). Procedia Eng. **118**, 489–497 (2015)

261. Kracker, M.: European patent information and the CPC taxonomy as linked open data. In: SEMANTiCS Posters & Demos (2018)

262. Kravchenko, A., Fayzrakhmanov, R.R., Sallinger, E.: Web page representations and data extraction with BERyL. In: Pautasso, C., Sánchez-Figueroa, F., Systä, K., Murillo Rodríguez, J.M. (eds.) ICWE 2018. LNCS, vol. 11153, pp. 22–30. Springer, Cham (2018). https://doi.org/10.1007/978-3-030-03056-8_3

263. Kreps, J.: Questioning the lambda architecture (2014). https://www.oreilly.com/radar/questioning-the-lambda-architecture/

264. Krishnan, S., Gonzalez, J.L.U.: Building Your Next Big Thing with Google Cloud Platform: A Guide for Developers and Enterprise Architects. Springer, Berkeley (2015). https://doi.org/10.1007/978-1-4842-1004-8

265. Krompaß, D., Baier, S., Tresp, V.: Type-constrained representation learning in knowledge graphs. In: Arenas, M., et al. (eds.) ISWC 2015. LNCS, vol. 9366, pp. 640–655. Springer, Cham (2015). https://doi.org/10.1007/978-3-319-25007-6_37

266. Kubitza, D.O., Böckmann, M., Graux, D.: SemanGit: a linked dataset from git. In: Ghidini, C., et al. (eds.) ISWC 2019. LNCS, vol. 11779, pp. 215–228. Springer, Cham (2019). https://doi.org/10.1007/978-3-030-30796-7_14

267. Kuhn, H.W.: The Hungarian method for the assignment problem. Naval Res. Logist. Q. **2**(1–2), 83–97 (1955)

268. Kumar, A., Shankar, R., Choudhary, A., Thakur, L.S.: A big data MapReduce framework for fault diagnosis in cloud-based manufacturing. Int. J. Prod. Res. **54**(23), 7060–7073 (2016)

269. Kumar, S., Mohbey, K.K.: A review on big data based parallel and distributed approaches of pattern mining. J. King Saud Univ. Comput. Inf. Sci. **31** (2019)

270. Kumari, A., Tanwar, S., Tyagi, S., Kumar, N., Maasberg, M., Choo, K.-K.R.: Multimedia big data computing and internet of things applications: a taxonomy and process model. J. Netw. Comput. Appl. **124**, 169–195 (2018)

271. Laney, D.: 3D data management: controlling data volume, velocity, and variety. Application Delivery Strategies, Meta Group (2001)

272. Lange, C.: Krextor - an extensible framework for contributing content math to the web of data. In: Davenport, J.H., Farmer, W.M., Urban, J., Rabe, F. (eds.) CICM 2011. LNCS (LNAI), vol. 6824, pp. 304–306. Springer, Heidelberg (2011). https://doi.org/10.1007/978-3-642-22673-1_29

273. Lange, M., Focken, U.: New developments in wind energy forecasting. In: 2008 IEEE Power and Energy Society General Meeting-Conversion and Delivery of Electrical Energy in the 21st Century, pp. 1–8. IEEE (2008)

274. Langegger, A., Wöß, W.: XLWrap – querying and integrating arbitrary spreadsheets with SPARQL. In: Bernstein, A., et al. (eds.) ISWC 2009. LNCS, vol. 5823, pp. 359–374. Springer, Heidelberg (2009). https://doi.org/10.1007/978-3-642-04930-9_23

275. Lee, C.H., Yoon, H.-J.: Medical big data: promise and challenges. Kidney Res. Clin. Pract. **36**(1), 3–11 (2017)

276. Lee, J.H., Yilmaz, A., Denning, R., Aldemir, T.: Use of dynamic event trees and deep learning for real-time emergency planning in power plant operation. Nucl. Technol. **205**(8), 1035–1042 (2019)

277. Lee, M., He, X., Yih, W.-T., Gao, J., Deng, L., Smolensky, P.: Reasoning in vector space: an exploratory study of question answering. arXiv preprint arXiv:1511.06426 (2015)

278. Lefrançois, M., Zimmermann, A., Bakerally, N.: A SPARQL extension for generating RDF from heterogeneous formats. In: Blomqvist, E., Maynard, D., Gangemi, A., Hoekstra, R., Hitzler, P., Hartig, O. (eds.) ESWC 2017. LNCS, vol. 10249, pp. 35–50. Springer, Cham (2017). https://doi.org/10.1007/978-3-319-58068-5_3

279. Leibniz, G.W.: The art of discovery. In: Leibniz: Selections, p. 51 (1951)

280. Lenzerini, M.: Data integration: a theoretical perspective. In: Proceedings of the Twenty-First ACM SIGACT-SIGMOD-SIGART Symposium on Principles of Database Systems, Madison, Wisconsin, USA, 3–5 June 2002, pp. 233–246 (2002)

281. Lepenioti, K., Bousdekis, A., Apostolou, D., Mentzas, G.: Prescriptive analytics: literature review and research challenges. Int. J. Inf. Manage. **50**, 57–70 (2020)

282. Levy, A.Y., Rajaraman, A., Ordille, J.J.: Querying heterogeneous information sources using source descriptions. In: VLDB 1996, Proceedings of 22th International Conference on Very Large Data Bases, Mumbai (Bombay), India, 3–6 September 1996, pp. 251–262 (1996)

283. Lewis, J.: Microservices: a definition of this new architectural term (2014). https://www.martinfowler.com/articles/microservices.html

284. Lin, F., Cohen, W.W.: Power iteration clustering. In: Proceedings of the 27th International Conference on Machine Learning. Figshare (2010)

285. Liu, S., McGree, J., Ge, Z., Xie, Y.: 8 - big data from mobile devices. In: Liu, S., McGree, J., Ge, Z., Xie, Y. (eds.) Computational and Statistical Methods for Analysing Big Data with Applications, pp. 157–186. Academic Press, San Diego (2016)

286. Liu, Y., Wang, Q., Hai-Qiang, C.: Research on it architecture of heterogeneous big data. J. Appl. Sci. Eng. **18**(2), 135–142 (2015)

287. Lösch, U., Bloehdorn, S., Rettinger, A.: Graph kernels for RDF data. In: Simperl, E., Cimiano, P., Polleres, A., Corcho, O., Presutti, V. (eds.) ESWC 2012. LNCS, vol. 7295, pp. 134–148. Springer, Heidelberg (2012). https://doi.org/10.1007/978-3-642-30284-8_16

288. Loukides, M.: What is data science? The future belongs to the companies and people that turn data into products. An O'Reilly Radar Report (2010)

289. Lukasiewicz, T., Martinez, M.V., Pieris, A., Simari, G.I.: From classical to consistent query answering under existential rules. In: Twenty-Ninth AAAI Conference on Artificial Intelligence (2015)

290. Ma, J., Jiang, J.: Applications of fault detection and diagnosis methods in nuclear power plants: a review. Prog. Nucl. Energy **53**, 255–266 (2011)

291. MacDonald, M., Livengood, S.: Benchmarking residential energy use. In: Residential Buildings: Technologies, Design, and Performance Analysis, p. 12 (2020)

292. Makela, E., Hyvönen, E., Ruotsalo, T.: How to deal with massively heterogeneous cultural heritage data: lessons learned in CultureSampo. Semant. Web **3**, 85–109 (2012)

293. Makonin, S., Bajic, I.V., Popowich, F.: Efficient sparse matrix processing for nonintrusive load monitoring (NILM). In: NILM Workshop 2014 (2014)

294. Makonin, S., Popowich, F., Bajić, I.V., Gill, B., Bartram, L.: Exploiting HMM sparsity to perform online real-time nonintrusive load monitoring. IEEE Trans. Smart Grid **7**(6), 2575–2585 (2016)

295. Mami, M.N., Graux, D., Scerri, S., Jabeen, H., Auer, S., Lehmann, J.: Squerall: virtual ontology-based access to heterogeneous and large data sources. In: Ghidini, C., et al. (eds.) ISWC 2019. LNCS, vol. 11779, pp. 229–245. Springer, Cham (2019). https://doi.org/10.1007/978-3-030-30796-7_15

296. Manghi, P., Mikulicic, M., Atzori, C.: De-duplication of aggregation authority files. Int. J. Metadata Semant. Ontol. **7**(2), 114–130 (2012)

297. Manyika, J.: Big data: the next frontier for innovation, competition, and productivity. The McKinsey Global Institute, pp. 1–137 (2011)

298. Marchi, E., Miguel, O.: On the structure of the teaching-learning interactive process. Int. J. Game Theory **3**(2), 83–99 (1974)

299. Marr, B.: Big data and AI: 30 amazing (and free) public data sources for 2018 (2018). https://www.forbes.com/sites/bernardmarr/2018/02/26/big-data-and-ai-30-amazing-and-free-public-data-sources-for-2018

300. Martis, R.J., Gurupur, V.P., Lin, H., Islam, A., Fernandes, S.L.: Recent advances in big data analytics, Internet of Things and machine learning. Future Gener. Comput. Syst. **88**, 696–698 (2018)

301. Mathews, L.: Just how big is Amazon's AWS business? (2014). https://www.geek.com/chips/just-how-big-is-amazons-aws-business-hint-its-absolutely-massive-1610221/

302. Mauch, L., Yang, B.: A new approach for supervised power disaggregation by using a deep recurrent LSTM network. In: 2015 IEEE Global Conference on Signal and Information Processing (GlobalSIP), pp. 63–67 (2015). ISBN 978-1-4799-7591-4

303. McCarthy, J.: Circumscription–a form of non-monotonic reasoning. Artif. Intell. **13**(1–2), 27–39 (1980)

304. Chari, S., Gruen, D.M., Seneviratne, O., McGuinness, D.L.: Foundations of explainable knowledge-enabled systems. In: Tiddi, I., Lécué, F., Hitzler, P. (eds.) Volume 47: Knowledge Graphs for eXplainable Artificial Intelligence: Foundations, Applications and Challenges, pp. 23–48 (2020). ISBN 978-1-64368-080-4 (print), 978-1-64368-081-1 (online)

305. Michel, F., Djimenou, L., Faron-Zucker, C., Montagnat, J.: Translation of heterogeneous databases into RDF, and application to the construction of a SKOS taxonomical reference. In: Monfort, V., Krempels, K.-H., Majchrzak, T.A., Turk, Ž. (eds.) WEBIST 2015. LNBIP, vol. 246, pp. 275–296. Springer, Cham (2016). https://doi.org/10.1007/978-3-319-30996-5_14

306. Michel, F., Djimenou, L., Faron-Zucker, C., Montagnat, J.: xR2RML: relational and non-relational databases to RDF mapping language. Rapport de recherche, Laboratoire d'Informatique, Signaux et Systèmes de Sophia-Antipolis (I3S), October 2017

307. Michelfeit, J., Knap, T.: Linked data fusion in ODCleanStore. In: ISWC Posters and Demonstrations Track (2012)

308. Michels, C., Fayzrakhmanov, R.R., Ley, M., Sallinger, E., Schenkel, R.: OXPath-based data acquisition for dblp. In: JCDL, pp. 319–320. IEEE Computer Society (2017)

309. Mijović, V., Tomašević, N., Janev, V., Stanojević, M., Vraneš, S.: Emergency management in critical infrastructures: a complex-event-processing paradigm. J. Syst. Sci. Syst. Eng. **28**, 37–62 (2019). https://doi.org/10.1007/s11518-018-5393-5

310. Miller, R.: Facebook with more than two billion users on millions of servers, running thousands of configuration changes every day involving trillions of

configuration checks (2018). https://techcrunch.com/2018/07/19/how-facebook-configures-its-millions-of-servers-every-day/

311. Mohammadpoor, M., Torabi, F.: Big data analytics in oil and gas industry: an emerging trend. Petroleum **4** (2018)

312. Mohi Ud Din, G., Mauthe, A.U., Marnerides, A.K.: Appliance-level short-term load forecasting using deep neural networks. In: 2018 International Conference on Computing, Networking and Communications (ICNC), pp. 53–57 (2018). ISBN 978-1-5386-3652-7

313. Morsey, M., Lehmann, J., Auer, S., Ngonga Ngomo, A.-C.: DBpedia SPARQL benchmark – performance assessment with real queries on real data. In: Aroyo, L., et al. (eds.) ISWC 2011. LNCS, vol. 7031, pp. 454–469. Springer, Heidelberg (2011). https://doi.org/10.1007/978-3-642-25073-6_29

314. Motamedi, A., Zareipour, H., Rosehart, W.D.: Electricity price and demand forecasting in smart grids. IEEE Trans. Smart Grid **3**(2), 664–674 (2012)

315. Mundial, F.E.: Big data, big impact: new possibilities for international development. Foro Económico Mundial. Cologny, Suiza (2012). Disponible en: www3. weforum.org/docs/WEF_TC_MFS_BigDataBigIm-pact_Briefing_2012.pdf

316. Munir, K., Anjum, M.S.: The use of ontologies for effective knowledge modelling and information retrieval. Appl. Comput. Inform. **14**(2), 116–126 (2018)

317. Murphy, K.P.: Machine Learning: A Probabilistic Perspective. MIT Press, Cambridge (2012)

318. Murray, D., Stankovic, L., Stankovic, V.: An electrical load measurements dataset of United Kingdom households from a two-year longitudinal study. Sci. Data **4**(1), 1–12 (2017)

319. Murray, D., Stankovic, L., Stankovic, V.: An electrical load measurements dataset of United Kingdom households from a two-year longitudinal study. Sci. Data **4**(1), 1–12 (2017)

320. Mutharaju, R., Sakr, S., Sala, A., Hitzler, P.: D-SPARQ: distributed, scalable and efficient RDF query engine. In: CEUR Workshop Proceedings, pp. 261–264 (2013)

321. Mutton, P.: Cloud wars: Alibaba becomes 2nd largest hosting company (2017). https://news.netcraft.com/archives/2017/08/22/cloud-wars-alibaba-becomes-2nd-largest-hosting-company.html

322. Shabbir, M.N.S.K., Ali, M.Z., Chowdhury, M.S.A., Liang, X.: A probabilistic approach for peak load demand forecasting. In: 2018 IEEE Canadian Conference on Electrical Computer Engineering (CCECE), pp. 1–4 (2018). ISSN: 2576-7046

323. Nayyeri, M., Xu, C., Lehmann, J., Yazdi, H.S.: LogicENN: a neural based knowledge graphs embedding model with logical rules. arXiv preprint arXiv:1908.07141 (2019)

324. Ngomo, A.-C.N.: Parameter-free clustering of protein-protein interaction graphs. In: Proceedings of the Fourth International Workshop on Machine Learning in Systems Biology (MLSB), pp. 43–46. Citeseer (2010)

325. Ngonga Ngomo, A.-C., Schumacher, F.: BorderFlow: a local graph clustering algorithm for natural language processing. In: Gelbukh, A. (ed.) CICLing 2009. LNCS, vol. 5449, pp. 547–558. Springer, Heidelberg (2009). https://doi.org/10.1007/978-3-642-00382-0_44

326. Nickel, M., Murphy, K., Tresp, V., Gabrilovich, E.: A review of relational machine learning for knowledge graphs. arXiv preprint arXiv:1503.00759 (2015)

327. Nickel, M., Tresp, V., Kriegel, H.-P.: A three-way model for collective learning on multi-relational data. In: ICML, vol. 11, pp. 809–816 (2011)

328. Nickel, M., Tresp, V., Kriegel, H.-P.: Factorizing YAGO: scalable machine learning for linked data. In: Proceedings of the 21st International Conference on World Wide Web, pp. 271–280. ACM (2012)

329. Nikolaou, T., Kolokotsa, D., Stavrakakis, G.: Review on methodologies for energy benchmarking, rating and classification of buildings. Adv. Build. Energy Res. **5**(1), 53–70 (2011)

330. Nishani, L., Biba, M.: Statistical relational learning for collaborative filtering a state-of-the-art review. In: Natural Language Processing: Concepts, Methodologies, Tools, and Applications, pp. 688–707. IGI Global (2020)

331. Noy, N., Gao, Y., Jain, A., Narayanan, A., Patterson, A., Taylor, J.: Industry-scale knowledge graphs: lessons and challenges. Queue **17**(2), 48–75 (2019)

332. Noy, N.F.: Semantic integration: a survey of ontology-based approaches. ACM Sigmod Rec. **33**(4), 65–70 (2004)

333. Nurdiati, S., Hoede, C.: 25 years development of knowledge graph theory: the results and the challenge. Memorandum **1876**, 1–10 (2008)

334. Ogliari, E., Dolara, A., Manzolini, G., Leva, S.: Physical and hybrid methods comparison for the day ahead PV output power forecast. Renew. Energy **113**, 11–21 (2017)

335. Oguz, D., Ergenc, B., Yin, S., Dikenelli, O., Hameurlain, A.: Federated query processing on linked data: a qualitative survey and open challenges. Knowl. Eng. Rev. **30**(5), 545–563 (2015)

336. Oussous, A., Benjelloun, F.-Z., Lahcen, A.A., Belfkih, S.: Big data technologies: a survey. J. King Saud Univ. - Comput. Inf. Sci. **30**(4), 431–448 (2018)

337. Owen, S., Owen, S.: Mahout in Action. Manning, Shelter Island (2012)

338. Özsu, M.T., Valduriez, P.: Principles of Distributed Database Systems, 2nd edn. Prentice-Hall, Upper Saddle River (1999)

339. Palanisamy, V., Thirunavukarasu, R.: Implications of big data analytics in developing healthcare frameworks - a review. J. King Saud Univ. - Comput. Inf. Sci. **31**(4), 415–425 (2019)

340. K. Panetta. Trends emerge in the gartner hype cycle for emerging technologies. Retrieved November, vol. 4, p. 5 (2018)

341. Papailiou, N., Konstantinou, I., Tsoumakos, D., Koziris, N.: H2RDF: adaptive query processing on RDF data in the cloud. In: Proceedings of the 21st International Conference on World Wide Web, pp. 397–400 (2012)

342. Papailiou, N., Tsoumakos, D., Konstantinou, I., Karras, P., Koziris, N.: H2RDF+ an efficient data management system for big RDF graphs. In: Proceedings of the 2014 ACM SIGMOD International Conference on Management of Data, pp. 909–912 (2014)

343. Parker, C.: Unexpected challenges in large scale machine learning. In: Proceedings of the 1st International Workshop on Big Data, Streams and Heterogeneous Source Mining: Algorithms, Systems, Programming Models and Applications, pp. 1–6 (2012)

344. Parson, O., Ghosh, S., Weal, M., Rogers, A.: An unsupervised training method for non-intrusive appliance load monitoring. Artif. Intell. **217**, 1–19 (2016)

345. Pashazadeh, A., Navimipour, N.J.: Big data handling mechanisms in the healthcare applications: a comprehensive and systematic literature review. J. Biomed. Inform. **82**, 47–62 (2018)

346. Patrizio, A.: IDC: expect 175 zettabytes of data worldwide by 2025, 03 December 2018. https://www.networkworld.com/article/3325397/idc-expect-175-zettabytes-of-data-worldwide-by-2025.html

347. Paulheim, H.: Knowledge graph refinement: a survey of approaches and evaluation methods. Semant. Web **8**(3), 489–508 (2017)
348. Paulheim, H.: Knowledge graph refinement: a survey of approaches and evaluation methods. Semant. Web **8**(3), 489–508 (2017)
349. Pearl, J.: Fusion, propagation, and structuring in belief networks. Artif. Intell. **29**(3), 241–288 (1986)
350. Pennock, M.: Digital curation: a life-cycle approach to managing and preserving usable digital information. Library Arch. **1**, 34–45 (2007)
351. Pérez, J., Pichler, R., Sallinger, E., Savenkov, V.: Union and intersection of schema mappings. In: AMW, CEUR Workshop Proceedings, vol. 866, pp. 129–141. CEUR-WS.org (2012)
352. Persico, V., Pescapé, A., Picariello, A., Sperlí, G.: Benchmarking big data architectures for social networks data processing using public cloud platforms. Future Gener. Comput. Syst. **89**, 98–109 (2018)
353. Pfandler, A., Sallinger, E.: Distance-bounded consistent query answering. In: IJCAI, pp. 2262–2269. AAAI Press (2015)
354. Chen, C. Phan, S.: Big data and monitoring the grid. In: The Power Grid, pp. 253–285 (2017)
355. Pichler, R., Sallinger, E., Savenkov, V.: Relaxed notions of schema mapping equivalence revisited. Theory Comput. Syst. **52**(3), 483–541 (2013)
356. Poggi, A., Lembo, D., Calvanese, D., De Giacomo, G., Lenzerini, M., Rosati, R.: Linking data to ontologies. In: Spaccapietra, S. (ed.) Journal on Data Semantics X. LNCS, vol. 4900, pp. 133–173. Springer, Heidelberg (2008). https://doi.org/10.1007/978-3-540-77688-8_5
357. Popping, R.: Knowledge graphs and network text analysis. Soc. Sci. Inf. **42**(1), 91–106 (2003)
358. Porter, M.E.: Competitive Advantage Creating and Sustaining Superior Performance, pp. 167–206. Free Press, New York (1985)
359. Pujara, J.: Probabilistic models for scalable knowledge graph construction. Ph.D. thesis, University of Maryland, College Park, MD, USA (2016)
360. Pujara, J., London, B., Getoor, L., Cohen, W.W.: Online inference for knowledge graph construction. In: Workshop on Statistical Relational AI (2015)
361. Pujara, J., Miao, H., Getoor, L., Cohen, W.: Knowledge graph identification. In: Alani, H., et al. (eds.) ISWC 2013. LNCS, vol. 8218, pp. 542–557. Springer, Heidelberg (2013). https://doi.org/10.1007/978-3-642-41335-3_34
362. Pujara, J., Miao, H., Getoor, L., Cohen, W.W.: Ontology-aware partitioning for knowledge graph identification. In: Proceedings of the 2013 Workshop on Automated Knowledge Base Construction, pp. 19–24. ACM (2013)
363. Punnoose, R., Crainiceanu, A., Rapp, D.: RYA: a scalable RDF triple store for the clouds. In: Proceedings of the 1st International Workshop on Cloud Intelligence, pp. 1–8 (2012)
364. Punčochář, I., Škach, J.: A survey of active fault diagnosis methods. IFAC-PapersOnLine **51**(24), 1091–1098 (2018)
365. Quix, C., Hai, R., Vatov, I.: GEMMS: a generic and extensible metadata management system for data lakes. In: 28th International Conference on Advanced Information Systems Engineering (CAiSE 2016), pp. 129–136 (2016)
366. Radivojević, G., Lazić, B., Šormaz, G.: Effects of business intelligence application in tolling system. Int. J. Traffic Transp. Eng. **5**(1), 45–53 (2015)
367. Rahm, E., Do, H.H.: Data cleaning: problems and current approaches. IEEE Data Eng. Bull. **23**, 3–13 (2000)

368. Ravi, K., Khandelwal, Y., Krishna, B.S., Ravi, V.: Analytics in/for cloud-an interdependence: a review. J. Netw. Comput. Appl. **102**, 17–37 (2018)
369. Ray, P.: A survey on Internet of Things architectures. J. King Saud Univ. - Comput. Inf. Sci. **30**(3), 291–319 (2018)
370. Reali, G., Femminella, M., Nunzi, E., Valocchi, D.: Genomics as a service: a joint computing and networking perspective. Comput. Netw. **145**, 27–51 (2018)
371. Ribón, I.T., Vidal, M., Kämpgen, B., Sure-Vetter, Y.: GADES: a graph-based semantic similarity measure. In: SEMANTICS - 12th International Conference on Semantic Systems, Leipzig, Germany, pp. 101–104 (2016)
372. Rich, E., et al.: Users are individuals: individualizing user models. Int. J. Man Mach. Stud. **18**(3), 199–214 (1983)
373. Richardson, M., Domingos, P.: Markov logic networks. Mach. Learn. **62**(1–2), 107–136 (2006). https://doi.org/10.1007/s10994-006-5833-1
374. Ristevski, M., Chen, B.: Big data analytics in medicine and healthcare. J. Integr. Bioinform. **15**(3), 1–5 (2018)
375. Rocktäschel, T., Singh, S., Riedel, S.: Injecting logical background knowledge into embeddings for relation extraction. In: Proceedings of the 2015 Conference of the North American Chapter of the Association for Computational Linguistics: Human Language Technologies, pp. 1119–1129 (2015)
376. Rohloff, K., Schantz, R.E.: High-performance, massively scalable distributed systems using the mapreduce software framework: the shard triple-store. In: Programming Support Innovations for Emerging Distributed Applications, PSI EtA 2010, pp. 4:1–4:5. ACM, New York (2010)
377. Rospocher, M., et al.: Building event-centric knowledge graphs from news. J. Web Semant. **37**, 132–151 (2016)
378. Russell, J.: Cloudera Impala. O'Reilly Media Inc., Sebastapol (2013)
379. Saggi, M.K., Jain, S.: A survey towards an integration of big data analytics to big insights for value-creation. Inf. Process. Manage. **54**(5), 758–790 (2018)
380. Saleem, M., Khan, Y., Hasnain, A., Ermilov, I., Ngomo, A.N.: A fine-grained evaluation of SPARQL endpoint federation systems. Semant. Web **7**(5), 493–518 (2016)
381. Tan, W., Blake, M.B., Saleh, I.: Social-network-sourced big data analytics. IEEE Internet Comput. **17**, 62–69 (2013)
382. Sallinger, E.: Reasoning about schema mappings. In: Data Exchange, Information, and Streams, Dagstuhl Follow-Ups, vol. 5, pp. 97–127. Schloss Dagstuhl - Leibniz-Zentrum für Informatik (2013)
383. Santos, E., Faria, D., Pesquita, C., Couto, F.M.: Ontology alignment repair through modularization and confidence-based heuristics. PLoS ONE **10**(12), e0144807 (2015)
384. Schätzle, A., Przyjaciel-Zablocki, M., Berberich, T., Lausen, G.: S2X: graph-parallel querying of RDF with GraphX. In: Wang, F., Luo, G., Weng, C., Khan, A., Mitra, P., Yu, C. (eds.) Big-O(Q)/DMAH -2015. LNCS, vol. 9579, pp. 155–168. Springer, Cham (2016). https://doi.org/10.1007/978-3-319-41576-5_12
385. Schätzle, A., Przyjaciel-Zablocki, M., Skilevic, S., Lausen, G.: S2RDF: RDF querying with SPARQL on spark. arXiv preprint arXiv:1512.07021 (2015)
386. Schiano, C., et al.: Epigenetic-sensitive pathways in personalized therapy of major cardiovascular diseases. Pharmacol. Ther. **210**, 107514 (2020)
387. Schneider, E.W.: Course modularization applied: the interface system and its implications for sequence control and data analysis. HumRRO-PP-10-73 (1973)

388. Schultz, A., Matteini, A., Isele, R., Mendes, P.N., Bizer, C., Becker, C.: LDIF - a framework for large-scale linked data integration. In: International World Wide Web Conference (2012)

389. Schwarte, A., Haase, P., Hose, K., Schenkel, R., Schmidt, M.: FedX: optimization techniques for federated query processing on linked data. In: Aroyo, L., et al. (eds.) ISWC 2011. LNCS, vol. 7031, pp. 601–616. Springer, Heidelberg (2011). https://doi.org/10.1007/978-3-642-25073-6_38

390. Sebastio, S., Trivedi, K.S., Alonso, J.: Characterizing machines lifecycle in google data centers. Perform. Eval. **126**, 39–63 (2018)

391. Sejdiu, G., Ermilov, I., Lehmann, J., Mami, M.N.: DistLODStats: distributed computation of RDF dataset statistics. In: Vrandečić, D., et al. (eds.) ISWC 2018. LNCS, vol. 11137, pp. 206–222. Springer, Cham (2018). https://doi.org/10.1007/978-3-030-00668-6_13

392. Sejdiu, G., Graux, D., Khan, I., Lytra, I., Jabeen, H., Lehmann, J.: Towards a scalable semantic-based distributed approach for SPARQL query evaluation. In: 15th International Conference on Semantic Systems (SEMANTiCS) (2019)

393. Sejdiu, G., Rula, A., Lehmann, J., Jabeen, H.: A scalable framework for quality assessment of RDF datasets. In: Proceedings of 18th International Semantic Web Conference (2019)

394. Serale, G., Goia, F., Perino, M.: Numerical model and simulation of a solar thermal collector with slurry Phase Change Material (PCM) as the heat transfer fluid. Sol. Energy **134**, 429–444 (2016)

395. Shafer, T.: The 42 v's of big data and data science (2017)

396. Shahanas, B.M., Sivakumar, P.B.: Framework for a smart water management system in the context of smart city initiatives in India. Procedia Comput. Sci. **92**, 142–147 (2016)

397. Sharma, P.: Wireless sensor networks for environmental monitoring. In: IEERET-2014 Conference Proceedings (2014)

398. Sheth, A.: Panel: data semantics: what, where and how? In: Meersman, R., Mark, L. (eds.) Database Applications Semantics. IAICT, pp. 601–610. Springer, Boston, MA (1997). https://doi.org/10.1007/978-0-387-34913-8_26

399. Sheth, A., Padhee, S., Gyrard, A.: Knowledge graphs and knowledge networks: the story in brief. IEEE Internet Comput. **23**(4), 67–75 (2019)

400. Shoumy, N.J., Ang, L.-M., Seng, K.P., Rahaman, D., Zia, T.: Multimodal big data affective analytics: a comprehensive survey using text, audio, visual and physiological signals. J. Netw. Comput. Appl. **149**, 102447 (2020)

401. Singh, A., Sahay, K.B.: Short-term demand forecasting by using ANN algorithms. In: 2018 International Electrical Engineering Congress (iEECON), pp. 1–4 (2018). ISBN 978-1-5386-2318-3

402. Singh, L., et al.: NSF BIGDATA PI meeting - domain-specific research directions and data sets. SIGMOD Rec. **47**(3), 32–35 (2018)

403. Sirin, E., Parsia, B., Grau, B.C., Kalyanpur, A., Katz, Y.: Pellet: a practical OWL-DL reasoner. Web Semant.: Sci. Serv. Agents WWW **5**(2), 51–53 (2007)

404. Sivarajah, U., Kamal, M., Irani, Z., Weerakkody, V.: Critical analysis of big data challenges and analytical methods. J. Bus. Res. **70**, 263–286 (2017)

405. Sivarajah, U., Kamal, M.M., Irani, Z., Weerakkody, V.: Critical analysis of big data challenges and analytical methods. J. Bus. Res. **70**, 263–286 (2017)

406. Siła-Nowicka, K., Vandrol, J., Oshan, T., Long, J.A., Demšar, U., Fotheringham, A.S.: Analysis of human mobility patterns from GPS trajectories and contextual information. Int. J. Geogr. Inf. Sci. **30**(5), 881–906 (2016)

407. Slepicka, J., Yin, C., Szekely, P.A., Knoblock, C.A.: KR2RML: an alternative interpretation of R2RML for heterogenous sources. In: Proceedings of the 6th International Workshop on Consuming Linked Data (COLD) (2015)

408. Socher, R., Chen, D., Manning, C.D., Ng, A.: Reasoning with neural tensor networks for knowledge base completion. In: Advances in Neural Information Processing Systems, pp. 926–934 (2013)

409. Souza, D., Belian, R., Salgado, A.C., Tedesco, P.A.: Towards a context ontology to enhance data integration processes. In: ODBIS, pp. 49–56 (2008)

410. Sowa, J.F.: Semantic networks, pp. 1–25. Citeseer (1987). Chapter 1

411. Stadler, C., Sejdiu, G., Graux, D., Lehmann, J.: Sparklify: a scalable software component for efficient evaluation of SPARQL queries over distributed RDF datasets. In: Ghidini, C., et al. (eds.) ISWC 2019. LNCS, vol. 11779, pp. 293–308. Springer, Cham (2019). https://doi.org/10.1007/978-3-030-30796-7_19

412. Stadler, C., Unbehauen, J., Westphal, P., Sherif, M.A., Lehmann, J.: Simplified RDB2RDF mapping. In: Proceedings of the 8th Workshop on Linked Data on the Web (LDOW2015), Florence, Italy (2015)

413. Stepanova, D., Gad-Elrab, M.H., Ho, V.T.: Rule induction and reasoning over knowledge graphs. In: d'Amato, C., Theobald, M. (eds.) Reasoning Web 2018. LNCS, vol. 11078, pp. 142–172. Springer, Cham (2018). https://doi.org/10.1007/978-3-030-00338-8_6

414. Stonebraker, M., Robertson, J.: Big data is' buzzword du jour;'cs academics' have the best job'. Commun. ACM 56(9), 10–11 (2013)

415. Sui, D., Sejdiu, G., Graux, D., Lehmann, J.: The hubs and authorities transaction network analysis using the sansa framework. In: SEMANTiCS Conference (2019)

416. Sun, C., Gao, R., Xi, H.: Big data based retail recommender system of non e-commerce. In: Fifth International Conference on Computing, Communications and Networking Technologies (ICCCNT), pp. 1–7 (2014)

417. Sun, Z., Deng, Z.-H., Nie, J.-Y., Tang, J.: Rotate: knowledge graph embedding by relational rotation in complex space. arXiv preprint arXiv:1902.10197 (2019)

418. Park, W.K., Ku, T.Y., Choi, H.: Iot energy management platform for microgrid. In: IEEE 7th International Conference on Power and Energy Systems (ICPES), Toronto, ON, Canada, pp. 106–110 (2017)

419. Tabatabaei, S.M., Dick, S., Xu, W.: Toward non-intrusive load monitoring via multi-label classification - IEEE Journals & Magazine. IEEE Trans. Smart Grid 8(1), 26–40 (2016)

420. Tafti, A.P., et al.: bigNN: an open-source big data toolkit focused on biomedical sentence classification. In: IEEE International Conference on Big Data (Big Data), Boston, MA, pp. 3888–3896 (2017)

421. Tang, W.: Fog-enabled smart health: toward cooperative and secure healthcare service provision. IEEE Commun. Mag. 57(3), 42–48 (2019)

422. Tasnim, M., Collarana, D., Graux, D., Orlandi, F., Vidal, M.: Summarizing entity temporal evolution in knowledge graphs. In: Companion of The 2019 World Wide Web Conference, WWW 2019, San Francisco, CA, USA, 13–17 May 2019, pp. 961–965 (2019)

423. DBLP Team: Records in DBLP (2016). http://dblp.org/statistics/recordsindblp

424. Thalhammer, A., Lasierra, N., Rettinger, A.: LinkSUM: using link analysis to summarize entity data. In: Bozzon, A., Cudre-Maroux, P., Pautasso, C. (eds.) ICWE 2016. LNCS, vol. 9671, pp. 244–261. Springer, Cham (2016). https://doi.org/10.1007/978-3-319-38791-8_14

425. Thalhammer, A., Rettinger, A.: Browsing DBpedia entities with summaries. In: Presutti, V., Blomqvist, E., Troncy, R., Sack, H., Papadakis, I., Tordai, A. (eds.) ESWC 2014. LNCS, vol. 8798, pp. 511–515. Springer, Cham (2014). https://doi.org/10.1007/978-3-319-11955-7_76

426. Thusoo, A., Borthakur, D., Murthy, R.: Data warehousing and analytics infrastructure at Facebook. In: Proceedings of the 2010 ACM SIGMOD International Conference on Management of Data SIGMOD 2010, pp. 1013–1020. ACM (2010)

427. Tian, X., Han, R., Wang, L., Lu, G., Zhan, J.: Latency critical big data computing in finance. J. Finance Data Sci. 1(1), 33–41 (2015)

428. Ting, K., Cecho, J.J.: Apache Sqoop Cookbook: Unlocking Hadoop for your Relational Database. O'Reilly Media Inc., Cambridge (2013)

429. Torre-Bastida, A.I., Del Ser, I.L.J., Ilardia, M., Bilbao, M.N., Campos-Cordobés, S.: Big data for transportation and mobility: recent advances, trends and challenges. IET Intell. Transp. Syst. 12, 742–755 (2018)

430. Trouillon, T., Welbl, J., Riedel, S., Gaussier, É., Bouchard, G.: Complex embeddings for simple link prediction. In: International Conference on Machine Learning, pp. 2071–2080 (2016)

431. Tu, C., He, X., Shuai, Z., Jiang, F.: Big data issues in smart grid - a review. Renew. Sustain. Energy Rev. 79, 1099–1107 (2017)

432. Turing, A.M.: Computing machinery and intelligence. In: Epstein, R., Roberts, G., Beber, G. (eds.) Parsing the Turing Test, pp. 23–65. Springer, Dordrecht (2009). https://doi.org/10.1007/978-1-4020-6710-5_3

433. Ullman, J.D.: Information integration using logical views. In: Afrati, F., Kolaitis, P. (eds.) ICDT 1997. LNCS, vol. 1186, pp. 19–40. Springer, Heidelberg (1997). https://doi.org/10.1007/3-540-62222-5_34

434. Ullman, J.D.: Information integration using logical views. Theor. Comput. Sci. 239(2), 189–210 (2000)

435. Upadhyaya, S.R.: Parallel approaches to machine learning - a comprehensive survey. J. Parallel Distrib. Comput. 73, 284–292 (2013)

436. Urhan, T., Franklin, M.J.: Xjoin: a reactively-scheduled pipelined join operator. IEEE Data Eng. Bull. 23(2), 27–33 (2000)

437. Vagropoulos, S.I., Chouliaras, G.I., Kardakos, E.G., Simoglou, C.K., Bakirtzis, A.G.: Comparison of SARIMAX, SARIMA, modified SARIMA and ANN-based models for short-term PV generation forecasting. In: 2016 IEEE International Energy Conference (ENERGYCON), pp. 1–6 (2016)

438. Vahdati, S.: Collaborative integration, publishing and analysis of distributed scholarly metadata. Ph.D. thesis, Universitäts-und Landesbibliothek Bonn (2019)

439. Vahdati, S., Dimou, A., Lange, C., Di Iorio, A.: Semantic publishing challenge: bootstrapping a value chain for scientific data. In: González-Beltrán, A., Osborne, F., Peroni, S. (eds.) SAVE-SD 2016. LNCS, vol. 9792, pp. 73–89. Springer, Cham (2016). https://doi.org/10.1007/978-3-319-53637-8_9

440. van de Riet, R., Meersman, R.: Knowledge graphs. In: Linguistic Instruments in Knowledge Engineering: Proceedings of the 1991 Workshop on Linguistic Instruments in Knowledge Engineering, Tilburg, The Netherlands, pp. 17–18 (1991)

441. Van Emden, M.H., Kowalski, R.A.: The semantics of predicate logic as a programming language. J. ACM (JACM) 23(4), 733–742 (1976)

442. Van Oorschot, N., Van Leeuwen, B.: Intelligent fire risk monitor based on linked open data (2015)

443. Vater, J., Harscheidt, L., Knoll, A.: Smart manufacturing with prescriptive analytics. In: 8th International Conference on Industrial Technology and Management (ICITM), Cambridge, UK, pp. 224–228 (2019)

444. Vavilapalli, V.K., et al.: Apache hadoop yarn: yet another resource negotiator. In: Proceedings of the 4th Annual Symposium on Cloud Computing, pp. 1–16 (2013)

445. Verroios, V., Garcia-Molina, H., Papakonstantinou, Y.: Waldo: an adaptive human interface for crowd entity resolution. In: International Conference on Management of Data, pp. 1133–1148 (2017)

446. Vidal, M., Endris, K.M., Jazashoori, S., Sakor, A., Rivas, A.: Transforming heterogeneous data into knowledge for personalized treatments - a use case. Datenbank-Spektrum **19**(2), 95–106 (2019)

447. Vidal, M.-E., Endris, K.M., Jozashoori, S., Karim, F., Palma, G.: Semantic data integration of big biomedical data for supporting personalised medicine. In: Alor-Hernández, G., Sánchez-Cervantes, J.L., Rodríguez-González, A., Valencia-García, R. (eds.) Current Trends in Semantic Web Technologies: Theory and Practice. SCI, vol. 815, pp. 25–56. Springer, Cham (2019). https://doi.org/10.1007/978-3-030-06149-4_2

448. Vrandečić, D., Krötzsch, M.: Wikidata: a free collaborative knowledgebase. Commun. ACM **57**(10), 78–85 (2014)

449. de Vries, P.H.: Representation of scientific texts in knowledge graphs. Ph.D. thesis, Groningen (1989)

450. Vu, D.H., Muttaqi, K.M., Agalgaonkar, A.P., Bouzerdoum, A.: Intra-hour and hourly demand forecasting using selective order autoregressive model. In: 2016 IEEE International Conference on Power System Technology (POWERCON), pp. 1–6 (2016). ISBN 978-1-4673-8849-8

451. Vychodil, V.: A new algorithm for computing formal concepts (2008). na

452. Wan, C., Lin, J., Song, Y., Xu, Z., Yang, G.: Probabilistic forecasting of photovoltaic generation: an efficient statistical approach. IEEE Trans. Power Syst. **32**(3), 2471–2472 (2016)

453. Wan, C., Zhao, J., Song, Y., Xu, Z., Lin, J., Hu, Z.: Photovoltaic and solar power forecasting for smart grid energy management. CSEE J. Power Energy Syst. **1**(4), 38–46 (2015)

454. Wang, C., Li, X., Zhou, X., Wang, A., Nedjah, N.: Soft computing in big data intelligent transportation systems. Appl. Soft Comput. **38**, 1099–1108 (2016)

455. Wang, G., Yang, S., Han, Y.: Mashroom: end-user mashup programming using nested tables. In: Proceedings of the 18th International Conference on World Wide Web, pp. 861–870. ACM (2009)

456. Wang, L.: Heterogeneous data and big data analytics. Autom. Control Inf. Sci. **3**(1), 8–15 (2017)

457. Wang, P., Xu, B., Wu, Y., Zhou, X.: Link prediction in social networks: the state-of-the-art. Sci. China Inf. Sci. **58**(1), 1–38 (2015)

458. Wang, Q., Mao, Z., Wang, B., Guo, L.: Knowledge graph embedding: a survey of approaches and applications. IEEE Trans. Knowl. Data Eng. **29**(12), 2724–2743 (2017)

459. Wang, Q., Mao, Z., Wang, B., Guo, L.: Knowledge graph embedding: a survey of approaches and applications. IEEE Trans. Knowl. Data Eng. **29**(12), 2724–2743 (2017)

460. Wang, Q., Wang, B., Guo, L.: Knowledge base completion using embeddings and rules. In: Twenty-Fourth International Joint Conference on Artificial Intelligence (2015)

461. Wang, X., Feng, W., Cai, W., Ren, H., Ding, C., Zhou, N.: Do residential building energy efficiency standards reduce energy consumption in China? - A data-driven method to validate the actual performance of buildings energy efficiency standards. Energy Policy **131**, 82–98 (2016)

462. Wang, Z., Zhang, J., Feng, J., Chen, Z.: Knowledge graph and text jointly embedding. In: Proceedings of the 2014 Conference on Empirical Methods in Natural Language Processing (EMNLP), pp. 1591–1601 (2014)

463. Warrior, K.P., Shrenik, M., Soni, N.: Short-term electrical load forecasting using predictive machine learning models. In: 2016 IEEE Annual India Conference (INDICON), pp. 1–6 (2016). ISSN: 2325-9418

464. Weber, L., Minervini, P., Münchmeyer, J., Leser, U., Rocktäschel, T.: NLProlog reasoning with weak unification for question answering in natural language. arXiv preprint arXiv:1906.06187 (2019)

465. Wei, Z., Zhao, J., Liu, K., Qi, Z., Sun, Z., Tian, G.: Large-scale knowledge base completion: inferring via grounding network sampling over selected instances. In: Proceedings of the 24th ACM International on Conference on Information and Knowledge Management, pp. 1331–1340. ACM (2015)

466. Wen, L., Zhou, K., Yang, S.: Load demand forecasting of residential buildings using a deep learning model. Electr. Power Syst. Res. **179**, 106073 (2016)

467. Wilson, K.G.: Grand challenges to computational science. Future Gener. Comput. Syst. **5**(2), 171–189 (1989)

468. Wishart, D.S., et al.: DrugBank: a knowledgebase for drugs, drug actions and drug targets. Nucleic Acids Res. **36**(suppl-1), D901–D906 (2008)

469. Wolfert, S., Ge, L., Verdouw, C., Bogaardt, M.-J.: Big data in smart farming - a review. Agric. Syst. **153**, 69–80 (2017)

470. Woo, B., Vesset, D., Olofson, C.W., Conway, S., Feldman, S., Bozman, J.S.: Worldwide big data taxonomy. IDC report (2011)

471. Woods, D.: Big data requires a big, new architecture. https://www.forbes.com/sites/ciocentral/2011/07/21/big-data-requires-a-big-new-architecture/

472. Woods, W.: What's in a link: foundations for semantic networks. In: Representation and Understanding, pp. 35–82(1975)

473. Wylot, M., Hauswirth, M., Cudré-Mauroux, P., Sakr, S.: RDF data storage and query processing schemes: a survey. ACM Comput. Surv. (CSUR) **51**(4), 1–36 (2018)

474. Xia, F., Wang, W., Bekele, T.M., Liu, H.: Big scholarly data: a survey. IEEE Trans. Big Data **3**(1), 18–35 (2017)

475. Xie, R., Liu, Z., Sun, M.: Representation learning of knowledge graphs with hierarchical types. In: IJCAI, pp. 2965–2971 (2016)

476. Yang, B., Yih, W.-T., He, X., Gao, J., Deng, L.: Embedding entities and relations for learning and inference in knowledge bases. arXiv preprint arXiv:1412.6575 (2014)

477. Yao, M.: Artificial intelligence defined 5G radio access networks. IEEE Commun. Mag. **57**(3), 42–48 (2019)

478. Yaqoob, I., et al.: Big data: from beginning to future. Int. J. Inf. Manage. **36**(6, Part B), 1231–1247 (2016)

479. Yazti, D.Z., Krishnaswamy, S.: Mobile big data analytics: research, practice, and opportunities. In: IEEE 15th International Conference on Mobile Data Management, Brisbane, QLD, Australia (2014)

480. Zaharia, M., et al.: Apache spark: a unified engine for big data processing. Commun. ACM **59**(11), 56–65 (2016)

481. Zaveri, A., Rula, A., Maurino, R., Pietrobon, R., Lehmann, J., Auer, S.: Quality assessment for linked data: a survey. Semant. Web- Interoper. Usability Appl. **7**(1), 63–93 (2016)

482. Zhang, L.: Knowledge graph theory and structural parsing. Twente University Press (2002)

483. Zhang, S., Jia, S., Ma, C., Wang, Y.: Impacts of public transportation fare reduction policy on urban public transport sharing rate based on big data analysis. In: 2018 IEEE 3rd International Conference on Cloud Computing and Big Data Analysis (ICCCBDA), pp. 280–284 (2018)

484. Zhou, A.C., He, B.: Big Data and exascale computing. In: Sakr, S., Zomaya, A.Y. (eds.) Encyclopedia of Big Data Technologies, pp. 184–187. Springer, Cham (2019). https://doi.org/10.1007/978-3-319-77525-8

485. Zhou, C., Su, F., Pei, T., et al.: COVID-19: challenges to GIS with big data. Geograph. Sustain. 1, 77–87 (2020)

486. Zhou, J., Song, Y., Zhang, G.: Correlation analysis of energy consumption and indoor long-term thermal environment of a residential building. Energy Procedia 121, 182–189 (2016)

487. Zhu, Q., Ma, X., Li, X.: Statistical learning for semantic parsing: a survey. Big Data Min. Anal. 2(4), 217–239 (2019)

488. Zhu, X.: Machine teaching: an inverse problem to machine learning and an approach toward optimal education. In: Twenty-Ninth AAAI Conference on Artificial Intelligence (2015)

489. Zikopoulos, P., Eaton, C., et al.: Understanding Big Data: Analytics for Enterprise Class Hadoop and Streaming Data. McGraw-Hill Osborne Media, New York (2011)

490. Zohrevand, Z., Glasser, U., Shahir, H.Y., Tayebi, M.A., Costanzo, R.: Hidden markov based anomaly detection for water supply systems. In: 2016 IEEE International Conference on Big Data (Big Data), pp. 1551–1560 (2016)

491. Zou, Y., Finin, T., Chen, H.: F-OWL: an inference engine for semantic web. In: Hinchey, M.G., Rash, J.L., Truszkowski, W.F., Rouff, C.A. (eds.) FAABS 2004. LNCS (LNAI), vol. 3228, pp. 238–248. Springer, Heidelberg (2004). https://doi.org/10.1007/978-3-540-30960-4_16

492. Óskarsdóttir, M., Bravo, C., Sarraute, C., Vanthienen, J., Baesens, B.: The value of big data for credit scoring: enhancing financial inclusion using mobile phone data and social network analytics. Appl. Soft Comput. 74, 26–39 (2019)

Author Index

Printed in the United States
By Bookmasters